THE LONG MARCH OI

Born in 1926, Charles Whiting joined the army as a volunteer in 1943 and served with the 52nd Armoured Reconnaissance Regiment in Belgium, Holland and Germany. After the war he studied at the University of Leeds and later at London, Kiel, Cologne and Saarbrücken. In 1958 he became a university teacher, first in the USA and then in England and Germany where he was also the German correspondent for the *Times Educational Supplement*. He gave up full-time teaching in 1973 to devote himself to writing.

Charles Whiting's first novel *Frat Wagon* was published by Jonathan Cape while he was at university. Since then he has had nearly a hundred books published ranging from fiction, under the pen name of Leo Kessler, to military history, espionage and linguistics. His most recent publications include *Death of a Division, The Battle for Hitler's Wall, The German Home Front, The Siegfried Line, '44: In Combat on the Western Front from Normandy to the Ardennes, '45: The Final Drive from the Rhine to the Baltic* and *Britain Under Fire: The Bombing of Britain's Cities, 1940–45*.

THE LONG MARCH ON ROME

The Forgotten War

CHARLES WHITING

CENTURY
LONDON MELBOURNE AUCKLAND JOHANNESBURG

'It is going to be one of the greatest marches in all military history. A long narrow green country, full of handsome people who have been enslaved for twenty years and are now being liberated and know it. You will be greeted like water in the desert, like a circus on the Fourth of July, *like Clark Gable at Vassar!*'

A man in a Cairo Bar to Sergeant Irwin Shaw, 1943

'It is true, I suppose, that the Americans consider that we have led them up the garden path in the Mediterranean – but what a beautiful path it has proved to be! They have picked peaches, here, nectarines there. How grateful they should be!'

Winston Churchill, 1943

First published in 1987 by Century Hutchinson Ltd, Brookmount House, 62–65 Chandos Place, Covent Garden, London WC2N 4NW

Century Hutchinson Australia Pty Ltd, PO Box 496, 16–22 Church Street, Hawthorn, Victoria 3122, Australia

Century Hutchinson New Zealand Ltd, PO Box 40–086, Glenfield, Auckland 10, New Zealand

Century Hutchinson South Africa (Pty) Ltd, PO Box 337, Bergvlei, 2012 South Africa

Designed by Tom Deas
Maps by Ed Dovey
Picture Research by Ed Dovey

Set in 11 on 13 pt Monophoto Times

Printed and bound in Great Britain by Butler & Tanner Ltd, Frome and London

British Library Cataloguing in Publication Data

Whiting, Charles
    The long march on Rome: the forgotten war.
    1. World War, 1939–1945 —— Campaigns —— Italy
    I. Title
    940.54'21   D763.18

ISBN 0 7126 9582 6 (C)

ISBN 0 7126 14397 (P)

Acknowledgements

I am indebted to a great number of people for their help in the preparation of this book. Of the 'old sweats' who slogged it out in Italy, I should like to express my thanks, in particular, to Messrs Telford, Tucker, Pinder (deceased), Dennis, and naturally that 'reluctant hero', Percy Castle. I should also like to thank Madge Faulkner for her account of her brother's last days.

The *Navy News* was splendidly supportive. Dozens of ex-RN men wrote to me with their accounts of the landings at Sicily, Salerno and Anzio. Of their ranks I should like to thank Messrs Daniels, Braddock, Tyers, West, Curtis, Davenport, May, Jones, Docherty, Burnett, Bob Burns D.S.M., Whittaker, Ratcliffe and Mrs Reader, who still treasures her father's 'Sicily Diary', written in a battered exercise book. I can only hope that this book does a little to keep the memory alive of all those who fought so hard and gave so much in that forgotten war.

C. W., Wittlich/W. Germany. Summer 1985

Reference Notes will be found at the end of the book, giving the sources of material quoted from previously published works. All quoted passages not so ascribed are derived from personal communications to, or interviews with, the author.

Title page: U. S. troops on the outskirts of Rome.

CONTENTS

INTRODUCTION

'We're the D-Day Dodgers, out in Italy,
Always drinking vino, always on the spree,
Eighth Army skivers and the Yanks,
We live in Rome, we laugh at tanks.
For we're the D-Day Dodgers, in sunny Italy.

Looking round the mountains, in the mud and rain,
There's lots of little crosses, some which bear no name.
Blood, sweat and tears and toil are gone.
The boys beneath them slumber on.
These are your D-Day Dodgers, who'll stay in Italy!'

The great deception had started innocently enough in the Junior Carlton Club, in the heart of London's clubland. The smart young officer from Naval Intelligence, Commander the Hon Ewen Montagu, listened to the words of the white-haired pathologist who was perhaps the world's greatest authority in his field. Over coffee, while the ancient waiters creaked back and forth, Sir Bernard answered the young officer's questions in his somewhat pedantic manner that, in the past, had awed bewigged senior judges at the Old Bailey, not far from where the two of them were sitting now.

'Death would probably result from a lowering of the person's temperature, especially if the man in question were to float by means of a life-belt. First he would fall unconscious....' The old man droned on and on.

Montagu posed the key question. 'Would there be any outward signs of how the man had met his death, sir?'

Sir Bernard considered for a moment, cup poised at his thin lips. He wasn't given to answering questions of that nature lightly. Montagu waited. 'No,' he said finally, 'in my opinion, there would be no outward characteristics of the manner of death.'[1]

Montague's heart missed a beat. It was the answer he had been hoping for ever since the XX Committee had dreamed up *'Operation Mincemeat'*. All he needed now was the right body.

'But you can't get bodies just for the asking!' Sir William Bentley-Purchase, the coroner for the Borough of St Pancras, objected pompously. 'I mean, even with bodies all over the place, each one has to be accounted for.'[2]

But in the wartime winter of 1943, the men who played the 'double-cross game', the Twenty Committee,* were all-powerful in London. Pressure was discreetly applied on Sir William, who guarded his bodies so diligently,

although there were corpses enough from the air raids on London in his icy vaults.

Thus it was that Sir Bernard Spilsbury, Sir William and Montagu met behind the locked doors of St Pancras mortuary. A century after the last body-snatcher had been arrested and imprisoned in that same London borough, the three men set about finding the corpse that Montagu needed for the great deception. In the harsh light cast by the naked bulbs they viewed a number of corpses set out on their slabs in the tiled, old-fashioned Victorian house of death. Finally Sir Bernard settled on an unknown 30-year-old man† who had died in a London hospital of pneumonia. According to the pathologist any unsuspecting doctor examining the corpse would conclude that, due to the fluid in the dead man's lungs, he had died of drowning. Montagu nodded his approval, glad that the macabre business was over. Now all that remained to be done was to dress the naked man before he was tucked away again in his vault. Then an unexpected difficulty cropped up: the dead man's feet were frozen solid! But Sir William was equal to the occasion. He ordered one of the attendants to bring down his electric hot plate on which they boiled the water for the afternoon tea. The coroner plugged it in and stretched the burner close to the iron-hard feet. Montagu, sickened, turned away, but Sir William didn't bat an eyelid. 'We'll thaw the feet out,' he announced in a matter-of-fact way, 'and as soon as the boots are on, we'll pop him back in the refrigerator and re-freeze him.'[3]

On 19 April 1943, *Operation Mincemeat* was finally ready. The dead man, now transformed into 'Major Martin', carrying letters to General Alexander and Admiral Sir Andrew Cunningham, was carefully packed in dry ice in a container labelled 'Optical Instruments' and loaded on

* From the Roman numeral 'XX', designating the top-secret committee.

† Forty-two years later the name of the man has still not been released.

6

Officers and men on the bridge of HMS Seraph. Captain Jewell is second from the left.

to the British submarine, HMS *Seraph*, at Holy Loch. Thence the 'optical instruments' were transported down the length of Britain, along the French coast, until the *Seraph* came to rest off the Spanish coast near Punta de Umbria. Captain Jewell ordered the submarine to the surface and then cleared the deck of all save officers, where he told them what their mission was.

It was an eerie scene, as Major Martin was unpacked from his dry ice and they checked whether his papers were still there and made sure that the briefcase was securely fixed to his wrist by a little chain. Somehow they fitted the corpse with its 'Mae West'. Finally Captain Jewell clasped his hands together, lowered his eyes and murmured the committal ceremony for the body lying there on the wet deck. It must have been one of the strangest 'burials' in the history of the Christian Church!

Gently the body was thrust over the side. Jewell's voice rose a couple of octaves as he started rapping out orders. Once more he was the typical Royal Navy skipper. The engines began to throb as the sub swung around. The ripples grew into waves. Slowly but surely Major Martin was driven towards the faint outline of the Spanish coast – and the waiting Germans.

Operation Mincemeat was one of several plants carried out by British Intelligence, in places ranging from Spain to India, to convince the Germans that, now that the Allies had driven the enemy from North Africa, their next step would be the invasion of the Balkans. German reconnaissance over the African ports could plainly make out the hundreds of ships being assembled there, obvi-

7

ously intended for a landing. The question for the German *Abwehr** was – *where?*

In essence the men of British Intelligence wanted the *Abwehr* to believe that the primary objective of the Mediterranean campaign in the summer of 1943 was the Greek mainland. The build-up for this attack would take place in Egypt and the Levant, withdrawing troops from Persia and Iraq. Then the main assault would take place against the Greek Peloponnese, with the object of seizing Piraeus and linking up with the sizeable Greek partisan organization. In North Africa the British Eighth Army under Montgomery and the American Fifth under General Mark Clark would be held in reserve ready to exploit the success in Greece. That spring forty-odd years ago agents of British Intelligence laboured mightily on three continents: in New Delhi, where information was planted on the Japanese (who would leak it to their German allies) about the Indian component of the invasion force; in Basra, where German agents were fooled into believing that British troops were being withdrawn for the coming assault, and in Damascus, where great camps were set up to welcome the 'invasion army' for the benefit of French spies in the pay of the *Abwehr*. Behind the scenes, as the tension mounted and the day of the great assault came closer, men of a dozen different nationalities deceived – and were deceived – in order to convince that old man in Berlin that the Allies' next objective was the Balkans.

'Father Christmas' they called him behind his back, on account of his snowy white hair, benign appearance and un-German habit of donning an apron and cooking dinner for his spies. But Admiral Canaris, the head of the German *Abwehr*, was no gentle old man in spite of his appearance. William Shirer has written of him: 'He was so shadowy a figure that no two writers agree as to what kind of a man he was, or what he believed in, if anything much.'[4]

Now it was Father Christmas's task to evaluate the papers found on Major Martin by a Spanish fisherman off the port of Huelva on the morning of 30 April, copies of which had been sent to him immediately by his spies in Spain, and to advise the Fuhrer on what the Allies' intentions were in the Mediterranean.

In the end he forwarded to Hitler the two letters to General Alexander and Admiral Sir Andrew Cunningham with an accompanying letter which read: 'There is no doubt about the genuineness of the captured documents. We are checking, however, whether they have been played into our hands deliberately and whether the enemy is aware of their loss or that we have gained possession of them. It is possible that the enemy has no knowledge of this fact.'[5]

Thereafter things moved fast. The First Panzer Division was moved from Southern France. Keitel, Hitler's Chief-of-Staff, ordered the strengthening of the German garrisons in the Balkans. The head of the German Navy, Admiral Doenitz, sent fresh naval units to the area and ordered increased mining of all coastal waters and the 'Desert Fox' himself, Field-Marshal Rommel, was sent hot-foot to Greece to inspect the German defences there. Montagu, who had even thought of placing a notice for 'Capt (A/Major) W. Martin' in *The Times*' 'List of Missing' just in case the Germans had an agent in London checking, was jubilant. *Operation Mincemeat*, and all the other plants of this exciting spring of 1943, had paid off. The Germans had been duped!

Only one senior German commander concerned with the defence of the southern flank of Hitler's 'Thousand-Year Reich' remained unconvinced. He was Field-Marshal Albert Kesselring, known by his troops behind his back as 'Smiling Albert', since he was always smiling. Once, when his staff car ran into a truck in Italy, his soldiers joked that 'Smiling Albert' had still come out smiling, though the 'smile had been wiped off the face of the truck for good'.

In the command of German forces in Italy, Kesselring dismissed Greece and the Balkans as the Allies' next objective, although Admiral Canaris had visited his headquarters to alert him to that possibility. As he wrote in his *Memoirs* after the war, 'The conglomeration of British and American forces in the Tunisian area indicated first and foremost that the Allies intended to prosecute their operations in the Western Mediterranean. Sicily lay within striking distance; the capture of the island would be an important step on the road to Italy.'[6]

But for the moment 'Smiling Albert' was in the minority. The Italian *Commando Supremo*, which had nominal command over Kesselring, was complacent and, in Kesselring's opinion, overly optimistic. 'On the maps everything was in order,' he wrote after the war. 'Their plans were cleverly thought out, in some respects too cleverly by half. But the construction work [in Sicily and the other Italian off-shore islands] done was mere eyewash. There were no prepared positions on the islands which were inadequately defended and had unguarded tank obstacles more likely to hamper the defenders than to check the enemy – *all so much gingerbread*.'[7] And it was exatly those 'gingerbread' defences which the Anglo-Americans were going to attack. Sicily *was* their objective, not Piraeus.

To Winston Churchill Italy and the Balkans were the Axis' 'soft underbelly'. For him and the British High Command it seemed self-evident that, after the victory in North Africa, the next step should be to attack Sicily and then Italy itself. In 1943 it appeared to him to be the easiest and most direct way into Hitler's *Festung Europa*. The Italians were war-weary and reluctant soldiers; Churchill reckoned that he could defeat them and knock them

* Intelligence.

'Smiling Albert' Kesselring.

out of the war. Besides, there was a year to go before the great cross-Channel invasion of 1944 and it was essential to keep the troops in North Africa busy in another operation. As Churchill told the House of Commons: 'We have to fight them somewhere, unless we are just to sit back and watch the Russians.'[8]

There was also another reason, one which Churchill could not tell Parliament in 1943. The Prime Minister's political instinct told him that the right place to meet the Russians advancing westwards was not in Germany but in Central Europe. The further away that threat to the future, namely the Russians, was kept from the West, the more it pleased Winston Churchill. But General Marshall and the American Chiefs-of-Staff thought otherwise. They thought that Nazi Germany should be finished by one single thrust to the heart, across the Channel and straight for Berlin. Nothing should be allowed to divert men and material from that main effort. Anything else would be a sideshow and Marshall, that stern unyielding figure in far-away Washington, was against side-shows.

'The Mediterranean,' Marshall told the Combined Chiefs-of-Staff as late as May 1943, 'is a vacuum into which America's military might could be drawn off until there is nothing left with which to deal the decisive blow on the Continent.'[9]

In the end Marshall was overruled by President Roosevelt and the US Army was committed – at least to the invasion of Sicily. But most of the US top brass remained unconvinced of the value of the new operation. One of them, General Wedemeyer, wrote a bitter letter to the head of the US Army's Operation Division, stating: 'We lost our shirts and are now committed to the *subterranean umbilious operation*'.[10] He was referring, of course, to that phrase so often used by Churchill when promoting operations against Germany's Mediterranean flank in Italy – 'the soft underbelly'.

In the end that 'soft underbelly' took two years to conquer, by which time it had become a 'tough old gut'. Throughout, Washington remained luke-warm about the Italian campaign and kept the American army there short of men and resources, so the Americans who fought in Italy could justifiably feel that they were, to a large extent, America's forgotten army. No wonder they and their comrades of the British Eighth Army sang bitterly after

D-Day, when they had already been fighting one year in Italy:

We're the D-Day Dodgers, out in Italy,
Always drinking vino, always on the spree.
Eighth Army skivers and the Yanks,
We live in Rome, we laugh at tanks.
For we're the D-Day Dodgers, in sunny Italy.

In October 1942, that same Royal Navy submarine, HMS *Seraph*, which had transported the dead 'Major Martin' to his destination, had taken another military man on an equally secret mission. He had been an American general, with a huge beak of a nose, General Mark Clark, the man whom Churchill consequently named 'his American Eagle'.

Landed secretly on the North African coast, Clark had met French military officers to sound them out on how they felt about a projected Anglo-American landing there. Disturbed by the French police, Clark had made a run for it back to the sub, during the course of which he lost his trousers, which were weighed down with gold for bribery purposes. When the news of the General who had 'lost his pants' on a daring secret mission was released to the US Press, it turned the hitherto obscure Regular Army officer in his mid-forties into a national figure whose name and photograph became widely known. Louella Parsons, the gossip columnist, called him 'America's dream hero'. A Boston newspaper maintained that every war America had fought had produced an act of personal daring which had given the person concerned a permanent place in US history. Nathan Hale had been the first such hero; Clark was the latest.

At his headquarters in Africa, Clark, whose sole combat experience hitherto had been one day in the trenches in 1918 before he had been hit by a shell splinter, received gifts and letters from all over the States. The Amalgamated Clothing Workers of America sent a telegram to Mrs Clark, who for the rest of the war worked assiduously as a one-woman publicity agent for her husband in the USA, stating, 'He lost his trousers honorably. He is a living example of the fact that a great hero need not lose his dignity thereby.'[11] The union then offered, if Mrs Clark would send them her husband's measurements, to make him 'as many pairs of trousers as he may need in bringing the war to the enemy'.[12] It was all very amusing and heady stuff, especially for a man like Mark Clark.

For forty-odd years he had lived in complete obscurity. Now his name was featured in banner headlines in newspapers such as the *New York Times* and the *Washington Post*. In late 1943 he was given command of the US Fifth Army and one year later command of the 15th Army Group, head of all the troops in Italy, including the British Eighth Army. During all this time he was a ruthless publicity hound, relentless in his quest for personal glory. Eric Sevareid, a US war correspondent in Italy, thought of him as vainglorious, self-seeking and driven by vanity and pride, 'the victim of the natural pressures of his position and fame'.[13] He noted that, when the Fifth Army Commander was photographed at the front, the pictures 'were always taken of the General's left profile. I noticed that, although an ordinary soldier risked a fine for not wearing his helmet in a combat area, the General was wearing his little overseas cap. When the pictures were finished and he had seen what he wished, he shook hands all round, mounted his jeep and turned back toward the pacified area. *Then he replaced the overseas cap with his steel helmet!*'[14] It was all show for the newspapers and movie theatres back home.

Most of his fellow officers also thought him a self-seeking phoney. General Jacob L. Devers, who worked with him for most of the Italian campaign, rated him as 'cold, distinguished, conceited, selfish ... very ambitious'.[15] Patton said, 'His [Clark's] mind is on Clark.... It makes my flesh creep to be with him.... Millions of pictures were taken ... all for the glory of F.D.R. and for Clark where he could get a chance. It was very disgusting.'[16] Once, when Clark had helped him, Patton praised him to Eisenhower. But in his diary, after the event, Patton wrote, 'I think if you treat a skunk nicely, *he will not piss on you as often!*'[17]

In the Second World War, the first war in history to be fought under the day-to-day scrutiny of the media, there were several American generals, such as Patton, who were as greedy for personal publicity as Clark was. On the British side General Montgomery was no exception. But these, on the whole, did not allow this greed for self-aggrandizement to dictate their strategy. Clark often did.

The overall command of the Italian campaign was weak. Washington was not particularly interested in the Italian backwater and there were no long-range goals for the campaign. From its very beginnings the Italian campaign had no specific strategic aim. The Allied commanders simply improvised. Without firm guidelines and objectives, they basically reacted and responded to German decisions. In essence, it was 'Smiling Albert' who determined what they did.

It was against this lax background, far away from direct American control, and with a British Supreme Commander, Alexander, who was reluctant or unable to control him, that Clark operated. Twice he failed to sack hopelessly incompetent American corps commanders who were personal friends of his patron back in Washington, General McNair. More than once he absented himself from his HQ or the battlefield and couldn't be found when important decisions were to be made, which could have resulted in bad publicity for him. As soon as the famous Benedictine abbey at Monte Cassino was bombed by the Allies and the world howled in protest and outrage, Clark went on record publicly and hurriedly to say that he had been against the bombing all along.

Always, throughout the campaign, he had his eye on

'We're the D-Day Dodgers, out in Italy, *Always drinking vino, always on the spree.'*

the media, worried whether his decisions would result in bad or good publicity. As the novelist Eric Ambler, who served in Italy at Clark's HQ briefly, noted: 'No World War II commander of men worked more assiduously in the field of public relations than General Clark.'[18] Ambler even thought that Clark had personally written a rousing ditty, known as the *'Sons of General Clark'*, which loyal staff officers at HQ sang lustily before the evening movie performances and which began *'Stand up and sing the praise of General Clark. Your hearts and voices raise for General Clark.'*[19]

None of Clark's attempts to gain publicity had such an effect, however, as his decision to let the retreating German 10th Army escape in order to capture Rome. He coveted the distinction of being the first general since Belisarius to capture 'Rome, the glittering prize', as he called it, from the south. General Jackson in *The Battle*

of Rome summarizes in scathing words what happened: 'It can be said that overnight he threw away the chance of destroying the right wing of von Vietinghoff's Tenth Army for the honour of entering Rome first.'[20]

So in the end, due to one man's greed for glory, there was no victory in Italy in 1944. The Germans continued fighting for another year and many more lives were sacrificed in the winter war to come. But many other thousands had already been thrown away in that long march on Rome. As one of them who survived wrote later, 'Deprived at the last of the full victory that would have made it worth while, it was in the end little more than a victory of the human spirit, an elegy for the common soldier, a memorial to the definitive horror of war and the curiously perverse paradoxical nobility of battle.'[21]

This is what *The Long March on Rome* is about.

I:
SICILY

'The indigent Sicilian,
With freedom in his belly,
Who once cheered Garibaldi,
Now yells for *caramelli!*

Anonymous G.I.

British troops receive a friendly welcome from Sicilian civilians.

12

Canadian troops aboard ship, on their way to Sicily.

'This lot can't even stand – never mind bloody well fight!'

It was Friday, 9 July 1943. For most of the voyage the sea had been calm, but during the dog-watch the wind suddenly started to freshen, growing in intensity by the second. On the bridge of the British destroyer HMS *Tetcott* the first lieutenant, D. Davenport, asked himself, 'Will it be too rough for the landing? Is the great expedition to be thrown away because of an unlucky change in the perfect weather of the last fourteen days?'

A terrible hot wind, straight from Africa, howled across the Mediterranean to strike the greatest seaborne force the world had ever seen. Within minutes the sirocco had begun tossing the landing-craft up and down as if they were on a giant roller-coaster. Valiantly the big troop transports strained to keep up to the all-important time table. They punched their way through the howling storm, laden with sea-sick British, Canadian and American troops, shipping tons of water.

Relentlessly the storm, which threatened to endanger the whole plan, grew in fury. The 2,500 ships of the invasion fleet were coming ever closer to the enemy's shore and still the gale rose in strength. Lieutenant Davenport, on the bridge of his destroyer, glanced at his instruments. The scale had risen from Force Two to Force Three and it was still rising. He had been through the débâcles at Dunkirk, Greece and Crete, where each time they had somehow managed to get the defeated troops away. Now he wondered, 'Is the Almighty on our side again or . . .?' He left the alternative unthought.

Desperately the huge convoys tried to keep together as the gale buffeted them mercilessly. Now it was blowing Force Seven!

The troopship *Derbyshire*, carrying the infantry of the First Canadian Division, sailing for their first combat action, wallowed like a drunken sow. Loose gear rolled back and forth as the big ship lurched from one trough to the other. A box of Mills grenades broke open and the deadly little bombs were hurtling back and forth like so many hard-pitched baseballs. Lieutenant Earley Mowat

15

of the Hastings and Prince Edward Regiment, recruited from south-eastern Ontario, known irreverently as the 'Hasty Pees', was relatively immune to seasickness and he struggled down to the troop decks to see how his men were getting on. He found 'many of the men still swung in their hammocks, green and groaning and unable or unwilling even to sit up. The smell of puke and engine oil was overwhelming.'[1] He managed to force his soldiers out on to the deck to get some fresh air, then set off to the officers' dining room in search of food. There he found his company commander, his face the 'colour of Gruyère cheese', slumped over a plate of boiled kippers. 'Sheer sadism!' the Major groaned. 'Only the Limeys would play a rotten trick like that on a dying man, and I'm dying, certainly.'[2]

It was no better in the ships carrying the British assault divisions. Some of them were being swept by the breaking seas so that they looked like half-awash submarines. Time and again huge waves washed over their heaving sterns. 'I've never seen the Med like it,' Corporal Pinder of the much-travelled British Fifth Division recalled forty years later. 'Half my platoon was lying in their own muck and past caring. The other half did manage to make the heads, but they were already choked with filth. Somebody said that the whole op was going to be cancelled if the weather didn't improve by teatime and I told the lads. But all they could groan was, "Just let us get our feet on land, it don't matter if it's frigging Germany!" '

A fellow Yorkshireman, Lance-Bombardier Castle of the 51st Highland Division was also relatively immune to the seasickness which reigned all about him. After nearly three years on the run in Occupied France, after the old 51st Highland Division had surrendered in 1940, he was a very reluctant soldier. Indeed he had told his C.O. just before the Division had embarked in North Africa that he would 'soldier no more', in spite of the stripe he had been given. Now, as he viewed the crowded seasick troops huddled together all about him, he told himself: 'It's going to be St Valéry* all over again. *This lot can't even stand – never mind bloody well fight!'*

The planning of the Allies' return to Occupied Europe had begun in London in January 1943. There it was decided that, once North Africa was cleared of the German and Italian enemy, the Allies would strike across the Mediterranean at the Italian island of Sicily. For six hard months the planners worked on this operation, code-named 'Husky', modifying it no less than eight times before presenting it to the Allied Supreme Commander, General Eisenhower in June. Eisenhower accepted this 'Husky Eight', but he had not reckoned with Montgomery, the victor of El Alamein, who was to command the Eighth Army in the great assault. Montgomery tackled General Bedell-Smith, Eisenhower's Chief-of-Staff, in the

* St Valéry, on the French coast, where the 51st had surrendered to the Germans in June 1940.

men's room in the St George's Hotel in Algiers, the Supreme Commander's headquarters, and convinced him that changes had to be made. 'We then left the lavatory,' Montgomery said later, 'and he went off to consult Eisenhower who liked the plan'.[3] Later, when Eisenhower, who had not been told where his Chief-of-Staff had been sold on the idea, visited Montgomery in Sicily, the latter asked the Supreme Commander, 'if he had ever been told that the final plan for Sicily had been put forward in an Algerian lavatory!'[4] Montgomery recorded that Eisenhower was much amused with the tale, but not many others were with the plan hatched 'in an Algerian lavatory'.

This, the largest amphibious assault in all history, bigger even than D-Day, envisaged the four divisions of General Patton's US Seventh Army and the four divisions of Montgomery's Eighth Army assaulting the coast of Sicily simultaneously along a front of one hundred miles. This great attack would be preceded by an airborne drop by elements of the US 82nd and the British 1st Airborne Divisions. The amount of detailed planning involved defied belief. Since every step in the invasion was related, one mistake by even a mere battalion commander would have repercussions throughout the whole operation. Facing the invaders in the triangular island the size of Vermont there were some ten Italian divisions and two German ones under the overall command of the Italian General Guzzoni. Patton's Chief-of-Intelligence, Colonel Koch, thought the Italians third-rate: 'Stick them in the belly and the sawdust will run out.' But the Germans he characterized as 'strictly hot mustard'.[5]

But in spite of the redoutable Germans, sixty thousand strong, plus nearly 200,000 Italians, it was thought the Allies with 478,000 British, Canadian and American troops, would have the advantage – *if* the weather held.

Now the weather had turned against the invaders. In Malta Eisenhower, feeling as if my 'stomach were a clenched fist', waited, knowing that if the wind continued blowing at forty knots it would ruin Patton's landing. Already his staff officers were suggesting that he should postpone the invasion before it was too late. Eisenhower conferred with the British Admiral Cunningham, head of the naval force, known on account of his initials as 'old ABC' and a veteran of four years of war in the Mediterranean. He assured Eisenhower that the velocity of the wind in that sea often changed after sunset. By midnight, two and three-quarter hours before the seaborne assault was due to start, conditions might have improved.

A little appeased, Eisenhower took Cunningham out for a walk to one of the island's airfields. Above them gliders and transports of the airborne attack were flying at only four hundred feet, their dim navigation lights just visible, looking like flights of great bats. But, as Admiral Cunningham recalled after the war, 'All the winds of heaven seemed to be roaring and howling round the control tower' and concluded that, in Eisenhower's pre-

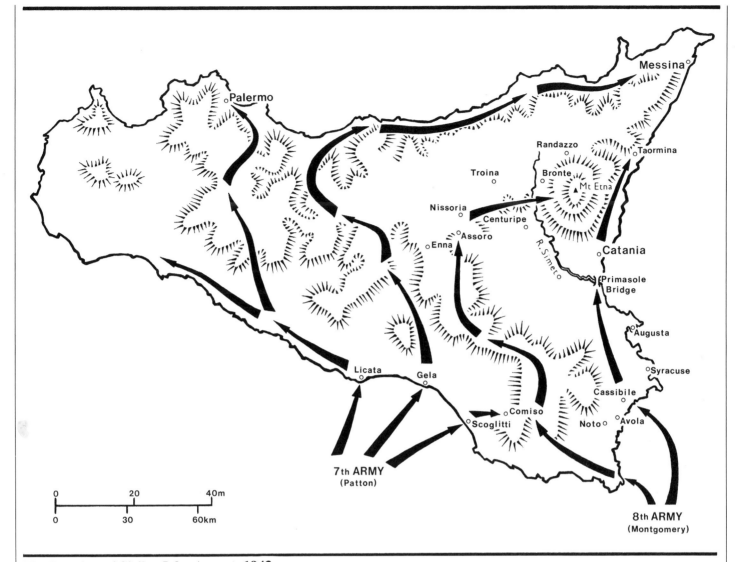

The Invasion of Sicily, July–August, 1943.

sent state, this 'was the last place we should have visited'.[6]

A wire came in from General Marshall, Eisenhower's boss in Washington: '*Is the attack on or off?*'[7] Eisenhower, who had just rubbed his seven lucky coins for the success of the passing airborne troops, wished he knew. All the same he decided that the operation must go on and radioed Marshall accordingly. As the long evening wore on and the wind velocity increased, Eisenhower felt 'there was nothing we could do but pray.'[8]

Now those airborne men whom Eisenhower had seen and wished success by turning over his seven coins in Malta were beginning to approach their objective – a dark smudge on the horizon in the silver quarter-moon. The wind was roaring from west to east at thirty-five miles an hour, an impossible speed for both gliders and parachutists. In the American Army a practice jump was always cancelled when the wind reached fifteen miles an hour!

The British 1st Air Landing Brigade's objective was the Ponte Grande, a road bridge near the town of Syracuse. But as they approached the island things began to go disastrously wrong. Major Chatterton of the Glider

Pilot Regiment, his head aching from the noise, his arms on fire after three hours of holding his glider in position, first became aware of the problem when, abruptly and to his horror, he saw he was flying side-by-side with his own tug! Hurriedly he hit rudder and aileron and jockeyed himself back in position.

The inexperienced American pilots, who were towing the British and who had never been in action before, started releasing the gliders without making any allowance for the tremendous headwind and the gliders began to stream towards the sea. Desperately the glider-pilots wrestled with their frail wooden and canvas planes, trying to keep them airborne, but to no avail. Glider after glider came down in the waves.

The Division Commander, General Hopkinson, who had less than six months to live, came down in the sea and swam for it. Chatterton, carrying his second-in-command, Brigadier 'Pip' Hicks, hit the water too. Together, the two senior officers and their staff swam ashore and lay there exhausted, impotent and unarmed, watching miserably as the surviving gliders were picked out by the Italian searchlights. Sixty-eight gliders had gone down in the sea, most of them disappearing without trace, leaving fifty-four to face the terrors of the land.

17

The American paratroopers of the 82nd Airborne Division were also approaching the island now, blown far off course to the east by the fierce winds. Again the American pilots were jumpy and only too eager to get rid of their human freight. Major Mark Alexander, commanding the Division's 2nd Battalion, was standing poised at the door of the Dakota, watching the sea below flash past, when the green light started to wink. It was the signal to jump. Immediately, his men, lined up behind him, started to shuffle forward. They decided that their C.O. had got cold feet and, as they had been trained to do in such a situation, they attempted to throw him through the door into the sea. He managed to fight them off and burst his way through them.

'What the hell are you doing?' he yelled at the pilot angrily.

'The co-pilot was in too much of a hurry,' the pilot apologized.[9]

Alexander ordered the pilots to fly on until they spotted land. But Alexander and his battalion were out of luck. They and the rest of the paras involved in this first night combat jump in the history of the US Army were scattered all over the island.

Their commander, Colonel 'Slim Jim' Gavin, who had worked himself up from private to colonel in twenty years of army service, now found himself commanding exactly five men instead of the thousands he had anticipated. Undeterred, the Colonel set off, slipping through the shadows cast by the olive groves, listening to the angry snap-and-crackle of small arms fire in the distance. Suddenly he heard a man whistling. As he recorded later, 'After twenty years of military service, I was about to meet The Enemy face to face!'[10]

The 'Enemy' turned out to be a terrified Italian soldier who had obviously heard the rumours spread by the Germans that the American paras were long-term convicts who had been granted their freedom if they became paratroopers. Now as one of the little band, a Captain Vandervoort, who had taken an Intelligence course and knew how to deal with prisoners, stepped forward to slice through the Italian's belt and then a fly button so that he would have to hold up his trousers and be unable to escape, the Italian quivered with fear. To Gavin, Vandervoort's knife glistening in the moonlight 'looked a foot long'. Vandervoort succeeded in cutting through their prisoner's belt but, when he reached for a fly button, the Italian began to scream so loudly that Gavin felt he could have been 'heard all the way to Rome'. The Italian thought the American 'criminals' were going to castrate him and fought back frantically, grabbing the knife from Vandervoort. Together they fell to the ground in 'a kicking, yelling, fighting mass'. But in the end the prisoner managed to escape, disappearing into the darkness, his manhood intact, leaving Gavin 'madder than hell'. His first taste of 'combat' after twenty years in the Army had been highly unsuccessful but soon he would be experiencing the real thing, storming the high ground at Biazza Ridge with 200 paras he had managed to round up and losing a staggering 165 men in the process.

The surviving gliders of the British 1st Airborne Division were now coming into land – straight into the Italian flak! One, hit in the wing, was spiralling down like a shot bird. Another, crashing on the rocky shore of the island, was set ablaze by an incendiary grenade. As the glider's ammunition started to explode the trapped pilot resolved he would rather commit suicide than burn to death.

'For God's sake, get me a rifle,' he cried out. His co-pilot tried to reach one, but at that same instant an ammunition box exploded and shattered his arm. Somehow, however, he managed to get his friend out of the wreckage and together they collapsed on the rocks. Virtually every one of the surviving gliders crash-landed as they smashed into the high stone walls typical of Sicily. Brakes shrieking, fuselage trembling frantically as two thousand pounds of men and equipment hit the stony soil, the pilots fought madly as their frail aircraft raced towards the ground. Gliders were upended. Others were ripped apart, scattering shattered bodies in their wake. Some slammed into the walls and crumpled like banana skins.

However, the survivors poured out of their wrecked craft and went into action, not knowing where they were, just heading straight for the sound of the battle. Colonel Henniker, the Division's Chief Engineer, rounded up other senior divisional officers and their batmen and led a spirited charge to capture an Italian coastal battery. Even the divisional padre joined in the attack! Some of those who had ditched in the sea also joined in. One glider which had landed 250 yards aware from the shore came under vicious Italian machine-gun fire but the men it contained of the South Staffordshire Regiment swam ashore. There they crawled under twenty feet of barbed wire with tracer bullets from an Italian pillbox only 100 yards away cutting the night sky just above their heads. By the time the six survivors returned to their battalion the following day they had captured two pillboxes and three machine-guns, and taken twenty-one Italian prisoners, complete with their anti-tank gun.

In the end, of the 2,000 soldiers who had set out with the largest gliderborne force ever launched from North Africa, only a mere handful, a platoon of the 2nd South Staffordshires, reached the objective – the bridge at Ponte Grande. But they succeeded in capturing it intact and holding it until the next morning. At the cost of three hundred men, most of them dying alone and far out at sea without having fired a single shot, the route to Syracuse had been cleared for Montgomery's Eighth Army.

The loudspeakers crackled into life: 'Attention Serial One. To your boat station – move!' Everywhere in the fleet which was carrying the Eighth Army the seasick soldiers

Landing craft approaching the beaches.

began to struggle into their equipment. This was it. They were going to land. Hearts beating faster, they began to file obediently up on to the decks. But there had been a sudden transformation. The storm had vanished. The sirocco, which had started hundreds of miles away in the Sahara Desert, had ceased as abruptly as it had started. Now a breeze gently ruffled the surface of the water under a heaven full of stars.

The serials began to move in a stiff-legged gait to the boats, each man's fingers hooked in the web belt of the man in front of him, platoon linked to platoon until a whole company coiled in and out across the deck like a human snake. Laden like pack animals with rifles, automatics, picks, shovels, packs – almost a hundred pounds in all – the clambered down the swaying rope ladders and cargo nets to the bobbing landing barges below.

Already the commandos, spearheading the Eighth Army's assault, were ashore, *on the wrong beach*, disappearing into the darkness to find an elusive Italian enemy, crying the password 'Desert Rats' to one another, followed by the bloodthirsty countersign, 'Kill Italians'. Behind them the infantry of the 50th, 51st and 5th British Infantry Divisions, plus those of the Canadian 1st Division, followed. The future Sir Alec Guinness, then a lieutenant in the Royal Navy in charge of a landing barge, ferried men of the 51st Highland Division ashore: 'Argyll and Sutherland Highlanders – men who had been in the desert since El Alamein, wonderful types physically and full of charm and guts.'[11]

Bombardier Castle, who had been imprisoned by the Germans (twice), French and Spaniards during his long odyssey through Occupied Europe, was not so entranced by the infantry of his Division. 'I had a hole in my shorts pocket and as we filed to the boats I heard something fall through it on to the deck. It was my lucky half-crown which I'd had with me all the time I'd been on the trot. Before I could bend down to pick it up, it had gone. Some Jock had nicked it. Keen hearing those infantry had in them days!' Disgruntled, he followed the rest of his serial to the boats, a reluctant hero if there ever was one.

Lance-Corporal Pinder of the Fifth Division, who had spent a good night after a generous rum ration issued to all ranks in the Fifth, was entranced by the view. Straight ahead he could see the majestic outline of Mount Etna, making a fitting backdrop for the flak spurting into the sky above Syracuse and Augusta. 'I forgot all about what was to come. After all, the Canadians had been slaughtered at the Dieppe landing the year before and Sicily could have been just as bad. I was just like a tourist in khaki, gawking at the view and going "oh", "ah"!'

By this time the Canadians of the First Division, already in the water, were more concerned with finding their way than with the fear of being slaughtered as their unfortunate compatriots had been in 1942. Many of their boats were lost and Lieutenant Mowat found himself steering his barge, after the cockney sailor in charge had given up. Surprisingly enough, the 'Hasty Pee' found a beach and prepared for action. 'This was the moment toward which all my years of army training had been building. It was *my* moment and, if I seized it with somewhat palsied hands, at least I did my best.'

'Revolver in hand, Tommy gun slung over my shoulder, web equipment bulging with grenades and ammo, tin hat pulled firmly down around my ears, I sprinted to the edge of the ramp shouting, "Follow me, men", and leapt off *into eight feet of water!*'

Later, however, the fun evaporated from that comic landing. Trying to dry himself out on shore, Mowat saw one of his men, who had been terrified of the assault, marching off the barge as if on ceremonial parade at Aldershot, 'except that his eyes were screwed tight shut'. At that instant a cluster of mortar bombs fell out the sky and the frightened soldier was hit 'marching blindly to Valhalla'.[12]

But, after that initial shock, the going proved exceedingly easy. As the Canadians cautiously approached the little town of Pozzallo, weapons at the ready, they were surprised to hear the sound of cheering and singing, as if some kind of Sicilian festival was taking place. In a way it was, for the Sicilians were celebrating their own surrender. Minutes before, a small party under the command of RN Lieutenant Peter Griffiths had come ashore from the two small destroyers anchored off the coast, HMS *Blankney* and HMS *Brissenden*, the naval men also expecting trouble. Instead they were welcomed by the local postman, who, being the only Sicilian present in uniform, promptly surrendered the place to the Royal Navy.

As the Canadians advanced to the centre of Pozzallo to the accompaniment of the civilians' cheers, their officer was received by a smiling Griffiths who formally handed over the town to the Canadians, though, as Griffiths said later, 'The ceremonial lost a bit of dignity through my having a couple of water melons and a glass of wine in my hands!'

Now the British divisions were streaming ashore, hindered only by the Italians' artillery fire and the mines. So far the two battalions of the Black Watch in the first wave of the 51st Division's assault had suffered only one casualty – a lance-corporal of the First Battalion who had died of seasickness! A landing craft of the Seventh Battalion discharged its cargo right in the midst of a nest of Italian anti-personnel mines and an officer and ten men were wounded. But these were the only casualties. Some while later the Black Watch's 5th Battalion followed, without a single casualty. The Italians had fled. As the Black Watch's history records, 'No enemy willing to fight was found for four days'.[13]

Indeed the opposition was so light that, like the Black Watch, some units deliberately looked for trouble. A group of commandos, accompanied by a pioneer detachment, finally thought they had found it in the shape of an Italian pillbox. The commando officer said to his pioneer colleague, 'All right, old man, I think we can manage this one without your chaps.'

'I beg your pardon,' the pioneer replied. 'It looks like a job for us.'

In the end they tossed for the 'honour' of assaulting the pillbox and the pioneer officer won. But as the pioneers finished their preparations for the assault a white flag appeared and a group of Italian soldiers came out.

'Damn,' the pioneer officer cursed. 'The windy bastards! All that training and all this gelignite and look what they've gone and done!'

The commando officer suggested, 'Tickle 'em up with the Bren, old boy, and see what happens.' This was duly done and the Italians fled back inside once more and the assault could go ahead as planned. While the disappointed commandos brewed up on the hillside above, the pioneers duly blew up the 'defenders' and their pillbox most efficiently before clambering up the hill to join their green-bereted comrades for breakfast.[14]

Thus by the end of that Saturday Montgomery's Eighth Army had taken all its objectives. The veteran 50th Division had captured Avola and Noto. The Canadians and the Highlanders were pushing out of the bridgehead, suffering only a few casualties. The 5th Division, after capturing Cassibile with the help of the 3rd Commando, was now entering Syracuse, the greatest prize of all, a key port completely undamaged, ready to accept the next wave of invaders and their supplies for the campaign that lay ahead of them. For less than one thousand men, killed, wounded and captured, the British Army had returned to Europe once more, three years after being chased out so ignominiously at Dunkirk in June 1940.

The American invasion beach at Gela presented a dismal sight. More than two hundred assault craft wallowed in the surf after burning out their engines while coming ashore. Bulldozers chugged back and forth moving supplies. More than seven hundred DUKWS plied from ship to ship fetching more supplies which would be urgently needed once the march inland started.

A few hours before, the US Army's premier division, the 1st Infantry, the Big Red One*, as it called itself proudly, had landed here in mass confusion. In one landing craft, in charge of a Major Grant, not one single man had moved when the ramp had clattered down.

'Jump off!' Grant had yelled. 'You want to get killed here? *Get on the beach!*'

He leapt ashore, followed by a single GI, but the others held back stubbornly, waiting to see what happened. When nothing did, they followed the irate Major.

*From its divisional insignia which was a large red one.

Troops of the 51st Highland Division coming ashore.

Left: A British M. P. directs armoured traffic, advancing inland from the beach-head.

Right: Audie Murphy, America's most decorated combat soldier of World War Two.

Now they and their comrades of this highly individualistic division, commanded by General Allen and his deputy, General Roosevelt, who had a bad case of arthritis and was drinking heavily to kill the pain, started to straggle up the beach. No one seemed to know what to do. There were no Italians and no Germans. So far not a single shot had been fired in anger. The invasion had hardly begun and Italian resistance, or so it seemed, was collapsing all along the Sicilian coast. But trouble was on the way. General Guzzoni at his Headquarters at Enna had ordered Italian and German tanks to attack the Americans who had taken Gela. The men of the 'Big Red One' straggling inland in large unruly bunches were heading straight for serious trouble.

The situation was little different on the beach at Scoglitti where General Middleton's completely green 45th Infantry Division had landed. The landing itself had been total confusion, with units split up and landing on the wrong beaches. Some fifty per cent of the landing craft used were lost, but there were few signs of the enemy, apart from some scattered machine-gunning. But the 45th's engineers now got completely out of hand. As the infantry started to trudge inland, they neglected their job of clearing the beach. Instead they started to loot the stores, even rifling personal kits. Later General Patton court-martialled their commanding officer, but, in the meantime, the conditions on some of the 45th's beaches became so clogged and uncoordinated that all operations there had to be suspended. Unknowingly the 'Thunderbirds', as the men of the Division were known on account of their Indian thunderbird insignia, were marching into the coming battle without any logistical support. Not that it seemed really to matter; the opposition seemed laughable.

1st Lieutenant Thomas Akers and his driver Private Weaver were first into Scoglitti, but as they entered the small seaside town all they could see were Italian soldiers. 'Oops,' said the Lieutenant, 'turn around, Weaver!'

They disappeared down the coastal road once more until they found twenty-five more dusty Thunderbirds. With these men Akers returned to the town, where, as he recorded at the time, 'I went to the centre of the square and drew a swastika in the dirt. Then I stamped it out with my foot. The people came running out of the houses, waving white handkerchiefs and soon the soldiers came too. They threw down their guns and surrendered. We brought back about fifty of them and they all seemed glad to be with us.'[15]

Subsequently the *45th Division News*, which boasted it was the first 'US newspaper to be printed in Nazi Europe', headlined the Lieutenant's tale as 'Dance in Dirt Captures Prisoners'. To the average American soldier coming off the beaches this first invasion of Hitler's *Festung Europa* all seemed a bit of a joke.

It seemed little different on the Third Division's beaches near Licata. Advancing with the forward infantry, newspaperman Jack Belden, crouched behind a stone wall, listened to the roar of motors getting closer. 'We waited in ambush beneath the wall, taut and silent. Like a crackling fire, rifles and machine guns split the air. Lined in the shooting light of tracer bullets we saw wheel spokes and the red flashes of bullets shooting through them.

'A louder explosion shook the wall where we huddled. Lieutenant Thomas Rodgers was firing his anti-tank gun.

A flash of flame tore the darkness and spot-lighted the careering truck and the white frightened face of the driver.... The night was upside-down with shouts, bullets and moving figures. We could not know what was happening. A private clapped his hand on somebody's shoulder and said, "What unit you from buddy?"

A voice answered, "*Mein Gott!*"

A shot rang out. Someone howled, then gurgled.'[16]

Later that morning a group of the Third Division's men, the 'Rock of the Marne' men*, was taking a break, enjoying the sunshine on a hill overlooking the beach, when a shell landed on the next hill, sending up a mushroom of black smoke. It was too far away to frighten the soldiers and one man, imitating Jack Benny's gravel-voiced black servant Rochester, shouted, 'Hey, boss a cahgo of crap just landed on Pigtail Ridge!'

The sally was greeted by a burst of laughter. One who laughed was a small, freckled-face youngster, the son of poor Texan share-croppers, who was burning to get into action in spite of the fact that he looked more like 14 then the 19 years of age he was.

The second shell was different. The boy suddenly felt 'something terrible and immediate about its whistle which makes my scalp start prickling. I grab my helmet and flip over on my stomach. The explosion is thunderous. Steel fragments whine and the ground seems to jump up and hit me in the face.'

Then there was silence again and the company wag began in his Rochester voice, 'Hey boss ...' He stopped

* A title gained from the 3rd Division's stand on the Marne in 1918.

dead. A redheaded soldier had tumbled from the rocks. Blood was trickling from his mouth and nose.

Later the boy from Texas asked who he was and was told he was 'a guy named Griffin. I got likkered up with him once in Africa. Told me he was married and had a couple of kids.'

'He could have stayed out,' someone else said. 'But he volunteered. Had to get into the big show.'

As the baby-faced boy plodded on he pondered on the first violent death he had seen. 'So it happens as easy as that. You sit on a quiet slope with chin in hand. In the distance a gun slams and the next minute you are dead'.[17]

Before the war was over the innocents of the 3rd 'Rock of the Marne' Division would see many, many more violent deaths. In fact, by May, 1945, the Division would experience a staggering 30,000 battle casualties! The baby-faced boy, burning for action, would become America's most decorated soldier. Wounded three times, holder of the USA's most coveted decoration, the Medal of Honor, Audie Murphy would survive to become a Hollywood star. But he, just like the rest of the innocents, would pay the price. To the day he died – violently, just like he had lived – he could never sleep without a loaded pistol beneath his pillow. 'There was the nightmare, the recurrent nightmare. I would dream I am on a hill and all these faceless people are charging up at me. I am holding a Garand rifle, the kind of a rifle that I used to take apart blindfolded. And in the dream, every time I shoot one of these people, a piece of the rifle flies off until all I have left is the trigger guard!'[18]

So it had been easy after all. The Americans had fought their first battle in Europe, if it really could be called a battle, and won it without even trying. It looked as if it was going to be 'roses, roses all the way', as that bar-fly in Cairo had sung to Sergeant Irwin Shaw just before the invasion.[19] But the roses were to be seldom and well-scattered. Not many of the victorious young Americans, Canadians and Britons, who had landed on the coast of Sicily that day would ever see the end of the road. By then they would be long dead, wounded or captured. Others would follow them, Frenchmen, Poles, Greeks, South Africans, Rhodesians, New Zealanders, Sikhs and Hindus, Brazilians, even Japanese, in the shape of the American Nisei regiment. For two years to come the battle in Italy would be waged. As one of the best of the war correspondents who accompanied them on that long haul up the boot of Italy, Eric Sevareid, depicted them: 'They understood the war's meaning no more than others – which is to say, hardly at all. Their country, their families were not in mortal danger now, and yet they plodded on.... They did not hate Germans.... They did not hate the concept of Fascism because they did not understand it. But they struggled on, climbing the hills, wading the rivers until they dropped ... and died in ignorant glory.'[20]

'This is the first time in this campaign I earned my pay'

It was Sunday, D-Day plus one. Just after six Brigadier-General Roosevelt, who would be dead within a year, went to visit one of the forward command posts of the 1st Infantry Division. It was another beautiful July morning, already very warm, and the heat haze was rippling in waves over the burnt hills. But General Roosevelt had other things on his mind than the weather and the scenery that morning. He was worried about the enemy. Yesterday the Italians had attacked the 'Big Red One' with light tanks, but had been beaten off easily. Now there were rumours that the Germans themselves were bearing down upon the American bridgehead in Sicily and as yet there were only two tanks ashore in the First Division's area; and most of the Division's anti-tank guns had been lost the previous day when a landing ship carrying them had exploded.

General Roosevelt had barely reached the command post of Colonel Bowen's 26th Regiment when the balloon went up. At 6.35 Italian dive bombers began to fall out of the clear blue sky and bomb Gela. Ten minutes later a hurried phone call from his 3rd Battalion informed Bowen that German medium tanks were attacking the unit and had already succeeded in breaking through in several places. Roosevelt acted immediately. He called the Divisional Commander, General Terry Allen.

'Terry, look,' Roosevelt said urgently, 'the situation is not very comfortable out here. The 3rd Battalion has been attacked by tanks and has been penetrated. If we could get that company of medium tanks, it sure would help.'

Allen promised he would do everything he could and hung up.

An hour passed and no tanks appeared. The situation began to deteriorate rapidly. Roosevelt called the Divisional Commander again.

'Situation not so good,' he told Allen. 'Out of communication with our 3rd Battalion. Terry, any news of what's to be expected? Now, what about those medium tanks? Goddamnit. I'll come back and pull 'em out myself! I'll return as soon as the situation becomes clarified.'[1] As he laid down the phone, unaware that most of the US 2nd Armored Division, to which the tanks belonged, were still at sea, soon to be subject to the second phase of the German counter-attack, General Roosevelt realized that something had to be done before the 'Big Red One' was torn to pieces – *and done soon!*

The Commander of the US Seventh Army, to which the 1st Infantry Division belonged, General George Patton, now made his celebrated landing on enemy soil. Immaculately dressed in tailor-made riding breeches, tie knotted, pistol in open holster, binoculars (naturally jumbo-sized), with a big cigar stuck between his tight lips, he waded to the shore – *backwards*! He was shooting the memorable scene of his landing with his own camera!

But, in spite of the histrionics, Patton soon made his presence felt. Almost immediately he realised just how dangerous the situation was on the American beaches. As he later told 'old ABC' Cunningham, 'Admiral, I was no longer in command of an Army, but merely a reconnaissance unit.'[2]

Arriving in Gela, already under German attack, he could see a horizon packed with the squat black shapes of Mark III German tanks and seven of them seemed to be bearing down on him personally.

Patton spotted a young naval ensign with a radio and shouted above the roar of the gunfire, 'Hey you with the radio!'

The sailor called, 'Can I help you, sir?'

Patton, who had little respect for the US Navy, bellowed, 'Sure as hell. If you can connect with your goddamn Navy, tell them for God's sake to drop some shellfire on the road.' He pointed to the dusty white road ahead.[3]

The ensign started to call the ships.

Meanwhile the 1st Division's front was crumbling rapidly. Colonel Bowen signalled that he was 'dispersing' his command post. In truth he was forcing cooks, clerks, drivers – anyone capable of holding a rifle – into the line with his First Battalion to meet the renewed German onslaught. Behind him the Division's artillery commander lined up every gun he had on the dunes. They would fire until their ammunition was exhausted.

Then the Division's 18th Infantry Regiment was attacked by forty German tanks. A little later it was the turn of the 16th Regiment. Most of the regimental staff were hit. Two battalion commanders became casualties and the 3rd Battalion was now being commanded by a 28-year-old captain, Boyce Denno, who was barely three

A German Mark III tank moves up against Allied positions.

24

years out of the US Military Academy, West Point. Someone signalled the regiment's harassed commander, Colonel Taylor, 'We are being overrun by tanks!' Taylor signalled back, 'Everybody stays just where he is! Under no circumstances will anyone be pulled back. Take cover from tanks. Don't let anything else get through. The Cannon Company is on the way. *Everyone is to hold present positions.*'[4] But the Cannon Company did not come and the German tanks had almost reached the beach. General Bradley, II Corps Commander, who was running the battle from a jeep sitting on a rubber cushion on account of his piles, called Allen and asked, 'Are you in trouble, Terry?'

Bravely General Allen radioed back, 'We haven't begun to fight. Our artillery hasn't been overrun yet.'[5]

But by this time the German tanks were within 500 yards of those guns and they were beginning to run out of ammunition. All naval personnel on the beach unloading supplies were ordered to grab a gun and flesh out the First Division's line. Then, when it seemed that the last American positions would be overrun by the German tanks, the guns of the US cruiser *Boise* thundered into action out to sea. The enemy tanks reeled to a stop as the navy gunners picked them off one by one.

By noon US tanks started to arrive at the hard-pressed Gela bridgehead and a relieved Patton told himself that the crisis was over. Later he would write in his diary, 'This is the first day in this campaign that I think I earned my pay.'[6]

On that day when the flamboyant Seventh Army Commander felt he had earned his pay, the first war crimes occurred on Sicily, crimes which could have been attributed to Patton and which, in the end, were.

Just before the green 45th Division had sailed for Sicily

Patton had given them one of his typical 'blood and guts' pep talks, full of good advice and profanity. He quoted a friend of his, the diminutive General Scott who was fond of boasting, 'By God, I could lick Joe Louis if he wasn't permitted to attack me!' and pointed out that 'the way to prevent the enemy from attacking you is to attack him.... Keep right on attacking him. This prevents him from getting set.'[7]

He also warned them, as one of his listeners, Albert Wedemyr, recalled, 'To be very careful when the Germans or Italians raised their arms as if they wanted to surrender. He stated that sometimes the enemy would do this, throwing our men off guard. The enemy soldiers had on several occasions shot our unsuspecting men or had thrown grenades at them'.[8] He went on to warn the 'Thunderbirds' to watch out for treachery and to 'kill the S.O.B.s' if they were not certain of their intentions during a surrender.

Now, after breaking out of the bridgehead at Scoglitti, the men of the 45th Division met the German tankers head-on. The fighting was as rough and tough as Patton had predicted. Soon rumours of atrocities began to circulate throughout the first regiment in the assault. According to Lieutenant George Appell, 'German atrocities were rampant and so were ours in retaliation. My driver was captured, was tied to a tree and shot by the Goerings*. They would rise without weapons, waving their hands in the air and shouting 'Kamerad'. Then, when we went to round them up, they would fall flat and other Germans concealed behind them would open up on us. We lost many men due to this. Casualties were severe – and the procedure of taking prisoners was abandoned on both sides.'[9]

In the case of the 45th Division that certainly seemed to be true. British war correspondent Alexander Clifford saw men of 45th mow down a truckload of German prisoners that day as they climbed down at Comiso airfield, killing all but two or three. Then he saw them kill sixty Italian prisoners the same way. Clark Lee reported further incidents. However, these war crimes were never followed up.

On 14 July, though, one was. On that day a company of the 45th's 180th Regimental Combat Team was ambushed by the Germans. After a bitter fight, which lasted three hours, the surviving forty-five Germans were rounded up, five allegedly in mufti. The officer in charge, a Captain Jerry Compton, was so overwrought and angry that he had the prisoners lined up against a barn and machine-gunned to death.

On the same day a Sergeant Barry West was ordered to take thirty-six German prisoners to the rear. It was getting dark and the sergeant grew nervous. He machine-gunned them by the roadside, killing the lot.

The two incidents couldn't be hushed up and were reported to the Corps Commander, General Bradley. He, in his turn, reported them to Patton. Patton noted

cynically in his diary that Bradley said Captain Compton had shot the prisoners down 'in cold blood and also in ranks, an even greater error'.[10]† Airily Patton dismissed the matter, 'Tell the officer,' he told Bradley, 'to certify the men were snipers or had attempted to escape....'[11]

Later, when General Bradley ordered an offical investigation, Patton wrote scornfully to his wife, 'Some fair-haired boys are trying to say I kill too many prisoners. Yet the same people cheer at the far greater killing of Japs. Well, the more I kill, the fewer men I lost, but they don't think of that. Sometimes I think that I will quit and join a monastery.'[12]

He didn't, and a year later the two incidents caught up with him when both soldiers pleaded at their courts-martial that Patton had incited them to commit the atrocities in his pre-Invasion speech. Somehow Patton weathered the ensuing storm, as he was to do successfully in that other scandal that was soon to take place in Sicily. As for the two accused, they were finally let off and expunged their shame by allowing themselves to be killed in action.

But it was not only the Americans who were committing atrocities. Four hours after the Germans began their counter-attack on land, the *Luftwaffe* began bombing the huge invasion fleet out at sea, which stretched for *over forty miles!* A God-given target for the German pilots.

'The enemy's favourite trick,' Lieutenant Davenport on the *Tetcott* recorded in his diary, 'seems to be for fighter-bombers to sweep down from behind the hills and drop their bombs on the shipping, then machine-gunning along the line and make off before our own fighters can reach them. Spitfires from Malta are very much in evidence and there are usually one or two flights overhead.'

Gunner 'Sunny' Hale, aboard HMS *Nubian*, noted in his 'Sicilian Diary': 'The ack-ack from the ships and shore was terrific and the bombs dropped did little damage to shipping. One ammunition ship was set ablaze and four aircraft brought down.'

The Stukas fell out of the skies like evil black hawks, hurtling down at 300 miles an hour, sirens howling. At the same time, Junkers 88s zoomed in at mast-top level, torpedoes flashing from their bellies. The escort ships took up the challenge. The sky was peppered with anti-aircraft shells. But still the *Luftwaffe* pilots pressed home their attacks. A US destroyer was hit and started to sink rapidly. A Junkers 88 fell out of the sky and plunged into the water, sending up a great spout. Ships of the British, Indian, American, Dutch, Greek and Polish navies kept up the tremendous barrage, sending more and more enemy planes into the sea. Some German pilots decided

† Shot thus, it could not be argued later that the prisoners had been killed in battle.

* The Hermann Goering Armoured Division.

it was time to look for easier targets and found them in the hospital ships which had been loading both Allied and enemy wounded all afternoon. As dusk approached the hospital ships, well defined by red crosses, turned on their lights, as required by international law, as well as the electrically-illuminated red crosses on their sides and decks. Nevertheless a flight of German planes turned their attention to the 8,000-ton British hospital ship *Talamba*, two miles off the coast south of Syracuse.

The correspondent of the *Daily Telegraph* watched in horror as the ship received a direct hit and 'saw the *Talamba* go under ... her nursing sisters, her wounded and her crew crying out in the night for help.... As we twisted and turned we passed close to the *Talamba*. Between bomb bursts and gunfire I could hear the shrill calls of women and hoarse shouts of men in the water.'[13]

A surgeon had just completed the amputation of a soldier's leg when the ship was rocked by explosions. Hastily binding the stump, he secured the unconscious man to a stretcher and lowered him into the water. Meanwhile the British matron, Violet Innes, shepherded all the wounded in her care into a lifeboat, 'without even wetting her veil' as one eyewitness put it. In spite of a broken leg, another sister, Miss Makepeace, managed to keep afloat for ninety minutes until she was rescued. Then the *Talamba* suddenly reared out of the water by the bows and slid to the bottom.

After such a day the ships' gunners were understandably trigger-happy. Thus it was that, forty minutes after the last German raid, another tragedy took place, when 504th Airborne Regimental Combat Team, commanded by Colonel Reuben Tucker, started to fly over the beachhead to reinforce Colonel Gavin's hard-pressed paras further inland. There were 144 Dakotas carrying 2,008 men heading for their first combat mission, led by a fire-brand of a commander who knew no fear. As they grew close to their objective the commander gave the order to his men to stand up and prepare to jump. Suddenly, down below in the Allied fleet, a single machine gun opened up. It seemed to act as a signal, for suddenly guns started firing everywhere, not only on the ships, but on the shore as well. The heavy transports tried desperately to take evasive actions. Signal flares lit the night sky, but the gunners were too carried away to notice. The first planes were hit and plunged towards the sea in flames. Troopers bailed out frantically. Some were shot as they dangled at the ends of their chutes. Others plummeted straight into the sea. In the end twenty-three American planes were shot down and thirty-seven were badly damaged. Of the 2,000-odd men involved, 318 became casualties in thirty minutes.

'Why did I have to go on deck?' a distraught Machinist's Mate Herbert Blair told the press later. 'Hit after hit we

American airborne troops and a British officer confer in Avola.

score until ship [aeroplane] after ship bursts into flames or falls spiralling into the sea. But something is wrong. From the wounded ships parachutes come fluttering, some to fall in flames into the sea ... others to billow out in slow descent. Then some trigger-happy gunner aboard another ship decides to pick off the supposedly helpless Jerries. Soon every gunner is firing away at the troopers who dangle limply beneath the umbrellas of their chutes. "Cease firing. Cease firing! Stand by to pick up survivors. Stand by to pick up survivors."

Only then does the dreadful realization descend like a sledgehammer upon us. We have wantonly, though inadvertently, slaughtered our own gallant buddies ... I feel sick in body and soul.'[14]

That night one troop-carrier pilot was reported to have said, 'Evidently the safest place for us over Sicily tonight would have been over enemy territory.'

He was only too right; there was more to come.

Now Montgomery's Eighth Army prepared to break out of their bridgehead, but in order to do so a bridge had to be secured across the River Simeto. This bridge, the Ponte di Primasole, carried the main road across the river

Primasole Bridge, the scene of bitter fighting during the advance on Catania.

towards the town of Catania, which had to be captured as a vital base for the final advance on the city of Messina on the northern tip of Sicily. If Messina were taken before the enemy could retreat across the Straits, a great victory would be achieved and the enemy's position in Southern Italy would be seriously weakened. In spite of the fact that so far all airborne operations conducted in Sicily had ended disastrously, it was now decided to capture the Primasole Bridge by a *coup de main*, using parachute troops. Thus it was that on 13 July 113 transports and sixteen gliders of Brigadier Lathbury's 1st Parachute Brigade, in all 1,866 men, most of them veterans of the fighting in North Africa, set off with high hopes for Sicily.

Again, as the airborne armada approached the island, the trigger-happy gunners of the fleet anchored below opened up. Lieutenant Stanforth of the Royal Engineers, flying in a plane called by its American crew '*Miss Carriage*', found himself in the middle of the barrage.

'Wham! Our world suddenly turned upside down and then blew up with a roar, opening a yawning chasm beneath our feet. Everything was momentarily black ... revolving planets ... plunging meteors ... the sound of tinkling glass ... the acrid smell of high explosive.... Then my vision cleared and we were lying together in a heap on the matted floor.'[15]

Somehow the pilot managed to right the plane and they flew on through their own fire. But not all the American planes managed it. Private Mick Tucker of the 2nd Parachute Battalion recalled forty years later seeing 'a Dakota simply fall apart. It was caught in a cone of searchlights and the buggers below – we didn't then know they were our own people – concentrated on it. The ack-ack shot it to bits. The wings came off, the nose crumpled and it went straight down into the drink. Nobody got out.'

Not only were the Allied planes shot down by the nervous gunners below, but the intense flak put the American pilots off target. Again they started to drop their loads too short or over the sea. In the end, of the 1,856 men who had set out that night from Africa, a mere 295 reached the bridge which was their objective. Under the command of a Colonel Pearson, the paras hastily set up their defences on and around the bridge. Then a panting para struggled up to Pearson with a strange story. He had dropped just short of the Italian-held airfield of Catania not far away and in the confusion he had bumped into another paratrooper who was carrying a German Schmeisser machine-pistol!

Not far away Lieutenant Stainforth was making a similar strange discovery. 'We stumbled across two square-shaped containers, painted white, but quite unlike any British type. One lay open and had a tubular steel towing-handle and two rubber-tyred wheels. That struck a familiar note! I turned it over and read "*V Fallschirmjaeger Regt*".'[16] They were German. What did it mean?

Dawn came. The sun was rising in the east, a blood-red ball. Slowly it started to burn away the mist over the river. Near the bridge the weary paras were 'stood down'. Taking off their smocks, they warmed their stiff bodies in the sun's rays. The heat increased. Water became a problem. The paras sought the shade. Still no sign of the enemy.

At ten o'clock precisely two Focke-Wulf 190 fighters appeared. They circled the bridge slowly, obviously trying to find out what was going on down there. Suddenly 'the leader dipped his wing and came streaking down and we hastily shrank into the cover of our holes. A long crackling burst ploughed into the farm building opposite. Then the other plane followed in for about half-a-dozen runs. Sometimes they dived and concentrated on the farm, at others they came racing up the river bank, plastering the vineyards and approaches to the bridge. A thick cloud of dust rose and hung motionless in the air. A haystack caught fire and crackled merrily.'[17]

In the end the two enemy fighters disappeared in the direction of Catania and, as Lieutenant Stainforth recorded, 'Life went back to normal and the drowsiness of the morning returned upon us all.'[18]

'They started to stonk us about eleven, I think,' Private Tucker remembered long afterwards. 'The mortar bombs began to creep towards us across the river. Didn't worry us much. We were well dug-in. Then the Spandaus opened up. Bullets were flying everywhere. We just ducked, kept our heads low and then there they were – *Jerries*! But they weren't wearing the usual coal-scuttle helmets. They were wearing rimless ones like our own and they were dressed in smocks just like us. Next to me my mate yelled, "*Christ, Mick, they're Jerry paratroopers*".'[19]

They were indeed. In the night the Germans had dropped a parachute brigade near the river, intending to block the British advance into the plain. Now the men on the bridge were to be attacked by the élite of the German Army, Colonel Heilmann's 3rd Parachute Regiment of the 1st German Parachute Division.

Two hours after the Red Berets had beaten off Heilmann's first attack on the bridge one of the few wireless sets which had managed to survive the drop crackled surprisingly into life. Its short resurrection lasted only four minutes, but it was enough time to let them know the British 4th Armoured Brigade was battling its way along the road to link up, but the opposition was tough. Then the set went dead and stayed obstinately dead for the rest of the action.

The hours passed. Still the tanks did not arrive. Time and again Heilmann's *Fallschirmjaeger* attacked with desperate bravery. In the breaks the weary Red Berets, short of water and with no appetite for food, lay at the bottom of their littered trenches panting like weary dogs.

'The day passed slowly,' Peter Stainforth recalled. 'Sometimes the enemy held off to draw breath, giving us a respite of an hour or so before battle opened once more. But they always came on again as fiercely as before, crawling down the avenues of grapevines and working closer and closer towards the bridge. As the afternoon wore on their attacks gained weight as reinforcements arrived and heavier and heavier support weapons were brought into play.'[20]

On the northern side of the bridge the Germans were slowly but surely gaining the upper hand. Brigadier Lathbury, the Brigade Commander, himself wounded in the leg and buttocks, ordered the survivors to withdraw and help defend the southern end. He could already hear the clatter of German tanks rolling up. Reluctantly the Red Berets began to pull back. As Corporal Stanion, one of the hundred or so survivors of the defending force, began to withdraw he was hit in the neck and knocked out. When he came to he found he was surrounded by Germans. He dashed into some reeds and again bumped into two Germans who took him prisoner.

'I sat there for an hour or two while they argued among themselves as to who was to take me back. Then apparently our chaps started firing into the reeds. Two Jerries got hit in the head straight away. The others ran back and I crawled through the reeds which were smouldering in parts. I got down to a point where they went into the water, into which I slipped and dog-paddled over to the other side. I lay there waiting for darkness to come.'

It was only a matter of time before Heilmann's *Fallschirmjaeger* recaptured the bridge. Still, the defenders hoped desperately that the Eighth Army would arrive and relieve them. Captain Gammon of the 1st Parachute Battalion, defending a pillbox, watched the German 88mm cannon work over the pillbox next to him.' To this day I swear as each round of solid shot struck it, it heeled over and bounced up again. At any moment the 8th Army must come! At any moment their armoured cars would sweep down the road and up to the bridge, but time wore on and no Eighth Army came.'[21]

Finally Lathbury, who would soon be evacuated due to wounds and loss of blood, gave his final order.

'The Brigadier has given the order to abandon the bridge,' Peter Stainforth noted at the time. 'Collect as many men as you can and make your way back to our own forces over the hills to the south. Our tanks can't be very far away now. Clear out of here and go like hell before the enemy comes through!'[22]

The survivors needed no urging. They vanished into the evening gloom and Primasole Bridge was German once more. In just over a year's time the weary survivors of that day – Lieutenant Stainforth, Private Tucker, Brigadier Lathbury – would go through the same horror, the same frustration, the same sense of let-down once again, but this time none of them would escape. The Bridge at Arnhem in September, 1944, would see the end of them all.

On the third night of the American landing Colonel 'Monk' Dickson reported to General Bradley that an Italian soldier had been captured near Bradley's Command Post wearing civilian clothes.

'Not an agent, I hope?' Bradley asked, barely interested.

'No sir,' Dickson replied. 'Not this bird, General. He's just a little *paesano* and he's scared to death. Told us he was home on furlough when the Americans came and it seemed like a good time to stay home on furlough.'

'Can't blame him for that,' Bradley said.

'No. There are probably thousands of others that would like to change places with him. They don't care about the war. They'd much sooner go home and get to work.'

'Then why do we bother to lock them up?' Bradley asked.

'Beats me, General.'

'Monk, why don't we see what happens if we pass the word around that any Sicilians wishing to desert may go back to their homes? We won't pick them up as prisoners of war.'[23]

Patton, who thought the Sicilians worse than the detested 'A-rabs', didn't approve of the plan, but already it was too late. In their thousands the disgruntled Sicilians deserted the Italian Army and went home to get on with the job of living once more, leaving the foreigners to carry on their silly war. The summer grain was ripening and they had been without their women for too long. War and violent death was for the foreign conquerors, as it had always been in that much-fought-for island.

This was one of the first official contacts with the Sicilians on the part of the invaders. Now, however, the officers of the Allied Military Government were coming ashore to run the conquered territory and they didn't much like what they saw of the local population.

'They all acted like a bunch of spoiled brats,' said one official later. 'From somewhere they got the idea that the American troops would come marching in, loaded down with clothes and food and money. Some were expecting new donkey carts, cigarettes, new homes. It took a while before they understood.'[24]

Poor they were, these Sicilians, the result of centuries of neglect by absentee landlords. Commando Douglas Grant, entering one 'farm' after a skirmish, found a Sicilian family huddled together. 'The grandmother, whose toothless face was withered like a mummy's shrunken skull by sun and labour, and the mother knelt with the children kneeling before them, their hands raised in supplication to the Virgin Mary; and the father, his lips also mumbling a prayer but his eyes fixed on our every movement, stood in the middle with an arm round the neck of a shabby moth-eaten donkey, clearly the one possession for which they were prepared to die. They were bundles of rags; poor scarecrows, riddled with disease and undercut by starvation; angular bones and stringy flesh showed through the gaps in their clothing. The whole place stank of excreta and it was as much as we could bear even to glance into the huts. We left the family still praying about their donkey, but a corporal, turning round in the gateway, tossed a packet of cigarettes into their midst; others followed suit with more cigarettes and bars of chocolate.'[25]

In the end contacts between the poverty-stricken Sicilians and the invaders remained strictly mercenary. Both sides, the conquered and the conquerors, were exploited. It was strictly goods exchanged for goods.

'There was this gal, see, and she was really stacked, I mean lovely,' one GI recalled afterwards. 'And we didn't have to find her. She came to us. Her English wasn't too good, but we got the message. She was staying at this hotel in town and we could come in one at a time. She didn't want money, she said. She just wanted food. There were eight of us and we were *ready*!'

'But, you know what? She was a great piece of ass and all that, but it was all spoiled for me. You see, she had her kid asleep in the other room. Just a little baby. I've got a kid of my own back home.'[26]

Some had fewer scruples about their relationships with the local women. A young Englishman who had run away from his public school at seventeen to join the Army found himself, slightly wounded, in a makeshift hospital. One of the cleaners was a mature woman who took his fancy. 'I have never lusted for anyone so much before or since.'

In due course the randy teenager 'got her standing up against the door'. Thereafter he 'had' her frequently in his bed when the coast was clear, keeping her supplied with the goodies he had burgled from the kitchen and the canteen. Later, when he could leave the hospital, he shared her bed. 'We slept naked for three wonderful nights, sharing the room with the sleeping children in the other beds, fucked during the day when alone and she refused me nothing.' Afterwards 'I lay in bed, proud to have filled that woman so full, no doubt the worst kind of chauvinistic pig at 17.'

But, while the opposition in front of Patton's Seventh crumbled rapidly in that first week of the invasion, as the Sicilians, who made up most of the Italian Army on the island, deserted in their thousands (by the end of the week, the Americans had taken 22,000 of them), and the Germans concentrated on stopping the British breaking out into the plain, the battle at Primasole Bridge raged on.

Left: Italian soldiers emerging from the rubble of a ruined house to surrender.

Right: Tanks and infantry mop up pockets of resistance in the Catania area.

The 8th Battalion of the Durham Light Infantry, part of the 50th Division, had begun the attack after a forced march which had exhausted them. Then they ran full-tilt into the paratroopers hiding in the reeds and the grim game of hide-and-seek began. As the D.L.I.'s regimental history says: 'It was very difficult to distinguish friend from foe in the shadows and it meant every man for himself with no quarter asked or given on either side.'[27]

Some of the Durhams were shot down at point-blank range as they blundered into the paras' positions. Others stalked the Germans and shot them in the back where they lay. To the advancing infantry it seemed as if there were Germans behind every bush. Men on both sides fired at trees thinking they were enemies. Both flung grenades recklessly, though they caused more casualties to their own side than to the enemy.

In twenty minutes both sides had fought themelves to a standstill. Both the leading attack company and the Germans facing them suffered nearly one hundred per cent casualties. As if by some strange form of mental telepathy, both sides now broke off the action and withdrew, leaving the area strewn with their dead and dying.

The 6th and 9th Battalions of the Durham Light Infantry then moved up to support their hard-pressed comrades. Time and again the German paras rushed their positions, but were broken up each time by heavy mortar fire. Once an Allied Sherman tank made its appearance. The Durhams held their fire. When it was 200 yards from their positions, the figure in the turret suddenly disappeared and a shell came howling towards them. The Germans had captured the tank only hours before and had quickly pressed it into their service. As the regimental history says: 'The paratroopers did not miss a single opportunity of inflicting casualties. They were first-class fighting troops and fanatics to the man.'[28]

The two fresh battalions counter-attacked at one-thirty the following morning. The paras fought back savagely. In the tangled chaos of the vineyards they stood and fought it out until, as an eyewitness put it, 'they either shot down their enemies or were shot down themselves'.[29] The Durhams rushed up their six-pounder anti-tank guns and started to winkle out the Germans individually at point-black range. Shermans followed, plunging into the vineyards. At last the German resistance started to crumble. White handkerchiefs were held up all along the line by the surviving paras. They came streaming in, hands raised above their heads, being urged on by the bayonets of the sturdy little men from the north.

What a terrible sight the road that led beyond the bridge now made as the Durhams pushed forward. It was a shambles of broken rifles and machine-guns, littered with bundles of blood-stained clothing, overturned guns, shattered anti-tank cannon – and dead soldiers. They lay everywhere, crumpled in the white dust. As the Durhams' history says: 'Men who had experienced the fiercest fighting of the North African campaign at Alamein and Mareth said they had never seen so much slaughter in such a small area.'[30] The three battalions had lost 500 killed and wounded.

That afternoon, just before the captured battalion commander of the German *Fallschirmjaeger* was led away to the cage, Colonel Clarke of the 9th Durham Light Infantry stopped him and stretched out his hand. For a moment the German stared at him in bewilderment; then it dawned upon him what he wanted. He put out his hand too, and they shook hands.

'My God, Georgie, you can't allow him to do that!'

On the same day that the British attacked the Primasole Bridge, the US Seventh Army was readied and poised for its own attack. Its artillery and armour were ashore. Supplies were running smoothly across the beaches. The troops were aggressive and willing; morale was at its peak. The only problem was – what was the Seventh Army's objective going to be?

In all the months of planning for the invasion of Sicily, the backroom boys had concentrated mainly on landing the troops. Little consideration had been given to future strategy once that objective had been attained. The Italo-German defences had been overcome with surprising speed, especially on the American front. Who now was going to make the race for what had to be the only real strategic objective on the island, the city of Messina on the northern-east tip of Sicily? The problem was complicated by the fact that the strategic commanders of the whole operation were so far away from the battlefield and were located in headquarters spread over two continents. Cunningham, in charge of the Allied Navies, was in Malta; the Supreme Commander, Eisenhower, and Alexander, in charge of all ground forces, were in Algiers; and Air Marshal Tedder, in command of Allied Air Forces, was in La Marsa on the Tunisian coast. Throughout the whole of the Sicilian campaign, these varied commanders never once came together to discuss operations.

Thus it was that the campaign in Sicily was virtually conducted on a strategic level by the two Army commanders, Patton and Montgomery, each of them prima donnas, eager to grab the glory of capturing Messina for himself.

Montgomery managed to have his plan accepted by Eisenhower first. Realizing that his advance was meeting the bulk of the German forces in Sicily and was being effectively blocked on the coastal highway, he decided to make a left hook around the west side of Mount Etna. Using one corps, he would head north-east from there to Messina. But to do so he would have to use the main road allotted to Patton's Seventh Army, Route 124.*

Surprisingly enough for a man who had such a short fuse, Patton accepted the new role given to his Seventh Army, which was now virtually a flank guard for Montgomery's Eighth Army. His Corps Commander, Bradley, protested, 'My God, Georgie, you can't allow him to do that!'

According to Bradley, Patton replied, with curious lameness, that it was too late to change orders.[1]

One American General, John Lucas, flew to Algiers to protest about the secondary role given to the Seventh Army. He told one of Eisenhower's staff that 'the British were determined to put us in a secondary role.... That

* At that time there were only three routes leading to Messina, one along the eastern coast, one across the northern western coast, and a central one across the plain. This was Route 124.

Generals Montgomery and Patton in unusually friendly mood.

this could not be accepted, that the two armies must be treated alike, and that neither we nor the American people would stand for our being pushed into the background.'[2]

Later he repeated his argument to Eisenhower. As always, the Supreme Commander failed to make a clear decision. He told Lucas, who was a ditherer himself and would later be sacked because of it, that, 'He agreed and said, however, that he had never found a case where the British had deliberately tried to put anything over us. I didn't answer that. He also said that I must try to put myself in Alexander's place. He first came in contact with American troops when the fighting in Kasserine* and Gafsa was going on. That they were so inexperienced that the British command completely lost confidence in them as offensive troops. That these same divisions did

* The Battle of Kasserine Pass in North Africa, where the US troops were routed by Rommel. See C. Whiting: *First Blood*, Secker & Warburg, for further details. (US title: *Kasserine*, Stein & Day.)

well in Tunisia but that now, in Sicily, there were two new divisions, one, the 45th, that had no combat experience at all, and the other, the 3rd, with very little. Alexander should not be blamed too much for being cautious.... He told me to see that Patton was made to realize that he must stand up to Alexander. He didn't mean he was not to obey, orders, of course.'[3]

In the event Patton accepted the new plan, but, desperate for glory as he was, he drafted a new plan for his forces which gained them territory and prestige, but little military advantage. Patton's campaign in Sicily would be typical of most of his subsequent battles and campaigns. They would grab the headlines – Patton was always good for copy and the war correspondents knew it – but they would not contribute much to the termination of the war. In the parlance of our time, they would become, all too often, 'ego trips'.

Patton now formed a provisional corps consisting of what was left of the 82nd Airborne, General Truscott's

Third Division and General Gaffey's 2nd Armored Division, nicknamed 'Hell on Wheels'. Under the command of General Keyes, this corps was to race north-west – well away from the real strategic target, Messina – and capture Palermo. As Patton radioed to Truscott, *'I want you to be in Palermo in five days!'*[4]

It was a tall order. Truscott's men and those of the 82nd Airborne were going to have to walk the whole way – one hundred miles under the burning hot sun of mid-summer Sicily! Although, according to the Offical US History of the War, it was 'little more than a road march', it was a strange business, 'unlike anything else I encountered during the war,' as Colonel Gavin of the 82nd Airborne recalled. 'Suddenly a machine gun or anti-tank weapon would open up and then the white flags would appear. A shot had been fired for "honor", but it was just as likely to cause casualties as a shot fired in anger.'[5]

It certainly was.

Audie Murphy, the future movie star, had seen two of his comrades shot by a machine gun the previous day, before the enemy surrendered. Now he was at the head of his company with the scouts. A couple of Italian officers were flushed out by the infantry of the Third. 'They should have surrendered. Instead they mount two magnificent white horses and gallop away madly.'[6]

Murphy had been brought up with a rifle. If he didn't shoot straight, the family didn't eat. Dropping on one knee, he fired twice. The Italians dropped from their horses, rolled over and lay still. Murphy's officer didn't like what the young soldier had done. 'Why did you do that?' he demanded.

'What should I have done?' Murphy retorted. 'Stood there with egg on my face, waving them goodbye?'

'You shouldn't have fired.'

'That's our job, isn't it?' Murphy said. 'They would have killed us if they'd had the chance. That's their job. Or have I been wrongly informed?'

The lieutenant let it go and Murphy wrote later: 'Now I have shed my first blood. I feel no qualms, no pride, no remorse. There is only a weary indifference that will follow me throughout the war.'[7]

But it was not only the demoralized Italians who suffered casualties. So did the Americans, as the sweat-lathered GIs slogged their way down the dusty roads of the interior, heading for Palermo.

Sergeant Martin of the US Army newspaper *Stars and Stripes* sailed in with the first American hospital ship to pick up those wounded on the drive to Palermo and saw 'a kid sipping Coke with an unbelieving look in his right eye. His left eye had been knocked out by a piece of shrapnel just 24 hours ago.'

'From hell to heaven in less than a day. That's pretty damned good, isn't it, bud,' said the kid.

Martin watched as more boats bearing wounded came alongside. 'By this time the sea was rocky and rough and they got the patients aboard by the single pulley stretcher dropped down from the side of the ship. One of the wounded soldiers laughed and yelled, "Better not drop me or I'll really make a big splash." The kid had one of his legs smashed in.'

In the passageway he bumped into a bleary-eyed medical attendant who had been working all night dragging up the wounded. Martin asked him how he felt.

"What the hell," he said. "Those guys are up there fighting and dying. This is the least we can do."

'The ship was moving fast now but you could still hear the guns blasting away at the Axis planes. Below deck the wounded were sleeping between clean white sheets. Tomorrow the war would be even further away for them: they were going to have bacon and eggs for breakfast.'[8]

Ernie Pyle, 'the GI's reporter', an earnest grey-haired newspaperman who the 'doughfaces' called 'Pop', was in one hospital tent when some men were brought in who would never reach the hospital ship. 'Their death rattle silenced the conversation and made all the rest of us grave. When a man was almost gone, the surgeons would put a piece of gauze over his face. He could breathe through it but we couldn't see his face well. Twice within five minutes chaplains came running. One of these occasions haunted me for hours. The man was still semi-conscious. The chaplain knelt down beside him and two ward boys squatted alongside. The chaplain said, "John, I am going to say a prayer for you." Somehow this stark announcement hit me like a hammer. He didn't say, "I'm going to pray for you to get well." He just said he was going to say a prayer, and it was obvious he meant the final prayer. It was as though he had said, "*Brother, you may not know it but your goose is cooked?*"

'The dying man mumbled a prayer; the chaplain said, "John, you're doing fine," and then dashed off to deal with another dying man. John was left utterly alone, just lying there on his litter on the ground, lying in an aisle because the tent was full. Of course, it couldn't be otherwise, but the awful aloneness of that man as he went through the last few minutes of his life was what tormented me. I felt like going over and at least holding his hand while he died but it would have been out of order and I didn't do it. I wish now I had.'[9]

Two years later Ernie Pyle himself would be dead, ripped apart by a burst of Japanese machine-gun fire on an obscure island in the Pacific. But for General Patton, as his aide Colonel Codman recorded it, 'every day continues to be a pippin'.[10]

One day before Patton's deadline, Truscott's Third and Colonel Darby's Rangers reached the outskirts of

Allied troops are welcomed as they enter a Sicilian town.

Palermo. The Americans caught the defenders by complete surprise. Although the handful of Germans in the place managed to escape, the Italians simply waited passively to be mopped up. So swift was the American advance that only two ships in the crowded harbour managed to escape.

That night Patton began to make his descent into the city down the mountain road running along the side of the cliff, the route lit by huge fires surrounding the city like a flaming wreath. The *Sicilianos* rushed out to meet the little cavalcade. 'Down with Mussolini!' they cried and 'Long live the Americans!' The Sicilians had long experience in how to change sides swiftly. But the cheers and the flowers didn't elate Patton. Rather they disgusted him. The Sicilians went to the bottom of his proverbial 'shit list', even below the 'A-rabs'.

It was past midnight when the procession reached the Quattro Canti in the centre of the city. Here Generals Keyes and Gaffey awaited Patton and guided him to Piazza della Victoria, commemorating the victories of former conquerors of the island.

At the so-called Royal Palace nearby, Patton set up his headquarters, noting in his diary for that day that he 'had it cleaned by prisoners for the first time since the Greek occupation'.[11]

It must have been a very dirty headquarters beforehand. The Greeks had left Palermo over two thousand years before – in 254 BC to be exact!

Patton's 100-mile dash to Palermo against weak opposition, mostly Italian, had been great theatre. It generated the headlines he craved and established him in American eyes, at least, as the United States' most dashing commander, a general in the model of the dashing cavalry commanders of the Civil War. Even Eisenhower was impressed. His personal aide, Lieutenant-Commander Butcher, wrote at the time: 'Patton's great progress gives Ike a warm glow.'[12] Soon Eisenhower was going to experience other, less warm, feelings for Patton. For the Americans playing games was now over. Soon they, like the British, were going to be involved in weeks of unrelieved combat, and Patton's nerves would not prove equal to the strain.

The fields were seared by past eruptions. Lava was everywhere, twisted into grotesque shapes like the claws of prehistoric monsters. Beyond lay the mountains, baked brown and devoid of vegetation in the July heat. And over all towered Mount Etna, a faint wisp of smoke coming from its summit, forked streams of lava trailing down its rugged sides. This was the killing ground on which the Eighth Army must fight and win its battle, if it wished to reach Messina.

Opposing Montgomery's four infantry divisions – 1st Canadian, 5th, 50th and 51st Highland – the Germans had the Herman Goering Division, Colonel Heilmann's paras and elements of six other battalions of infantry. In essence, the Germans were hopelessly outnumbered, but the terrain was on their side. There were few roads, and those passed through gorges and around cliffs, so that they could be easily defended or demolished – and above all there was the observation post of Etna, which allowed the Germans to watch any Allied movement on the plain below. For the first time the Allies had encountered a mountain position which would be devilishly difficult to take; it wouldn't be the last. A year later it would cost them 185,000 casualties to take a similar mountain fortress named Cassino.

The day after Patton had ordered his men to dash for Palermo the British attack started. The 15th Brigade of the Fifth Division tried to extend the 8th Army's bridgehead through what was called 'Dead Horse Corner'. All day the Germans had been watching the build-up. Now, when the British barrage ended and the infantry moved into the attack, they poured withering machine-gun fire into the Green Howards and the King's Own Yorkshire Light Infantry who led the assault. The infantry simply melted away. In hand-to-hand fighting Yorkshire's finest left-arm spin bowler Captain Hedley Verity, commanding B Company of the Green Howards, fell severely wounded. As he lay dying, he ordered the survivors back to safety. Later he was picked up by the Germans and died in an ambulance on the way to hospital. The attack fizzled out.

Next the 51st Highland Division was sent into the attack. The Division, reformed after the surrender of the original 51st in France in 1940, had become a very cocky and self-sure formation. Indeed one could have taken it for an American unit, such was its penchant for self-advertisement. Throughout the campaign in North Africa it had plastered its divisional insignia, the 'HD', on everything it captured, so much so that it was known scornfully by the soldiers of other formations as the 'Highway Decorators'.* But the 51st were no more successful than the Yorkshiremen who had preceded them.

'It was obvious, wasn't it?' Bombardier Castle recalled scornfully. 'Even a bloody staff officer should have seen that! Old Jerry was looking down our throats. He could see what we had for breakfast. The troops moved out at night, but the Jerries had been watching us all day. They knew we were coming all right!'

Two battalions of the Black Watch and a battalion of the Argyll and Sutherland Highlanders began the attack, but, as the regimental history of the Black Watch records, the going was 'disastrous. One company ... was lost to the man. One by one the tanks were knocked out by self-propelled guns.... The battle gradually came to a standstill.'[13]

The Commanding Officer of the 1st Battalion the Black Watch was standing next to the Brigade Commander, Brigadier Rennie, who had escaped from St Valéry in 1940

* Over forty years later the white-painted 'HD', albeit faded, can still be seen on buildings along the Libyan coast.

A 25-pounder gun in action in the foothills of Mount Etna.

and was to be killed in action commanding the 51st on the Rhine five years later, debating what to do next. A shell exploded nearby and he went down, his leg nearly severed. Rennie hurried off to 'borrow' a further battalion to continue the battle; but while he was away the new commander of the 1st Battalion, who was now the senior officer on the spot, decided that there was only one way out – to pull back to the irrigation ditch from which the brigade attack had started. This was done under heavy fire, one company being shot to pieces and returning with only eight men of its original 120-odd unwounded.

That afternoon Montgomery decided that the main axis of the advance to Messina would be moved further west. In essence, the outnumbered Germans had stopped the veteran Eighth Army dead.

Now, while a hasty appeal for more infantry was sent to North Africa, the First Canadian Division was ordered to break the dead-lock by making a left hook which would threaten Catania from the north-west. As part of

this new attempt to break the stalemate the Hastings and Prince Edward Regiment, the 'Hasty Pees' as they called themselves, were given the task of capturing the mountain village of Assoro.

'Very tough nut, I do believe,' the battalion's English Intelligence Officer briefed the assembled Canadians in his clipped, professorial style. 'Key to the whole position though. First fortified by the Sicels about a thousand years B.C. Been a citadel against invasion ever since. Old Roger the Norman built a cracking great castle there when he conquered Sicily. Supposed to have been impregnable in his time. Shouldn't wonder, eh? Need a goat with wings to scale that bloody thing!'[14]

The 'Hasty Pees' moved up through the Loyal Edmonton Regiment and the Royal Canadian Regiment, but they had hardly started when the Intelligence Officer and the battalion C.O. were killed by a German shell from the heights. Major the Lord Tweedsmuir, son of John Buchan the novelist, took over command and the approach march continued through the trackless gullies to the foot of the great cliff. The battalion would scale

the precipitous wall in darkness and attack the summit at dawn. Privately the general in charge of the brigade to which the 'Hasty Pees' belonged thought Tweedsmuir's plan 'arrant madness. The likelihood that Tweedsmuir would lose the whole battalion seemed almost a dead certainty. But then I thought, "My God, he just *might* pull it off." So I let him go, but I sweated blood for the next twelve hours.'[15]

Somehow the Canadians managed to reach the base of the cliff on time, their boots cut to pieces by the rugged terrain, one man even marching without boots at all! Now, under a pallid crescent moon, they started to climb the rock, edging their way up from ledge to ledge, those who faltered being heaved up from behind, their weapons passed up hand-to-hand so that no sound would alert the German defenders. By dawn they had reached the top, still unobserved. But as the sky began to lighten to the east the silence was suddenly broken by a burst of Tommy-gun fire.

'The voice of God Himself announcing the world's end could not have terrified me more,' Lieutenant Mowatt recalled years later. 'I was certain that the harsh staccato, reverberating back and forth from cliff to cliff, would assail the ears of every German within a hundred miles.'[16]

But Mowatt, up front with the lead formation, was wrong. Surprisingly enough the burst of fire hadn't alerted the defenders. 'To our amazement we beheld clusters of German soldiers strung out along the road, gathered around their morning fires in a scene of cheerful, almost domestic tranquillity. Through my binoculars I could see some of them shaving. Others stood, stripped to the waist, enjoying the first warmth of the sun.'[17]

Next to Mowatt, an amazed Sergeant Bates gasped, 'Shit a brick! Will you look at that! Let's clobber the sons o' bitches quick!'

Before Mowatt could give the order, one of his bren-gunners had opened up. Almost immediately sixty rifles and several 2-inch mortars joined in.

But the Germans were veterans of the 15th Panzer Grenadier Division who had fought for two years in the desert. They had been ambushed before and they reacted with surprising speed. Almost at once they organized a counter-attack and soon heavy guns started to fire on the lightly-armed Canadians at point-blank range. The 'Hasty Pees' had sown the wind. Now the whirlwind burst upon them.

Watching the top of the mountain from below one of the officers thought 'It looked absolutely ghastly! The whole top of the mountain seemed to blow up. I was sure I'd have to indent for a brand-new battalion. I didn't see how any of the poor sods could possibly survive.'[18]

On top of the mountain some 500 Canadians now crowded among the rocks, trying to find shelter as the German artillery pounded their hiding places. But the desperation of their situation sharpened the trapped men's wits. Someone found an artillery spotter's telescope and with its aid Tweedsmuir and a Major Kennedy, who had been trained in artillery spotting, began to radio down the enemy's gunpit positions to their own artillery at the base of the mountain. One by one the German gunpits disappeared in a sudden flash of flame and another gun ceased firing, until the Canadian gunners had disposed of all of them.

The Canadians dragged their wounded into a big cave, so that it soon 'looked and stank like a slaughterhouse. Blood was everywhere, glaring from torn, dust-whitened clothing, naked grey flesh and yellow straw'.[19] In spite of the fact that the only doctor present had nothing but the men's first aid kits to work with and could do little but staunch the blood, there were no complaints. The men were still too shocked to notice their agony.

The survivors moved forward to probe the German positions, their main objective the village of Assoro, but they didn't get far. Suddenly there was an eerie rasping and scraping noise like a flint being rubbed along a glass window, a metallic shriek, rising swiftly into a tremendous baleful howling that seemed to fill the whole world. Six plumes of black smoke spread across the sky and in an instant the advancing Canadians were buffeted by tremendous explosions that blasted the air from their lungs and made the ground beneath their feet tremble. For the first time they had encountered that terrifying German mobile mortar, 'the Moaning Minnie', a six-barrelled electrically-fired mortar on wheels which could be easily concealed in a ditch or behind a wall, could be easily moved and which was devilishly hard to locate.

Lieutenant Mowatt had been afraid a couple of times in the previous few days, but now 'what I felt was undiluted terror. As salvo after salvo screamed into our positions and the massive explosions and shuddering blast-waves poured over me, my whole body grew rigid, muscles knotting so tightly they would no longer obey my orders.'[20]

When the mortar bombardment ceased the shaken Canadians began to advance once again, getting ever closer to the village. It lay silent and brooding in the hot afternoon sun, no sign of life anywhere. Had the Germans abandoned it? Out of nowhere a tired old donkey appeared, two heavy wickerwork panniers slung across its moth-eaten back. The Canadians halted. What did it signify? Was it some sort of trick? But, as the donkey ambled peacefully on, the Canadians' thoughts turned to food. They had not eaten since the previous night. Perhaps there was food of some kind in those panniers. But before they could find out, there was a sudden hard crack like a twig being snapped underfoot.

'Goddamn!' a Canadian cried, 'the donk's being hit!'

But the donkey did not seem to notice. It continued to struggle on, dragging its left hind leg behind it.

Another shot rang out from the village. There was a thump as the donkey was struck again. Another leg was hit and, a moment later, the third. The unseen German sniper shooting at the beast was either amusing himself or demonstrating his marksmanship to the Canadians. By now the donkey was completely immobilized. It lay on the ground braying pitifully.

'That rotten fucking Kraut,' a soldier cried. 'I'd like to blow his fucking brains out!'

Lieutenant Mowatt could not stand it. 'For God's sake,' he cried, talking to the unseen German sniper, 'kill the bloody thing!'

The man next to him thought he was being addressed. He raised his rifle, aimed and pressed the trigger. The butt slammed against his shoulder. The donkey jerked convulsively and moved no more.

Just before sunset the Germans attacked. A whole battalion of Panzer Grenadiers came charging in. Thanks to their radio link, the 'Hasty Pees' were able to call down the fire of three regiments of guns. The Germans were stopped in their tracks. Valiantly they made another counter-attack and were again torn to pieces. They came for the third time, but, after the guns had pounded them yet once again, they gave up. That night the Germans evacuated Assoro and the Canadians achieved their objective.

But the cost had been high, not only for the 'Hasty Pees', but also for the other Canadian regiments involved. The Royal Canadian Regiment attacking Nissoria, supported by tanks, had been ambushed and suffered severe casualties. They didn't take their objective. In the end it took two full battalions of the 1st Canadian Division's Second Brigade, supported by massive artillery fire and fighter-bombers to clear the Germans from Nissoria.

The Canadians had lost, on average, about a fifth of each battalion of infantry involved in the fighting within three weeks of their first going into action and were now withdrawn from the line. Behind them they left a bitter lunar landscape. John Gunther, the American correspondent, who had seen them go into action 'high-strung and over-confident', toured the battlefield they had just left behind them and found 'bodies everywhere. The shelling had been so intense from both sides that there has been no opportunity for burial parties. We saw charred lumps of men, bodies without faces, a heap of old clothes with a leg protruding upwards like a signpost, and bloated corpses melting blackly into the earth. The smell was sharp and obscene.'[21]

Now the Canadians streaming back out of the line, their uniform often in tatters, boots cracked and with flapping soles, were no longer 'high-strung and over-confident'. Instead they were bitter and angry – not only at the Germans who had inflicted such grievous losses at them in their first battle, but at the 'folks back home' as well. They were seriously short of reinforcements, yet Premier Mackenzie King's Liberal Government continued to avoid introducing conscription, which would bring them the new men they desperately needed (so far all Canadian soldiers overseas were volunteers). The news from home was all about anti-war riots led by fascist sympathizers, strikes by war workers for higher pay and the 'sacrifices' of the civilians who were now going to be subjected to the horrors of sugar rationing! Slowly the survivors, preparing for the battle to come in Italy, began to realize that they were forgotten men. Bitterly they would sing to the tune of *Lili Marlene*, 'We're the D-Day Dodgers, out in Italy, Always drinking vino, always on the spree,' ending with that harsh final verse, 'Looking around the mountains, in the mud and rain,

There's lot of of little crosses, some which bear no name.

Blood sweat and tears and toil are gone.

The boys beneath them slumber on.

These are your D-Day Dodgers, who'll stay in Italy.'

'... These are your D-Day Dodgers, who'll stay in Italy.'

'I ought to shoot you myself – right now!'

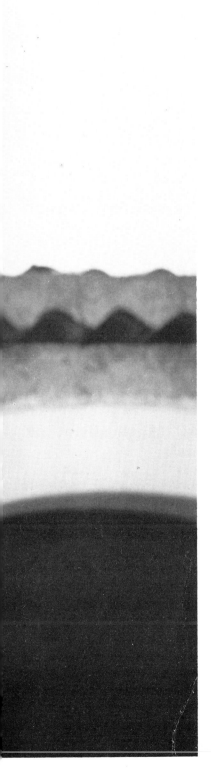

General George S. Patton.

For Patton the trouble started on the first of August. Ever since he had captured Palermo and had learned to his glee that Montgomery was stalled to the west, he had aimed at seizing Messina himself. After all, it was the key objective and would bring him the headlines he craved. For days now, therefore, he had been pushing the 1st and 45th Infantry Divisions along the coastal roads towards Messina. Both divisions were spent and needed a rest badly, but before the 1st Division was withdrawn, its aggressive little commander, General Terry Allen, wanted to have the honour of capturing the pivot of the German defences in his sector, the town of Troina.

All that long hot day, Patton waited impatiently for news of the 'Big Red One's' progress. But, unknown to the Army Commander, Allen had 'flubbed badly', as General Bradley was to put it later. He had miscalculated the enemy's strength and had been thrown back with heavy losses. By midday many of the Division's companies were being commanded by sergeants, with corporals commanding platoons, as the Germans went over to the counter-attack. (By the time the action was over, one regiment alone, the 26th Infantry, had held fast against thirteen sallies by the enemy.)

So when Patton telephoned Bradley at sunset to inquire how the battle at Troina was going, Bradley told him, 'Terry was hit by a powerful counter-attack and thrown back to his line of departure.'[1]

'Goddamnit!' Patton swore, 'it's just like Allen.'

Bradley tried to defend his Divisional Commander. 'No, General,' he said. 'Allen can't be blamed for the setback. Troina was going to be tougher than we thought. The Kraut is touchy as hell there.'

That was not the only bad news that Patton received that evening. He also learned that Middleton's 45th Division was stalled and that once again the Division had been bombed by its own air force, a frequent occurrence in Sicily. Middleton's Division was seriously understrength as well and now he discovered that there were only a few reinforcements coming from North Africa to fill the gaps in the ranks of the 45th.

After saying his prayers, which he did every night kneeling at the bottom of the bed, Patton fell into a troubled sleep, realizing that, for the first time, the battle was going against him. At four-thirty the next morning he was rudely awakened by a tremendous explosion, as German and Italian planes sneaked in to blow up an ammunition ship anchored in nearby Palermo habour. Thereafter, he couldn't sleep any more and got up, depressed and edgy.

Often, when Patton was in such a mood, he collected a basketful of Purple Hearts and went off to the nearest military hospital to decorate his wounded soldiers. He did so this morning, accompanied by his aide, Colonel Codman, distributing some forty medals, stopping and chatting with each wounded soldier. Stopping by the bed of one very black Negro, he asked his customary question, 'And where did you get it, boy?'

Perfectly serious, the Negro answered: 'In de bivouac area, sah!'

That raised quite a laugh from the other patients, but when Patton came to the last soldier, unconscious, oxygen mask strapped to his face, who, he was told, would not live, 'the boss pulled one of those quick switches of his,' as Colonel Codman described the incident after the war, 'took off his helmet, knelt down, pinned the medal on the pillow, whispered in the guy's ear and then stood to attention. I swear there wasn't a dry eye in the house.'[2]

A little more cheerful, he went to the front to put some spirit into the infantry and their commanders. After all, he was, as he stated to Bradley on more than one occasion, 'the best damn butt-kicker in the whole United States Army'.[3] But he could do little with Terry Allen's men. The soldiers of the 'Big Red One' had always regarded themselves as being different from the rest of the US Army. They had been the first American troops in action in the First World War and they had been the first to fight in North Africa in the Second. For them there was the 'Big Red One' and then the rest of the US Army. As one officer of another division complained, 'Trouble with them is they think the US Army consists of the 1st Division – *and ten million replacements*!'

At that moment the sorely hurt Division thought it had been over-used, left to do all the fighting. The men were obviously indulging in self-pity at their present plight. Patton began to feel troubled and nervous again, very definitely on edge, especially when he was told that there were more and more men of the Division breaking down and refusing to fight, pleading that they couldn't stand it any more. 'Combat fatigue', as the doctors now called it (in Patton's day it had been 'shell-shock') was something that the Seventh Army Commander could neither understand nor sympathize with.

So on the following day, when Patton spotted a sign at the roadside reading '15th Evacuation Hospital', he told his driver, Sergeant George Mims, 'Take me to that Evac.' He was going to find out for himself how many of these malingerers, as he undoubtedly thought them, there were. After visiting some of the wounded, he came across a boy in his mid-twenties who was squatting on a box near the dressing station. There were no bandages on him to indicate how he had been wounded. The boy, Private Charles Kuhl, eyed the General with what Patton thought was a 'truculent look', as the latter asked him what was the matter.

'I guess I can't take it,' Kuhl replied.

What happened next was described by Kuhl in a letter to his father afterwards: 'General Patton slapped my face yesterday and kicked me in the pants and cussed me. This probably wont get through [the censorship]. Just forget about it in your letter.'[4]

Patton, boiling with rage, then turned to the Hospital Commander, Colonel Wasden, and yelled, 'Don't admit this sonovabitch. I don't want yellow-bellied cowards around here, stinking up this place of honour!'[5]

Turning back to Kuhl, Patton shouted, 'You're going back to the front – *at once!*'[6]

Kuhl was hurriedly spirited away by some orderlies and examined. They found that he had a temperature of 102, that he suffered from malaria and that he had been suffering from chronic diarrhoea ever since he had joined the 'Big Red One' at the front.

And there the incident ended. Patton, the hospital staff and the unfortunate Kuhl got on with the business of war, though later Patton did issue a memorandum to all commanders urging them not to send men suffering from combat fatigue for treatment: 'You will take measures to see that such cases are not sent to hospital but are dealt with in their units. Those who are not willing to fight will be tried by court-martial for cowardice in the face of the enemy.'[7]

Seven days later, however, Patton was again a sorely troubled man. General Truscott of the Third Division was not happy with an amphibious landing Patton had planned to break the German resistance on his front. He wanted it postponed for twenty-four hours, but Patton would have none of it because, as the US Official History states, he 'did not relish' having to 'tell the war correspondents the operation had been delayed'. He overruled Truscott. The landing would go ahead, with disastrous results – nearly one third of the attacking force was killed or wounded and the Germans got away.

Then, too, there was the problem of Generals Allen and Roosevelt of the 1st Infantry Division. Patton had had enough of the posturing of the 'Big Red One' and its two commanders. He decided to tell Bradley to fire both of them straightaway. So he set off in a highly agitated mood to pass on his order to Bradley and chanced again on an evacuation hospital, this time the 93rd, behind Truscott's Division. Here he found another unwounded soldier suffering from combat fatigue, and an almost exact replay of the previous incident took place. The soldier, Paul Bennett, was squatting shivering on his bunk when Patton asked him what his problem was.

'It's my nerves. I can hear the shells come over, but I can't hear them burst,' Bennett replied.

Patton exploded. 'Your nerves, hell! You're just a goddamned coward, you yellow son of a bitch. You ought to be lined up against the wall and shot! *In fact, I ought to shoot you myself right now, goddamn you!*'

Whereupon the enraged General pulled out his pistol and waved it in Bennett's face, shouting to the nearest doctor, 'I want you to get that man out of here right away. I won't have these other brave boys seeing such a bastard babied!'[8]

Patton thrust his pistol back in his holster and started to leave the tent, but when he saw Bennett was beginning to cry he rushed back and hit the soldier so hard that his helmet liner flew off. And there the second slapping incident ended, forgotten almost immediately by Patton as he went off to deal with the problems of the landing and the 'Big Red One'.

But at that time Sicily was full of well-known, powerful journalists who soon came to hear that the Army was hushing up two incidents which involved the Commanding General slapping private soldiers who had been evacuated because they were ill or wounded. Two of them took the story to General Eisenhower in Algiers and Eisenhower appeared deeply shocked, although he already knew what had happened via the report of hospital's commander which had been submitted to him.

When Quentin Reynolds, a well-known radio journalist of the time, dined with him and his aide, Commander Butcher, a few days later, the naval officer told Reynolds that Ike hadn't slept for two nights worrying about the problem of Patton.

'It is a difficult situation,' Eisenhower told Reynolds and the other journalists present. 'General Patton made a great record in the Tunisian campaign. It would be dreadful to have this one incident undo all of that work and nullify his excellent record. On the other hand there is the boy to be considered and the other men. I have asked General Patton to apologize. The army needs General Patton.'

'This would be a nasty story to get out,' Reynolds suggested. 'Goebbels could do a lot with it. Every mother in America would think her son was being subjected to this sort of treatment.'

'I know, I know,' Eisenhower said wearily. 'But I will not impose any censorship on the story. No security is involved.'

The journalists assured Eisenhower that it was up to the Army to handle the 'story' as it wished.

'I appreciate that, boys,' Eisenhower said, and added, perhaps tongue in cheek, for he believed he had already effectively stopped the story being leaked to the States by taking the journalists into his confidence, 'but still I won't order any censorship ban.'

According to Quentin Reynolds, 'We left completely satisfied with Eisenhower's decision. He had taught Patton a lesson and had humbled the proud General, and yet he had not lost his service to the Allied cause which a court-martial or an "official" reprimand might have done.'[9]

Of course, the story was broken. Journalists, especially American ones, know a scoop when they see one. On 21 November, 1943, the well-known journalist and radio commentator Drew Pearson 'revealed all' in his regular Sunday evening broadcast from New York. In the ensuing scandal Patton was to lose command of his army with the result that the Fifth Army (as his divisions had been renamed) landed in Italy led by a man whom Patton cordially disliked, General Mark Clark.

In retrospect, the slapping incidents can be seen as the first examples of the growing newsworthiness of America's top brass. In this, the first war to be fought under the relentless glare of the media, all these American generals, who two years previously had been obscure middle-aged colonels considering retirement, had suddenly become aware of their public image. Headlines meant everything, and 'a bad press' had to be avoided like the plague. Time and again they would sacrifice strategy for the sake of publicity gained by the capture of glittering but strategically or politically unimportant prizes.

Bradley, who himself was no exception when he became an army commander, was still shocked by Patton's attempts to beat Montgomery to Messina: 'Toward the end Patton became nearly irrational in his determination to beat Monty. He stopped me on the road and exhorted: "I want you to get to Messina just as fast as you can. I don't want you to waste time on these maneuvers, even if you've got to spend men to do it. *I want to beat Monty into Messina!*"'[10]

Bradley recorded, 'I was shocked. The orders sickened me. I ignored them. I continued to maneuver and refused to waste lives merely for the sake of winning a meaningless race.'[11]

Now General Montgomery, that other headline-catcher, with his many military hats, his 'gamp' and his civilian slacks, was also putting on the pressure to get his army to Messina first. In Africa he had told the assembled 78th Infantry Division, known after its divisional insignia as the 'Battleaxe Division', that the campaign ahead of them was going to be easy. He had said that he never went into the attack without having more than he really needed in troops and air support. He had urged them in that high-pitched squeaky voice of his, to *'Kill the wops! Kill the wops! Kill the wops!'*

But men of the 78th now found themselves in Sicily advancing through the baking hot hills, preparing to fight

Traffic control. British style. Signpost erected by the 78th Infantry Division on the Bronte road.

not the easy 'wops' but the very hard Germans!

Leading his company of the 5th Northamptons, Lieutenant Eric Telford, a veteran of the North African campaign, moved up to the start line from where they would attack and capture a rocky hill overlooking the village of Catenanuova, to be assaulted by the Canadians.

'It had been a long, weary march, passing through orange orchards and olive groves pitted with shell-holes and derelict vehicles, corpses sprawled everywhere. I remember a Canadian captain lying half out of the turret. He had no head. There was only the red meaty stump of his neck. And there was that sickly, all-pervading smell of unburied dead. Black-faced like negroes, putrefying by the roadside, bloated and puffed up by the gases within. One of my platoon went over with a knife to cut off a German's belt. He must have punctured the skin or something, because the corpse gave off a wheezing sound which made the young lad dash back in terror.'

At dusk they passed the start line and set off for their objective, laden like pack animals. The climb was back-breaking as they stumbled ever upwards, gasping and panting with the strain, streams of sweat running down into their smarting eyes.

'There were several brief halts. At first we stood bent forward on our knees, panting loose-tongued like dogs,' Telford remembers. 'But soon that was no good. When we stopped we collapsed on the ground. And when we were ordered forward again, it was sheer agony to drive our stiffened legs forward.'

With startling suddenness the first German shell exploded nearby. Behind them scarlet flame stabbed the gloom as British guns took up the challenge. In a flash the night was made hideous with the frightening thunder

of the artillery. Fatalistically, like dumb animals being led to the slaughter, the infantry stumbled from rock wall to rock wall, praying they would make it safely. That night they did.

But it was a different matter the next morning when they continued their advance over that barren, sun-baked landscape. Telford's platoon was edging its way cautiously down a narrow valley in single file when suddenly there came the high-pitched sound of a German machine gun. 'We fell flat at the same time as a terrible cry came from the second section commander, "Mother of Mercy pray for me!" I have never forgotten it. Corporal Dooley had been wounded, a row of bloody holes stitched along the front of his shirt. The first aid kit was in my section. Nobody wanted to risk the bullets to take it back. I had to do it. I was not being brave, just scared of appearing scared.'

Dooley appeared to the 21-year-old officer to be dying. With the last of his strength he gasped. 'There's thirteen pounds in my paybook credit, sir. Please make sure my mother gets it, sir. She's a widow in Liverpool.'

Telford promised, but he never found out whether the money ever reached Dooley's mother. He, too, was wounded and evacuated back to hospital.

On 30 July Catenanuova fell to the Canadians and men of the 78th Infantry. Two days later Montgomery launched his attack on Centuripe, a heavily defended position on a high mountain pass, reached by a single steep mountain road which twisted dizzily up until it reached the top. For two days the British attacked and attacked and were, in their turn, counter-attacked by the Germans. The Northamptons alone lost forty-six men in their first attack up the road, including two officers who had just joined. Of one of them all that could be found was a gas cap attached to the rear of a belt, which held what was left of his torso. As Lieutenant Telford helped to bury them, listening to the padre droning on, 'I am the resurrection and the life', he told himself, 'No one is really listening. All are thinking, it doesn't always happen to the other chap. *Am I next?*'

That night Centuripe fell. One at a time the men of the Inniskilling Fusiliers, commanded by Colonel Butler, rushed the terraced ridges that ran up the mountainside. It was almost *Boy's Own Paper* stuff, the infantry attacking in the face of withering German machine-gun fire, clawing their way up the walls which were five foot high and faced with cactus.

By midnight one company of the Irishmen had managed to penetrate the little town, dodging in and out of narrow alleyways stinking of manure, with civilians poking their heads out of their windows and yelling something about the *Tedeschi** being here or there. As if the troops didn't know. The 'Teds' were everywhere, firing at the advancing Irishmen. In the darkness con-

* Italian for 'Germans'.

Men of the Inniskilling Fusiliers clear a house in Centuripe.

fusion reigned. Fire was pouring from doorways and smashed windows on all sides. It was hard to distinguish friend from foe. The slightest movement attracted fire from both sides. The wounded lay dying in the darkness, crying out for stretcher-bearers. In the end the medics of both sides took off their boots and crept out silently to save them.

By morning the news bulletin could announce that the town was 'partially taken'. But, as always, the butcher's bill was high.

The men of the 78th then began to move through the positions of the 51st Division. They were to advance along the central road that led to Messina, winding around the west side of Etna, through Bronte and Randazzo, moving in a large loop until they joined the coastal road again at Taormina.

Again the Northamptons were in the lead. Lieutenant Telford spotted an old lady lying by the roadside with what he thought was a yellow carnation in the middle of her face. When 'I was a pace or two nearer, I saw it move and writhe. A mass of heaving maggots spread in a thick circle where her mouth and nose had been!'

The Colonel came up. Telford's platoon wasn't moving fast enough for him. As if this was some kind of competition, the Colonel snapped, 'You're not going to let the Surreys take Bronte, are you? It's only round the next bend. Move on.'

Telford moved, but not very far. Round the next bend the Germans were waiting for them. There was the rattle of machine guns. The infantry dropped, trying to press themselves into the ground, as the tracer zipped above their heads.

'There was a brilliant light. Clods and stones and sparks seemed to fly around my face. Something smashed into the back of my shoulder. Another burst chipped the rock around my knee. I clawed the ground. I prayed. The burst went to the next man and the next. As each one finished, I wondered if the next would come to me again. Then all went silent. Boots came running up. It was all over for me for a few months.'

It was almost over now. On the evening of 16 August, thirty-eight days after the Allies had landed, the first elements of the US Third Division started to enter Messina. The following morning the local dignitaries offered to surrender the city to General Truscott, the commander of the Third. But Truscott had been ordered to leave that honour to Patton. The Third would undertake a formal surrender, complete with parade, but they would be led in by General George S. Patton Junior himself!

Angrily the men did as ordered, watching helplessly as the Germans ferried ever more troops across the Straits of Messina to the mainland of Italy. Bradley was 'so angry at Patton's megalomania, that I was half tempted to enter the city myself and greet him on a street corner when he arrived.'[12]

At ten o'clock on 17 August Patton drove up in his command car and demanded, 'What in hell are you all standing around for?'[13] The Americans started to enter Messina.

'Messina no longer had anything left worth bombing,' one eyewitness recorded later. 'It was just a pile of rubble where people used to live. But, as we came in, life had come back to the rubble. The people were streaming out of their caves, marching through the streets, yelling and cheering, drowning out their small bands whose members were fiercely playing on their battered instruments. In the back streets we could see old people and kids and pregnant women loaded down with sacks of flour and boxes of canned goods. Too long starved, they had broken into an Italian warehouse, almost rioting, grabbing as much as they could carry. The slow-moving human convoy was a picture of the worst of war.'[14]

The conqueror, Patton, did not seem to notice. Standing upright in his command car, immaculate as ever, he wore his 'war face number one', that stern imperious look which he practised assiduously in front of the mirror.

By now a token British force had arrived from the west. As General Truscott remarked maliciously, 'General Montgomery had no doubt been anxious to beat General Patton into Messina, for he had landed a patrol a few miles down the coast for the purpose of being there before us.'[15]

The British had failed and the British officer in charge, Brigadier Currie of the 4th Armoured Brigade, treated his 'defeat' gallantly. He extended his hand and said, 'I congratulate you, sir. It was a jolly good race.'[16]

'That jolly good race' had cost the Allies some 30,000 men, dead, wounded and missing. At the time it was thought this high cost in young men's lives had been worth it, because the generals claimed they had killed a large number of Germans. The contrary was the truth. The Germans had, in fact, succeeded in evacuating a large part of their army, leaving behind only a few thousand dead. The only real achievement of the Sicilian campaign was that it had led to the downfall of Mussolini, the Italian dictator, on 25 July, and would soon result in the breaking-up of the German-Italian coalition.

But the Sicilian campaign had been no advertisement for the Anglo-American coalition either. Neither ally showed much tact. General Alexander sacked American General Huebner from his staff because he was 'too American'. The BBC broadcast that, while the Eighth Army was bearing the brunt of the fighting in the east, Patton's Seventh Army was lazing about 'eating grapes and sitting under the shade of pine trees'. When the Eighth Army suffered its reverses near Etna, Patton wrote to General Hughes, the American deputy theatre commander, 'Our cousins got a bloody nose!'

Indeed, by the time the campaign ended, with Patton boasting (according to Eisenhower) that he had ruined Montgomery's career by capturing Messina first, a bitter feud raged between the two Allied commanders. It was a feud similar to the ones which would dog Allied leadership for the rest of the battle in Italy. British officers, conventional, stiff-upper-lip and upper class, would be appalled by the American generals' style. They'd be baffled, too, by the American officers' delight in skirt-chasing. 'We did not have the same primeval need to prove our manhood,' said one British officer of the Americans' womanizing.

The Americans, for their part, thought the British effete, snobbish and supercilious. The British, or so it seemed to them, always got their own way, due to Eisenhower's weak handling of the British generals. Mostly, it appeared to them, the Americans were fobbed off with unimportant, secondary roles as they had been in North Africa and Sicily, while the British grabbed the headlines. As one American officer, Colonel Ben Sawbridge, summed up the US Army's attitude just before Independence Day, 1943: 'We should celebrate July the Fourth as our only defeat of the British. We haven't had much luck since.'[17]

As the first American shells began to land at Villa San Giovanni, a rail and ferry terminus on the mainland, the men who had done the fighting stared across the three miles of water which separated the island from Italy and wondered what was to happen now. The British and American infantrymen were not concerned with the rivalries of senior officers and their silly headlines. Too many of their friends had died during the 'race for Messina' for them to be interested in such things. Lieutenant Telford, recovering in hospital, thought, 'It wasn't going to be as easy as all the base wallahs were proclaiming the crossing into Italy would be. After all, *they* weren't going to do the fighting.' Bombardier Castle, still obstinately refusing 'to soldier' told himself, 'I've got to look around for a cushy number, a staff job with my feet under the table.' Corporal Pinder of the Fifth Division thought it 'looked easy. We certainly had the Eyeties on the run. Some of the officers were saying that Germany would be out of the war by Christmas. But I wasn't so sure.' Corporal Pinder was right. He'd still be fighting Germans in far-off Lübeck on the Baltic coast two years later!

But the *Stars & Stripes*, the US Army newspaper, obediently produced a GI ready to go. As he stared out over the Straits at the mainland, blurred a little by a light mist, looking deceptively calm and peaceful that day of victory, Sergeant John Begovich was quoted as snorting: 'Hell, we might just as well go over right now.'

Go they would, but not many of them would come back.

American troops advance through Randazzo.

II: 'SOFT UNDER-BELLY... TOUGH OLD GUT'

'Then fare weel, ye banks o' Sicily,
Fare ye weel, ye valley an' shaw.
There's nae Jock will mourn the kyles o' ye.
Puir bliddy bastards are weary'.
The Highland Division's Farewell to Sicily

British signallers dive for cover during an artillery barrage.

'Vivere pericolosamente!'

At three in the morning of 3 September 1943, 600 guns in the hills above Messina opened fire with demonic fury. It was exactly four years since Chamberlain had announced in London, 'This country is at war with Germany. Now may God bless you all.' Now at last the British were returning to the mainland of Europe.

The mighty barrage, typical of all of Montgomery's barrages, descended upon the beaches where the Eighth Army would land, lifted from them to positions further inland and then 'walked' back to them once more. Meanwhile the old veterans of the First World War, the battleships *Warspite* and *Valiant*, steamed up and down the Straits slamming shell after shell into the Italian coastal batteries. Resistance from the enemy gunners was negligible. The Italians were totally demoralized and in no mood to play hero. In one battery, it was later reported, the adjutant was temporarily incapacitated when one of his artillerymen threw a brick at him in rage! As for his commanding officer, he was found by the attackers weeping softly in his dugout, the muzzle-covers still in position on his guns!

Afterwards, when the captain of the *Warspite* went ashore to discover how effective his guns had been he was told by a small boy, 'Marina. Bom-bom-plonk-plonk. *Soldati refugio*,' and the little Italian made running-away gestures. Evidently the whole battery thereabouts had 'refugioed'.

For the two brigades of the 5th Division, which would attack with the 1st Canadian Infantry Division, the main hazard was the darkness and the tremendous cloud of smoke and dust thrown up by the barrage across the Straits. Several indeed landed on the wrong beaches, but, for the time being at least, that was really the only trouble they encountered.

It was little different for the Canadians, but their mood

British Infantrymen entering Reggio observe some of the local graffiti.

had changed drastically from six weeks before when they had prepared to land in Sicily. As Lieutenant Mowat of the 'Hasty Pees' recorded, 'Only six weeks earlier we had plunged into battle with joyful abandon. Now we would continue to fight primarily because we had no choice.'[1]

But their landing proved to be an anti-climax. There were no Germans waiting to slaughter them as they came up the beaches and the Italians weren't inclined to fight. Indeed, as Mowat remembers, 'The Italian soldiers came down from the hills, not like members of a defeated army but in a mood of fiesta, marching raggedly along with their personal possessions slung about them, filling the air with laughter and song. For them the war was over.[2]

Small parties of commandos had been ashore on the mainland since the last week of August. Now 200-odd men of the SAS went ashore under the command of the bold Irish giant 'Paddy' Mayne, who, surprisingly enough, had been a solicitor before the war. Major

Mayne's task was to capture the town of Bagnara. Mayne personally cleared a house at the edge of town of enemy machine-gunners in order to set up his HQ. Then the men, whose cap bore the bold motto 'Dare and Win', started to assault the town, held by both Germans and Italians. But unlike Sicily, the local inhabitants stood their ground and even walked the streets while the fighting raged all around. It was a bizarre sight – the black-veiled women of the medieval town gliding along with pitchers on their heads, while their ragged menfolk lounged about, chatting and doing nothing. Now and again they broke off their conversations at the sight of the sweating bronzed SAS men to cry, 'Mussolini finito!'

By mid-morning most of the resistance in Bagnara was over, as it was on the other beaches, and it was time for no less a person than Monty to make a visit to his victorious troops, the first to land on the European mainland since Dunkirk.

As the little launch chugged its way through the great invasion fleet, Montgomery lectured the correspondents accompanying him: 'You must never let the enemy choose the ground on which you fight,' he barked in his high-pitched voice. 'You must never fight the battle *his* way. He must be made to fight the battle according to your plan. Never his plan. *Never!*'[3]

Little did the cocky British general know that from now onwards, with the Germans in sole charge in Italy, it would be *their* commander, Marshal Albert Kesselring, who would be dictating the coming battles to the Allies.

The soldiers spotted Montgomery as soon as the launch touched the sand. Their joy knew no bounds. They had massed for an assault landing and each man, the night before, had told himself that this time he might encounter 'one with his number on it'. Nothing had happened. They had landed with only a handful of casualties. Watching the scene that bright morning, Australian war cor-

respondent Alan Moorehead thought, 'It was, in a curious way, a heart-breaking scene. Just for a moment the man with the thin sharp face standing at the windscreen was the full expression of everything the troops had felt in the night and their elation in the morning. He represented the risk taken and the success. Young subalterns clinging desperately to discipline stood rigidly at the salute along the road. The soldiers themselves gave way to their emotions entirely. They bawled out anything that came into their heads. As each vehicle passed us on the road, the soldiers inside jumped to their feet. Someone would shout: 'Jesus, there's Monty!' And then the cheering and shouting would pass along the column!'[4]

Truly it was a happy day, perhaps the last day of happiness of the long bitter campaign to come. From now onwards Italy, for the Western Allies, would be disappointment after disappointment, defeat after defeat. Nothing would go right until the Germans finally gave up, but that was nearly two years away. As General Fuller characterized the war in Italy, it 'was strategically the most useless campaign of the whole war: it prolonged the war, wrecked Italy and wasted thousands of American and British lives.'[5]

Six days later two brigades of the 1st Airborne Division were landed at the Italian port of Taranto. Men of the 6th Parachute Battalion were mustered on the deck of the fast minelayer HMS *Abdiel* for disembarkation when there was a tremendous explosion. The *Abdiel* shuddered violently, began to list to port and then sink rapidly. She had struck a mine and this in turn had detonated the mines aboard the ship. Now she simply fell into two halves, both going to the bottom within two minutes.

Major J. Pearson, one of those rescued, jumped into the water, 'and as I did so, a searchlight swept the water and I caught a fleeting glimpse of two huge hulks slowly disappearing below the water. As the stern portion was sinking I saw flashes and sparks which, although most alarming at the time, I now presume to have been caused by live electric wires making contact with the water. Then I became conscious of many distressing calls for help around me and the nauseating smell of fuel oil.'[6]

The Major found a floating drum and clung on to it 'for grim death. I rested for a while, then paddled the drum about, and when a small Italian rowing boat loomed out of the darkness there were about ten of us hanging on to one another. . . . We had been in the water twenty to thirty minutes, but it seemed to us like hours.'[7]

He survived, but fifty-eight officers and men, including the Commanding Officer, were killed and another 120 were wounded. Virtually a third of the 6th Parachute Battalion had been wiped out in a single blow.

Next day the Divisional Commander was killed by a stray bullet near the front. The bad times were beginning for that ill-fated 1st Airborne Division which would be decimated at Arnhem a year later . . .

Coming ashore that first afternoon at Taranto, the Red Berets had chanced across a water-tower with a huge Fascist slogan in white letters painted across it. They burst out laughing when it was translated for them. '*VIVERE PERICOLOSAMENTE!*' it read. The paras could hardly believe that the 'wops', as they called them, would like to 'live dangerously'. As Lieutenant Stainforth recorded: 'They could hardly imagine the local peasants living other than the quietest of lives! Beyond lay the whole panorama of the bay, with a carpet of olive groves stretching away to the distant hills, a streak of violet against the sky. Drenched in the glow of a September afternoon, nothing could have been a less convincing background to the writing on the wall.'[8]

But the Italian scenery and the calm were deceptive. From now onwards, willingly or unwillingly, the men at the sharp end would surely have to 'live dangerously'.

The decision to invade Italy had been reached quite suddenly. On 18 July Eisenhower had advised General Marshall, his chief in Washington, that, after Sicily had been captured, Italy should be attacked. Surprisingly enough Marshall, who had been against American involvement in the Mediterranean, agreed. Although seven divisions were to be withdrawn from the theatre in the autumn for use in the invasion of France, the attack across the Straits of Messina could go ahead.

As August gave way to September and it became clear that, after the downfall of Mussolini, Italy would get out of the war, the Allied commanders agreed that a mere landing in the toe of Italy would be too tame a response to the opportunity being offered them. So, in addition to Montgomery's crossing in the extreme south, a much more daring operation had been planned. It was to land three divisions, two of them British, under the command of General Mark Clark, who had now taken over from the disgraced Patton, at Salerno. This force, once ashore, would strike north, its objective the important port of Naples. Montgomery hadn't liked the idea. He thought it too risky. With eighteen German divisions still in Italy, which could easily be rushed south, what chance did three Allied divisions stand, he reasoned. But after his own successful landing on 3 September, when the most serious opposition had come from a puma and a monkey which had escaped from the zoo at Reggio and attacked some Canadian soldiers, all doubts vanished. It was decided to go ahead with the bold operation, in spite of the fact that Montgomery's Eighth Army would be separated from the landing site at Salerno by 300 miles of very rugged terrain. If General Clark's newly created Fifth Army ran into trouble, which Montgomery thought it would, the Eighth would find it very difficult to go to its aid.

But General Clark was not worried. After thirty years as a soldier he now had his first combat command and was enjoying it. On 8 September, 1943, as the convoy carrying his troops to battle closed with the Italian main-

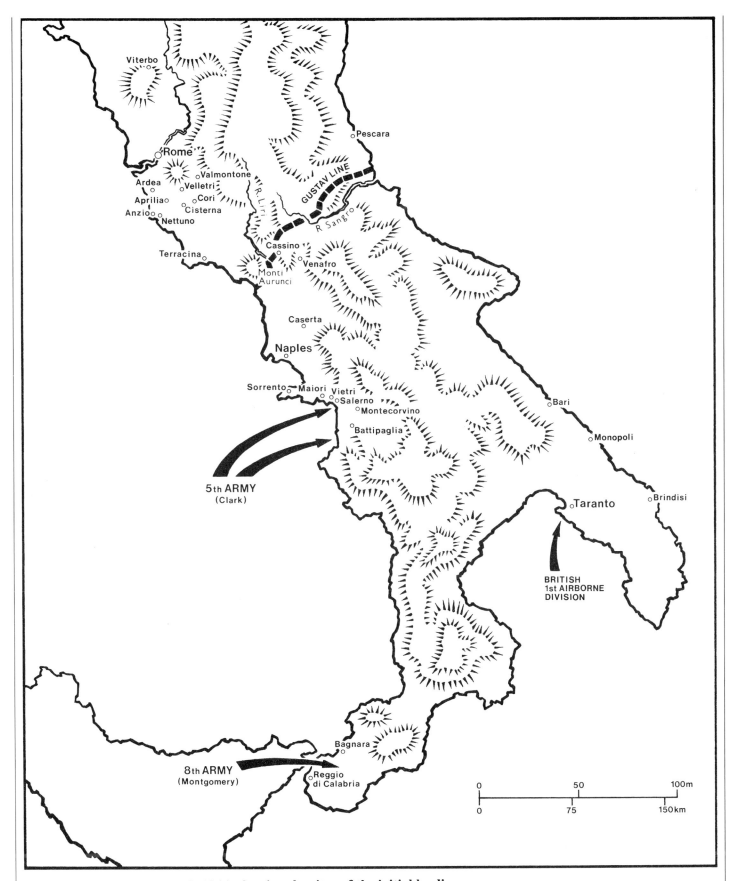

The Campaign in Italy, 1943–1944, showing the sites of the initial landings.

land, he read a prayer, as was his custom, just before he went to bed. It read: 'With Thee I am unafraid for on Thee my mind is stayed. Though a thousand foes surround, safe in Thee I shall be found. ... In the air, on sea or land, Thy sure protection is at hand.'[9] It was recorded that, thus comforted, the tall skinny American General slept soundly.

Ten miles off shore the 100,000 British and 69,000 American soldiers who would carry out the Salerno landing were mostly in a state of elation. Beer and bottles of Algerian wine passed from hand to hand. Officers consumed their monthly drink ration in one go. Sing-songs were being organized. On the American ships some of the troops had asked their padres for an impromptu service of thanksgiving. Everywhere there was laughter and happiness. The faces which had been tense and strained were now smooth and relaxed. The war was over!

At twenty minutes past seven the BBC had just announced some tremendous news. Italy had surrendered! It followed it with an extract from a speech made over Radio Algiers by Eisenhower: 'The Italian Government has surrendered its armed forces unconditionally. ... Hostilities will cease at once and the Italians can now have the assistance and support of the United Nations to expel the German oppressors from Italian soil.'[10]

For several seconds the infantrymen had simply stood there stunned, unable to comprehend the news. Then spontaneous cheering broke out. Men clasped each other and danced around. Bottles passed from hand to hand. 'The Eyeties have jacked it in!' they cried. 'The bleeding war's over!'

Some commanders were not so sanguine. Sir Mortimer Wheeler, then an artillery officer, collected his men and, speaking through a megaphone, said, 'Well that's that. Now I am going to ask you to do a little thinking. What does Italy's surrender mean to you and me? It means just this. It means that, instead of a reception committee of a few half-hearted Italians on the beach at Salerno, we shall find a first-class German armoured corps with its back up.'[11]

But few of them seemed to believe him. Even their commander remained over-optimistic. He concluded, 'At the best we could steam into Naples harbour unopposed; at worst we could have one hell of a fight'. Then, as an afterthought, he wrote in his memoirs: 'Anyway we were on our way and, at last, I had my first battle command.'[12]

On the day before Clark's Fifth Army landed 'Smiling Albert' had issued two orders: one, to disarm the treacherous Italian Army; the other, to prepare to repel an Allied landing in the area around Naples.

Already the *Luftwaffe* had spotted the invasion fleet back in its North African harbour at Bizerta and had bombed it repeatedly. Scandalously lax Allied security had aided the Germans further. It was recorded that onlookers seeing the invasion fleet off called jokingly, 'See Naples – *and live*, boys!'

A British major-general commanding one of the assault divisions was sent home in disgrace just prior to the departure because the censor caught him writing to his wife that he would celebrate their next wedding anniversary in Italy. The local Italians in the area of Salerno knew the invasion was coming too. They reasoned that, although the Allies had bombed Salerno, they had left the docks untouched. Wasn't that a clear indication that Salerno was the Allied objective? In those early days of September, the question asked by the locals was: 'When will the landing be?'

The command of the German 16th Panzer Division, closest to the beaches at Salerno, now issued the codeword '*Orkan*' (hurricane). Immediately the plan worked out several weeks before went into operation. A unit of the Division under the command of Major von Alvensleben drove to the headquarters of the Italian 22nd Coastal Division and swiftly disarmed the staff, thus inducing the surrender of the Division. Its commander, General Don Ferrante Gonzaga, refused to hand over his pistol to von Alvensleben. Alvensleben grabbed for it. The General stepped back, trying to pull out the weapon himself, crying, 'A Gonzaga never lays down his arms!' It was a dramatic gesture, but von Alvensleben's grenadiers had no sense of occasion. One of them jerked up his Schmeisser machine pistol and pressed the trigger. The burst hit the old Italian General in the head and he pitched forward dead.

Lieutenant Rocholl, of the Division's Reconnaissance Battalion, sped with his armoured cars past demoralized Italians straight through Salerno to take up his position above the beaches. There he would observe the Allies when they came into view and report back to the divisional artillery.

There were Italian artillerymen in position there with their guns. Rocholl told them Italy had surrendered and they could make their way home.

'It happened just as I had expected,' he wrote in the diary, which was found on his dead body three days later. 'They threw their weapons away and showed their joy that the war was now over for them.'[13]

The artillerymen's C.O., however, proved unexpectedly stubborn. 'I demanded the unconditional surrender to me of his artillery position. ... He did not seem at all keen to comply with my orders and I was forced to give him a short-term ultimatum – to hand over or be fired on by my men.'[14]

The officer surrendered and the Germans were able to take over their positions, as they were doing all round Salerno. The Germans were ready and waiting. The *Amis*, as they called the Americans contemptuously, and their Allies, the 'Tommies', were sailing straight into a trap.

German interrogating Italian Officers, following the Italian Government's armistice with the Allies.

General Clark had divided the thirty-six-mile coast of the Salerno Gulf into two sectors. The northern half, where the hills came very close to the beaches, which included Salerno, Montecorvino and the rail centre of Battipaglia, was to be assaulted by X Corps, commanded by General Sir Richard McCreery. The southern half was to be attacked by General Dawley's American VI Corps, composed of the inexperienced and ill-fated 36th Texas Division and, in reserve, the 'Thunderbirds' of the 45th who had seen action in Sicily. Kicking off the attack would be Colonel Darby's American Rangers, who had also fought in Sicily. They would land in the extreme north on the Sorrento peninsula at Maiori, their objective the Chiunzi Pass, one of the two passes leading to Naples. They would be followed by British commandos landing near the small port of Vietri, just north of Salerno. Their objective was the Molina defile, the second pass to Naples.

Now the great fleet of ships began creeping into Salerno Bay. Both sides, the waiting Germans and the unsuspecting Anglo-Americans, the euphoria of the previous day almost vanished, were tense and keyed up.

Overlooking the beaches in their hiding place, Rocholl and his observers were startled at midnight by the sound of planes breaking the silence. They looked upwards. 'They weren't British planes. German bombers. Flying out to sea. The moon shone in a weak crescent, very low on the horizon. We could recognize nothing at sea,' Rocholl scribbled in his diary. 'Suddenly on the horizon terrific AA fire opened up. A convoy. The broad curtain of AA fire showed us clearly the full length of the convoy.'[15]

He started to wind the handle of the field telephone to inform headquarters. The enemy was almost here now. Darby's men went in first. They landed without opposition and pushed on to the pass, where they would soon dig in, without incurring a single casualty.

Now it was the turn of the commandos. They, too, landed without difficulty and pushed on towards La Molina; again the objective was captured easily. But already, even as the main body of troops prepared to land, things started to go wrong. Brigadier 'Lucky' Laycock, commanding the Commando Brigade, bumped into the first German patrol. Laycock flattened himself next to the nearest house and began to edge his way round it. Suddenly, to his horror, he found himself staring into the muzzle of a German pistol. But he lived up to his nickname. Just as he fired, the German did the same – and they both missed!

Afterwards, someone asked him what he had done then. Laycock snapped, 'We both turned and bloody well ran, of course!'[16]

Not far away Colonel Tom Churchill was hurrying forward to reach his namesake, Jack Churchill, who always led his men into action, waving a huge and very sharp sword, when 'suddenly out of the road in front an enormous Hun rose up, muttering.'[17] In a flash another of the party dropped him with two quick bullets in the stomach. But the damage was done. German flares started to hiss into the night sky signalling the alarm and already the first angry bursts of German machine-gun fire could be heard quite clearly. The trap had been sprung!

On Clark's command ship, which had once taken the now disgraced Patton to Sicily, the USS *Ancon*, they waited. 'It was 3.30 and we held our breaths and hoped for the best. But nothing happened – at first,' Quentin Reynolds, the war correspondent, wrote later. 'Then from the north, where the British divisions were landing, came flashes of fierce light. No one had been surprised after all.'[18]

Clark, who had decreed that, in order to achieve surprise, there would be no preliminary naval bombardment, ordered the three American cruisers accompanying the US force to start firing.

But now 'to the south where the 36th of Texas was landing, we saw disturbing lights,' Reynolds wrote. 'Red tracer bullets firing low, scorched the black mystery of the night and we knew that the 36th was catching hell.'[19]

It was. The Texans, who would remain an unlucky division for most of their fighting career in Italy, had run straight into the waiting Germans. As one disgruntled Texan told novelist John Steinbeck after the assault, 'If we thought we were going to sneak ashore, we were nuts. They were waiting for us. They knew just where we were going to land. They had machine guns in the sand and 88s in the hills. We were out there all packed in an LCI and then all hell broke loose. The sky was full of it and the star-shells lighted it up and the tracers were criss-crossing. ... We saw the assault go in and then one of them hit a surf mine and went up and in the light you could see them go flying about. ... It didn't seem like men getting killed, more like a picture, a moving picture. We were pretty crowded up in there and then all of a sudden it came on me that this wasn't a moving picture. Those were guys getting the hell shot out of them!'[20]

On board the *Ancon* the bugles shrilled 'General Quarters'. The enemy dive-bombers were coming in now. Reynolds wrote later: 'We didn't hear them but suddenly four lovely chandelier flares hung in the soft night air two thousand feet above us. Then to our port side, our flak rose in brilliant red arcs. It rose from the right and from the left in symmetrical circles with the glowing chandelier flares trapped in the middle so that the whole effect was of some gaily-lit celestial Christmas tree.'[21]

The whine and thump of the exploding bombs soon brought Reynolds, who had been through the London blitz, down to earth again. He thought of the 'kids from Texas'. 'There were flares over them and bombs falling and I could visualize the kids there trying to keep their stomachs from tying into knots for it is like that when fear grips you.'[22]

On the *Ancon* tension began to rise rapidly. Casualties coming back to the hospital ships brought with them exaggerated accounts of the Germans' attack. Tanks apparently were cutting the invaders to pieces. Otherwise the messages from shore were infrequent and fragmentary. A rumour spread that the Commandos had lost their hold on Marina beach. A message was flashed to 'Lucky' Laycock: 'At all costs you must retake Marina beach!' The Brigadier radioed back: 'Impossible. *I have never lost it!*'[23]

Standing on the bridge of the *Ancon*, Clark had a 'helpless feeling – all out of my hands until we get reports.'[24]

The British, landing to the north, were doing no better than the Americans. Huge shells ploughed up the beach all around them. Wounded and dying lay everywhere. Machine-gun fire, low and lethal, scythed the exits. The German gunners couldn't miss. The beaches were packed with men and material and, high above in his observation point as dawn broke, Lieutenant Rocholl 'witnessed a magnificent spectacle: the entire allied landing fleet lay in the Bay of Salerno. ... It wasn't long before the daylight made things unpleasant for the Allies, which was very understandable, as the entire landing fleet lay before us as on a platter.'[25]

'Unpleasant' was hardly the word. The men fought their way across the beaches, taking casualties all the time, leaving behind them a khaki-coloured carpet of the dead. Snipers were everywhere, making the British infantry pay dearly for each inch of real estate they gained.

There was the rattle of German armour as the 16th Panzer sought to drive the invaders back into the sea. The Hampshires, advancing up a narrow coastal lane walled on both sides, were caught by the German tanks. They had no anti-tank weapons and they couldn't escape by clambering over the high walls so they stayed and fought it out. But not for long. Firing their turret machine guns, the Germans mowed the Hampshires down by the score, crushing both living and dead beneath their tracks. Later, officers inspecting the carnage in what became known as 'Hampshire Lane', came across a young radio operator, his lower half crushed, the earphones still receiving messages he would never acknowledge.

German tanks were also attacking on the American beaches. Two GIs, a sergeant and a private, crawled towards a German tank, trying to knock it out with their grenades. The sergeant was wounded and, as he lay there helpless, the German driver ran over him, crushing him to pulp.

Yet, even in the midst of all the horror and carnage, the human mind continued to work in mysterious ways. A GI, it was recorded, after being pulled out of an irrigation ditch where he had almost drowned, became worried about his precious photographs in his wallet. Despite the bullets and shell-splinters cutting the air all around him, he tried to wipe them dry on the grass and waved them back and forth in the air. Another stopped shooting long enough to crawl over to a vineyard and help himself to some grapes. Still another soldier suddenly stopped in the midst of combat to wash his feet in a stream and then, as an afterthought, he took off his socks again and began to wash them too.

Sergeant John Leonard in the early stages of the attack found himself in the barnyard of a deserted farmhouse. Leonard got out of his Sherman tank and wandered around, feeding the abandoned chickens and pigs. Later he explained that he had been a farmer at home and he had thought it appropriate to look after the animals.

But on the whole the American beaches were as chaotic and deadly as the British, in spite of the fact that a full-blown General, John 'Iron Mike' O'Daniel, was acting as beach master, a profane two-star traffic policeman.

Allied troops guarding German prisoners at Salerno.

John Steinbeck, the novelist, saw 'a small Italian girl with her stomach blown out ... and an American soldier standing over a twitching body crying ... the wreckage of houses, with torn beds hanging like shreds out of the spilled hole in a plaster wall. The stretcher-bearers come back from the lines, walking in off-step so that the burden will not be bounced too much and the blood dripping from the canvas. ... And the walking wounded coming back with shattered arms and bandaged heads ... and off to the right the burial squads are scooping slits in the sandy earth. Their charges lie huddled on the ground and before they are laid in the sand, the second of the two dog tags is detached so that you know that the man with that Army serial number is dead and out of it.'[26]

'We've got them just where they want us,' Major Brinkenhoff commented bitterly that day about the situation on the beaches.[27] But here and there were bold men who would not allow themselves to be slaughtered like dumb animals, who were determined to fight back. One such was Sergeant Kelly, known as 'Commando Kelly' because he had once received some Ranger training back in North Africa. Later, journalists dubbed him 'a one-man army'. And so he was. All that day he had fought a lone war against the Germans, running through two light machine guns and killing a dozen of the enemy. Now he was weaponless and in search of something with which he could continue killing Germans.

'I went back into the house where I found a third BAR* in the hands of a dead man on the third floor. He had been killed firing it. ... I worked that BAR until it began to smoke as if somebody had baked it in an oven. A Heinie shell hit the side of the building and made a big

hole in it, burying two men under the rubble. Snipers were touching them up down in the kitchen and someone sent for me to go down there and help. I started down the hallway, but when I got there, a group of dizzy GIs were cooking spaghetti, just as if they were chefs in a ravioli joint back home, and all they had to think about was food. They had spread tablecloths, laid out knives and forks, sliced bread, opened watermelon and honeydews and put grapes and tomatoes on the table. I don't mind people doing screwy things – it helps to let off the steam when things are so tight that otherwise you'd go off your rocker – but to see them readying that meal made me mad and I got off a few overheated remarks. Then I thought, "The hell with it, maybe they've got a good idea at that." I found a box of champagne, broke the neck off a bottle and wet my whistle. Then I took the straw off a basket and got out three or four eggs, broke them into an empty C-ration can and drank them raw. Nobody had time to give those snipers much attention. They had been having things pretty much their own way and had grown careless about concealment. I saw one of them in a tree and drew a bead on him. His rifle dropped from the tree first and after a few seconds he toppled to the ground after it. After working the BAR for a while, it began to heat up. I put it down and went over to lap up some more champagne. To me, it tasted like soda pop or 7-Up.'[28]

At the end of the day there were only thirty men of his company left hiding in the house and as darkness fell they decided to break out and try to get back to the beaches in twos and threes. 'Commando' Kelly was not going to run away. He volunteered to stay behind as rearguard. Whether they got through no one recalls. But 'Commando' Kelly was still alive and full of fight when they gave him America's highest award, the Congressional Medal of Honor.

* A light automatic.

57

'We stay here and we die here. We do not retreat!'

The day started with a minor victory for the British. As the troopers of the 46th Reconnaissance Regiment, who had bumped unexpectedly into the Germans further ahead, retired through Vietri they warned the waiting commandos that the Germans were coming. The men of the Marine Commando went to ground as they had been taught to do and waited. They hadn't long to wait. Down below in the defile they spotted the first of the German attackers stealing forward furtively, their faces painted with streaks of green, their bodies draped in camouflage nets. The commandos tensed. But instructions had been given not to fire until the Germans were only thirty yards away.

'Fire!' an officer yelled. The commandos needed no urging. They let rip with every weapon and at that range they couldn't miss. It wasn't war; it was a massacre. But the Germans refused to retreat. They continued their advance, stumbling and falling over the bodies of their comrades, only to drop themselves the next moment. Still they came on, urged on by the cries of their officers. The sheer weight of numbers began to tell as the Germans closed on the few score commandos. Hand-to-hand fighting broke out in which no quarter was given or expected.

Back at his headquarters Colonel Lumsden, their C.O., reacted swiftly. He ordered an immediate counter-attack to relieve his hard-pressed men on the height. The officer leading it fell dead almost immediately, but his 19-year-old second-in-command, Lieutenant Peter Haydon, continued the attack. Men fell all around him, but still he continued. Then he was hit in the hip and forced to stop. He had only seven men left, but he would not give up. He refused morphia and, seizing a dead marine's rifle, he rallied his minute force and started firing at the Germans. Three times he fainted from loss of blood, but he did succeed in holding the position and killing four Germans, personally.

Colonel Jack Churchill, waving his sword, now led

German 81mm mortar crew in action.

another counter-attack and drove the enemy back to their original positions. On the top of the hill he was still holding, they found young Haydon, wounded a second time, but determined not to surrender. Haydon was awarded the Distinguished Service Cross, a decoration for bravery rarely given to a young lieutenant, but he was killed in action before he was twenty-one.

All that morning the Germans kept up their pressure on the commandos. The Commander of the 46th Infantry Division, General Hawkesworth, came up and congratulated the commandos on their spirited defence. 'Lucky' Laycock asked for reinforcements. His losses were already very heavy. All that the hard-pressed General could send him was a company of Royal Engineers to act as infantry. Wisely, Laycock decided not to send them into the line but keep them as his last reserve.

Shells started to land on the HQ of the Royal Marine Commando, which had already lost eleven officers and seventy-four other ranks. Colonel Lumsden and some of his staff were wounded, and all the radio sets were knocked out. The Germans counter-attacked in force. A Sergeant Bullock saved the day. He rushed forward and set up his machine-gun. A vicious hail of bullets stopped the Germans in their tracks and they fled the way they had come, leaving the ground littered with their dead. But again the cost had been high. Sergeant Bullock was dead and the four men who had run forward with him were all wounded.

Now the attackers resorted to their usual dirty tricks in an attempt to break through the obstinate commandos. There were calls for help – 'Help me, mate, I'm wounded' – trying to lure the commandos out of their positions. A German would appear to be surrendering, hands above his head, crying the customary 'Kamerad!' But at the last moment the man would pull out a grenade and throw it at his would-be captors, or drop and let another man hidden behind him open fire.

Once the commandos spotted what appeared to be a reluctant prisoner being urged on by a soldier in battle-dress. 'Keep quiet, you little bastard,' the captor urged, 'or I'll cut yer throat. Shut up or I'll have yer liver for supper.' The commandos grinned and prepared to receive the unwilling prisoner. Suddenly, however, just as the two of them were only twenty yards away, they threw themselves to the ground and opened up with automatics. They were *both* German! Yet another German trick had almost succeeded and a short sharp battle ensued before both were killed.

Somehow the commandos held on, inspired by what was known at Laycock's HQ as an 'avalanche* of Churchills', namely the Prime Minister's son, Major Randolph Churchill, Laycock's Chief-of-Staff, Tom Churchill, and

* 'Avalanche' was the code name given to the Salerno landing.

Colonel Jack Churchill, commanding the Army Commando.

Randolph, big, boozy and an inveterate skirt-chaser, was not a popular man among some of his fellow officers, but he got on well enough with the commandos, whose unit had been formed on his father's orders. He had no specific appointment with the force, but helped out everywhere. Once he used his father's name to make a group of American mortarmen go into action to support his adopted unit, haranguing them as if from an imaginary soap-box in the florid style of the Great Man in Whitehall.

But if the other two Churchills did most of their work to the rear in HQ (though Laycock's Headquarters were really in the front line), Jack Churchill definitely led from the front. 'Mad Jack of Vaagso', as he was known to his soldiers on account of his actions in Norway back in the early days of the commandos, could not lay claim to one drop of Scottish blood. All the same he often went into action with pipes playing as if he had generations of wild Highland blood running through his veins. Laycock once spotted him going into action carrying a bow and arrow. Asked what the hell he was doing, he retorted, 'Show me a target!' Laycock pointed one out a couple of hundred yards away. As the arrow zipped through the air and hit its target with unerring accuracy, Mad Jack said, 'And think how frightened you'd be if a shower of arrows suddenly descended upon you.'[1]

As for the sword that he normally carried into action, he once told another officer who was foolish enough to enquire why he carried it, 'Any gentleman without a sword is improperly dressed.'[2]

As the situation grew more critical, Churchill decided to carry the battle into the enemy camp. With six troops, all well spread out, he advanced through a wooded valley as the daylight began to fade, each man crying as loudly as he could 'commando'. Not only did the call keep them in touch with one another, but it also made the Germans think there were many more of them than there were. Churchill, waving his sword, captured the first two Germans. Then he advanced on a mortar pit and caught the enemy mortarmen completely off guard. Another few Germans went into the bag. One man who knew the password was threatened with beheading there and then if he didn't lead 'Mad Jack' to each of the German outposts in the valley. With Churchill's sword poking into his back, he was trotted from post to post. Out tumbled the Germans to be greeted by 'Mad Jack' waving his sword. In this manner thirty or forty men were taken without a single shot having been fired. The pressure on the commandos eased – for a while.

The tanks hit the 201st Guards Brigade at dawn the next day. Up front, on the road to Battipaglia, a sentry of the 9th Royal Fusiliers suddenly yelled, 'Tanks!' His cry was taken up by other outposts as a column of Tigers and

British jeep entering Battipaglia.

Mark IV tanks came rumbling down the road towards the Fusiliers' position. The battalion's six-pounder anti-tank guns took up the challenge and armour-piercing shells zipped towards the German tanks; but they bounced off the Tigers' thick metal hides like ping-pong balls. There was no stopping them.

The Battalion Commander was badly wounded and his second-in-command, Major Delforce, took over. As the German pressure increased, he was forced to shorten his perimeter defences. His men began to get jittery and frightened. He reassured them that the Guards Brigade was on its way to relieve them and said, 'Although we are surrounded, we shall not be captured.'[3] But privately he told his officers to destroy all maps and codes.

The pressure increased still more. The men caught glimpses of large numbers of tanks, reckoned that they didn't have a chance and started to surrender. The wounded C.O. refused to be evacuated. He was going to fight to the end. All their anti-tank guns had been wrecked and the only thing they could do was to try to knock out the tank crews by firing through the visors.

Finally Major Delforce gave the order for the men to break out individually. It was the recipe for disaster in the average English infantry battalion. Without their officers and NCOs, the average British soldier of that time showed little initiative and was usually lost. It was no different now. Many surrendered straight away and a large number of them were marshalled under two officers, Majors van Gelder and Sandford, and were told by a German officer, 'You have fought well. This is our third counter-attack. If you had beaten us this time, we could not have launched another.'[4]

But some of the Fusiliers who did manage to escape the débâcle at Battipaglia now ran panic-stricken back to the sea crying, 'Back to the beaches! We're overrun! We've had it! The German tanks are right behind us!'[5]

Their panic was infectious and the morale of the Guards moving up to counter-attack through the shattered remnants of the Fusiliers sank lower and lower.

The Grenadier Guards, with three hundred years of tradition behind them, bumped into the German armour almost immediately. They had just begun to dig in when they were hit by German armoured cars and tanks. One platoon was overrun before the Guardsmen realized what was happening. One company bolted and fled back to the start line. Here they were stopped by officers and NCOs who pushed and shoved the fleeing soldiers back into some sort of order. In the whole history of the Grenadier Guards nothing like this had happened before and, as one Guards officer recorded after the battle, 'Nobody will really know what happened, and perhaps it is better to gloss over the rest of that day. The morale of the Grenadiers was not high and it is certain that small parties considered the only plan was to return to the beaches as quickly as possible. On their right, some Fusiliers ... had a similar idea. By mid-afternoon the small roads were full of frightened soldiers, many retiring pell-mell, regardless of officers.'[6]

But not all.

Young Lieutenant Bulteel of the Coldstream Guards was supervising loading some wounded into a jeep when another vehicle, filled with frightened Grenadiers, roared by, the men shouting, 'They're coming! They're through! Get back to the beaches!'

Bulteel reacted correctly. He sprang into the driver's seat of the jeep and, with a crash of gears and a snarl of the engine, swung it crosswide in the road, effectively blocking it. The he pelted to his Company Commander, Major Griffith-Jones.

The Major, playing the role of an urbane, unflappable

Guards officer, was on the phone and would not let himself be disturbed by the excited young officer. Finally he deigned to listen.

'Mervyn,' Bulteel blurted out, 'some of the Grenadiers have run away! We are to be ready for an immediate counter-attack!'

'Nonsense,' the Major retorted airily. 'Everything's quite all right. The Grenadiers have attacked again and now they're back where they started. I am going to have a sleep.' Which he proceeded to do immediately.[7]

Major Griffith-Jones was right. The Grenadiers had rallied and counter-attacked, but they had run straight into the armour of the 2nd Panzer Regiment. They hadn't had a chance. The Germans had mown them down mercilessly at small loss to themselves. Now is was decided to send yet another battalion of the Guards – the Scots Guards this time – to restore the position.

Stolidly the Scots plodded into the attack like countrymen returning home after a hard day's work in the fields. The sun shone down out of a perfect September sky. All was deceptively calm, save for the distant rumble of the permanent barrage, The Scots advanced through the bodies of the dead Grenadiers getting steadily closer to their objective, the Tobacco Factory. With their rifles at high port they advanced at a half-crouch, waiting for the first murderous burst of enemy fire.

It came with startling suddenness: first the howl of a mortar, followed almost immediately by the chatter of an MG 42. Then the feared German 88mm cannon added to the cacophony.

The Scots charged forward, cursing and cheering. Several Guardsmen fell as machine-gun fire scythed the lane down which they ran. Now they blundered through the scrub, the slugs cutting the air all round them. A high fence loomed up. It was the one which surrounded the Tobacco Factory. The six-foot tall Guardsmen weren't stalled long. Some almost high-jumped it. Others clambered across it on the backs of their comrades. Before them was a maze of small wooden huts, linked by corridors. The Battalion split up into little parties, firing from the hip, hurtling grenades as fire flashed from every window. The battle grew in intensity. Still the Scots pressed home their attack and it seemed that they were going to capture their objective, but Major Freiherr von Falkenhausen, Commander of the 2nd Panzer and the scion of an ancient Prussian military family, thought differently. He ordered an immediate counter-attack in full strength.

Like the Grenadiers before them, the Scots were now forced to withdraw. They pulled back to the fence, hard-pressed by the Germans. Lieutenant Fyfe-Jamieson stayed behind with his bren-gunners to give the retreating men covering fire. Then came his turn to clamber over. In the haste and confusion, with the Germans only yards away, he slipped and found himself caught on the fence by his trousers, German bullets cutting the air all around him. In other circumstances his plight would have been

thought funny, but not today. One of his sergeants ran back and swiftly sliced through the trapped officer's pants with his jack-knife. Fyfe-Jamieson and the sergeant, William Lumsden, ran to the shrub and dived in. They survived and Lumsden was later awarded the Distinguished Conduct Medal for his bravery.

The 201st Guards Brigade was now almost a spent force, having suffered very heavy casualties for gains in ground of only a couple of hundred yards. As one officer remarked to his colonel, 'If we don't hold these German counter-attacks, it will be just like Dunkirk again except this time there are no little ships to take us off.'[8]

Indeed, the fleet which had brought the soldiers to Salerno was under constant attack itself. Hour after hour the German planes came in straight from the sun, machine guns blazing as they zoomed in over the fleet at mast-top height, trying to get under the barrage with their bombs. And for the first time the Germans began to use a new and terrible weapon against the sitting ducks out in the Bay.

On the second day of the invasion the venerable HMS *Warspite*, which had fought at the Battle of Jutland in 1916, had enjoyed the great moment of seeing the Italian fleet sailing towards Malta to surrender. As the historian of the ship, Captain Roskill, recorded, 'To the ship which had so often sought for, pursued and engaged those self-same enemies, the moment must have seemed the climax of her long life, pregnant with memories of another fleet surrender she had witnessed twenty-five years earlier.'[9]

But that triumph lay behind the old ship, the seventh to bear the name*. Now the battleship was hotly engaged in aiding the hard-pressed troops on the beachhead with her great cannon, at the same time trying to stave off enemy air attacks. At midday, just as the *Warspite* was bombarding enemy ammunition dumps ashore, twelve German fighter-bombers fell out of the sun and raced across the glittering sea straight for her. Immediately the gunners went into action. The massed machine guns, known as 'Chicago Pianos', chattered frantically. The heavier guns peppered the sky with shells, and then the attackers were gone, zooming high into the sky, and gradually the firing died away. Wearily the sweat-lathered gunners slumped down on the decks littered with shell cases and waited for the next attack.

At 2.30, a few minutes after the fighter-bombers had disappeared, the ship's lookouts spotted something in the distance. Flying at 6,000 feet were three black spots, growing larger every instant. All the lookouts swung their glasses on them. Were they high-flying bombers? The 'bombers' slipped into the bright circles of calibrated glass and for the first time the watchers saw the new weapon, a primitive forerunner of our own space-age

* The present *Warspite* is a nuclear submarine.

instruments of destruction – the wireless controlled high-explosive bomb being steered to its target from an unseen controller, flying 20,000 feet up.

The ship's skipper, Captain Parker, said afterwards, 'The three bombs, when directly overhead, looked like three very white mushrooms as they turned vertically down and dived for the ship at very great speed. From the time of sighting to the time of the bombs' arrival was only some seven or ten seconds. The ship was making about ten knots through the water at the time and in the congested area avoiding action was not possible – and would in any case have been ineffective. One bomb came straight for the ship and penetrated to No 4 boiler room, where it burst. A second bomb was a near-miss amidships. ... It burst under water. The third bomb was a near-miss on the starboard side aft.'[10]

The 3000-pound bomb had penetrated right through *six* armoured decks to the warship's double bottom before exploding. All power went immediately and she was now a sitting duck for any further attacks. Never in all her long career through two wars had the *Warspite* been in such a dire predicament.

But her Captain was determined to get her back to Malta 300 miles away. Tugs were hurriedly whistled up and the *Warspite* began her long and dangerous voyage. With no lights and no machinery running, the silence inside the ship was eerie. On the upper deck the gunners looked like so many ghosts in their white anti-flash hoods. There was no water to drink, only a strictly limited quantity of lemonade. Food consisted of corned beef and biscuit. Five days later she made it, with the German planes searching for her all the time; but they never managed to find her. '*Belli dura despicio*,' was the *Warspite*'s motto, and never had she lived up to it better.

But some of the ships sailing in the Bay of Salerno were not as lucky as the *Warspite*, only nine of her men being killed out of 1,200-odd. Four days after the landing the British hospital ship *Newfoundland* sailed from Bizerta, carrying with it one hundred American nurses bound for the beaches. As they were expected to dig in on the beach, they were helmeted and carried with them picks and shovels. Later, it was suspected, they had been seen boarding the ship thus by a high-flying German reconnaissance plane and were taken for soldiers. This might account for the fact that as the *Newfoundland* approached Salerno that night she was attacked by German bombers and sunk. The ship's British matron and five of her nurses, plus all the ship's doctors, were killed outright. The hospital carriers *Leinster* and *St Andrew* went to the rescue. The *Newfoundland* was burning fiercely. Flames flickered from every porthole. Rescue boats slid over the dark waters, where tongues of flame licked upwards from the flood of escaping oil.

With a total of 460 wounded on board, the *Leinster* made for Bizerta, while the *St Andrew* managed to find all the American nurses and land them on shore, where the enemy was now so close that the hospitals themselves were under direct artillery fire. Indeed only the day before a shell had landed on the operating tent of No. 14 British CCS, killing a surgeon and his patient, plus most of the orderlies. For the crisis had come at Salerno and now the Germans were determined to 'Dunkirk' the British once again, this time with their American allies, and run them into the sea.

As the German pressure on the Americans mounted, some of the artillery units supporting the US 45th Infan-

HMS *Warspite*.

try Division began to pull back without orders. The Assistant Divisional Commander, General McLain, stopped the column on a bridge when it had withdrawn 3,000 yards and ordered, 'Turn those M-10s around. The fight's up front, not here!'[11]

McLain drove from one gun battery to another, personally supervising the digging in of the pieces, telling the men 'to prepare for anything'. Sergeant Hubert Gilliand of the Divisional Artillery remembers him 'looking solemn, and we decided the situation was critical'.[12]

It was, and the Divisional Commander now ordered, 'Put food and water behind the 45th. We're going to stay here!'[13] General Middleton's bold attempt to put spirit into his 'Thunderbirds' belied the fact that he was a very worried man, for already there were rumours coming from higher headquarters that General Clark was preparing drastic action on the American sector of the bridgehead at Salerno.

The rumours were correct. That day Clark had received a call from 6th Corps Commander, General Dawley, saying that the situation was critical. Clark asked what he was going to do about it.

'Nothing,' Dawley replied, 'I have no reserves. All I have is a prayer.'[14]

That shook Clark, who could see his first combat command falling apart. He began to prepare for the emergency and arranged for his headquarters to be evacuated at ten minutes' notice. If the worst came to the worst, he would be ferried by fast motor-launch to the area held by the British 10th Corps. He went even further, drawing up a plan for the evacuation of the whole of the American 6th Corps and landing it again on the British beaches so that he could retain a 'clawhold' on Italian soil!

It was in the midst of this near chaotic situation that Eisenhower's deputy, the overall Commander of Allied ground forces, Field-Marshall Alexander, arrived to review the position. Handsome, battle-experienced and courteous, but perhaps not too bright, he listened in silence as Dawley briefed him and Clark noticed that his voice trembled. When he pointed to the map, Dawley's hand shook. When Alexander asked him about his future plans, Dawley's reply was little short of embarrassing; he really didn't know. Clark's Chief-of-Staff, General Lemnitzer, recalled afterwards, 'General Dawley made a pitiful effort to explain the disposition of his troops and what he planned to do.'[15]

Afterwards Alexander told Clark, 'I do not want to interfere with your business, but I have had some ten years' experience in this game of sizing up commanders. I can tell you definitely that you have a broken reed on your hands and I suggest you replace him immediately.'[16]

But for the time being Clark held his hand. Alexander left it to him, but he *did* quash Clark's wild plan to evacuate the American beach. Normally an urbane man, perhaps even a lazy one, who was not in the habit of making swift and harsh decisions, he ordered Clark to drop the idea immediately. As General Lemnitzer remem-

bered, 'The Navy were trying to make sure that, if the Army had to withdraw, they at least had some kind of plan. But Alexander's view was that the news of this would spread like wildfire. If it were known among the troops ashore that they were even considering a withdrawal plan, it would be disastrous for morale.'[17]

Alexander had been at Dunkirk in 1940. He had seen how discipline had collapsed. Now he said grimly, as he had done at Alamein in August 1942, 'We stay here and we die here. *We do not retreat!*'[18]

If Dawley was pessimistic, McCreery, emaciated and tall, but still very dashing, the British 10th Corps Commander, was still cheerful and unworried. But, on the same day that Alexander told Clark there would be no retreat, he too was faced with a problem of morale that was dreaded by any senior officer. Returning to his HQ after a morning at the front, he was told by a staff officer that he was urgently needed on the beach; there was trouble with the reinforcements just landed from North Africa to replace the gaping holes in his two divisions.

McCreery raced there in his jeep to find an appalling situation. A huge crowd of soldiers, most of them wearing the balmorals of Scots regiments, were squatting on the sand, surrounded by hard-faced, armed military policemen. Swiftly the senior redcap filled the Corps Commander in. They were mostly men from the 51st Highland Division who had been wounded or were sick and had been left behind in North Africa when the Highland Division had moved to Sicily. They had been on their way to join the Division when they were switched to Clark's Fifth Army. They had protested they wanted to be sent to the Eighth Army and said they wouldn't fight here. Three times they had been ordered to pick up their kit and move off the beach and three times they had refused. Legally they could be tried by court martial and sentenced to at least seven years' penal servitude.

McCreery decided to give them one last chance. He drove his jeep closer to the sullen crowd and stood on the bonnet, inviting the mutineers to gather round him. He told them that he understood their problem. As soon as the situation at Salerno was clarified he would send them to their parent units in the Eighth Army. But first they would have to fight. His speech was greeted by boos, whistles and catcalls. Red-faced officers muttered angrily that the whole insolent lot of them should be placed under arrest and sent back to Africa forthwith. McCreery persisted, but he did not realize that the mood of the British Army in general was changing in these middle years of the war. The men had become 'bolshy'. They no longer accepted that officers were a privileged class who always knew best. Earnest young sergeants with socialist leanings had promised them a brave new world after the war. The *Picture Post* and the *Daily Mirror* had taught them that there was a way of airing their grievances, that they, too, had something called 'rights'.

A Sherman tank advancing inland.

Just before he left, McCreery told the officer in charge to give the mutineers a chance to talk it over. Then he left, praying that his words would have the right effect. The mood of the troops already fighting was shaky enough as it was.

In the end all but 192 said they would go into the line and fight. The mutineers were herded into a boat with German POWs, where the latter jeered and hissed the Scots as cowards. Back in North Africa all of them were sentenced to between five and twenty years. Sentence was suspended immediately and the prisoners were posted to the Eighth Army's front, but in the troopship taking them there they were separated from the rest of the reinforcements, who would not talk with them. In the end, many of them later deserted and were sent to prison.

Afterwards it was claimed that the prisoners had real grievances. But the truth was different. Most of them had heard through the soldiers' grapevine that several units of Montgomery's Eighth Army, including the Highland Division, were being sent to England for the invasion of France. That was the explanation of their eagerness to return to the Eighth, for the Eighth meant a return to Blighty and the possibility of not having to fight any more.

Thus the day of greatest crisis passed. There were four more days to go before 'Smiling Albert' decided he would withdraw his divisions opposing the Fifth Army and start the long fighting retreat, the length of the boot until the German Army could retreat no more. Salerno was Allied at last. It had been nip-and-tuck. Churchill sent Clark a message stating, 'Accept my hearty congratulations on the hard and brilliantly conducted battle which you have won on the beaches of Salerno in which British and American soldiers have shed their blood together and not in vain. Every good wish for further success.'[19]

His other message to General Eisenhower was more succinct. It read: '*As the Duke of Wellington said of the Battle of Waterloo, "It was a damned close-run thing."*'[20]

65

'Want some fun, Joe?'

Colonel 'Slim Jim' Gavin of the 82nd US Airborne Division was sleeping on the floor of an Italian farmhouse on the morning of 1 October 1943, when he was awakened by the British liaison officer. The Britisher was elegant and impeccable in appearance, almost as if he were about to go on parade. He told Gavin in a languid sort of way that the paras and his brigade, the British 23rd Armoured, had been ordered to fight their way into Naples, the largest Italian city the Allies had yet encountered. Gavin liked the young Britisher.

'From that moment on, I found my association with the British Army a most pleasant and delightful one. In many ways they took the whole war far less seriously than we, but on the other hand, in matters of discipline and combat effectiveness they set very high standards.'[1]

The British tankers and the weary paras, who had been dropped into the Salerno bridgehead at the height of the crisis, now started to advance towards the great port. At first the German resistance was fairly stiff on the twisting road that led to Naples. In one stretch of road, only 2,000 yards long, there were five mountain bridges, all blown by the Germans as they retreated. And there were snipers everywhere. 'Snipers were thicker than flies,' paratrooper Corporal Joseph Toporski told the reporter from the *Stars and Stripes* that day, 'and you know how thick the flies are around here. If there is something I don't like, it's snipers. So me and my pal, finding ourselves all alone, just went down the street shooting. We got quite a few of them and then they got my pal. I had no more carbine ammunition so I took his. I got a few more. Then it got too hot and I ducked inside a door. That's where I met my pal here.'

He indicated Trooper Sam Wagne of the 23rd Armoured. Wagne said, 'It was very hot indeed. Inside the building it was very cool. Two girls came down and we got to talking. One was named Joan and one Marisa. We went upstairs and they had a phonograph and American records too. All old-fashioned, but American music.

US troops receive an enthusiastic reception in Naples.

So we danced. We had a good time.'[2]

So while Toporski and Wagne danced and 'had a good time', the advance pushed on, with the German resistance weakening all the time until the city limits were reached. Here, as the British sent in a reconnaissance unit, Colonel Gavin waited with the advance guard of the 82nd. Now it was almost noon.

It was about then that his S-3, Major John Norton, came running up to report, 'Colonel, we are to wait until a triumphant entry is organized.'

'A triumphant entry!' Gavin exploded. 'How in the world can we organize such a thing? It takes the participation of the natives.'[3]

As Norton explained that General Clark would personally lead the troops into Naples as Patton had done back at Messina, a worried Gavin visualized not only the Italians 'tossing flowers' but 'Germans tossing grenades from the rooftops'.[4]

But orders were orders and Gavin set about making the route safe for the publicity-seeking Army Commander. He would enter in the lead jeep, followed by Clark in an armoured half-track. They would head for Garibaldi Square where one whole battalion would seal off the place so that Clark could make the 'customary conqueror's speech'.

All went according to plan, save that the streets were ominously empty. Clark was surprised too. Later he wrote in his autobiography: 'There was little that was triumphant about our journey. . . . I became aware that there was something besides the wreckage that impressed me. I felt that I was riding through ghostly streets in a city of ghosts. We didn't see a soul. . . . I made a quick survey of the area around Place Garibaldi and still saw no Italians, but I was becoming conscious of the eyes that peeked out on us from behind the closed shutters of every house and every building. It was still that way as we drove out of Naples.'[5]

So the conqueror was deprived of his triumph.

What neither the crestfallen Gavin nor the downcast Clark knew was that there were *thousands* of Italians waiting to welcome the conquerors only a mile away. At the city's Plaza Plebiscito the square was packed with expectant Neapolitans. For it was here that they traditionally welcomed victors, and over the last fifteen hundred years the citizens of the great port city had had plenty of practice.

So the Allies took over the first great European city they conquered in the Second World War. It was a city in ruins. The Germans had destroyed the flour mills, drained the reservoirs, blown up the main aqueduct, opened the prison doors, smashed the sewage disposal system and had planted time bombs in public buildings, timed for weeks ahead and which would kill hundreds of civilians.

But it was not only the Germans who had ruined the city. Corrupt Fascist officials had been systematically milking the place for years so that now most of its citizens were in rags and half-starved. And, in the midst of the bomb-wreckage and the starvation, a vast black market and an incredible network of corruption and bribery flourished. As more and more Allied soldiers passed through on their way to the new front, staring down at the hungry, dirty faces and the barefoot children crying, '*Pane, biscotti, sigarette!*' the sleek black marketeers rubbed their hands at the thought of all the new business these Anglo-Saxon innocents would bring them.

For the victor, of course, life in Naples was fine. The British, who had been strictly rationed since 1939, were astonished to find the shops stocked with all sorts of goods that had long vanished from the stores back home. There were radio sets, gloves, stockings, jewellery, non-essential goods of all kinds – at a price.

At the San Carlo Opera House, untouched by bombs, a good company played *The Barber of Seville*, *Lucia di Lammermoor* and *Il Trovatore*. The sun streamed down and you could lunch in the black market restaurants on the quays below the Excelsior Hotel on the kind of food not seen in London's restaurants for several years. There were even musicians strolling from table to table. As the black market flourished, the corruption began of the base troops as Naples became a great military port.

In the overcrowded old town, where typhus soon began to rage, the dead being spirited away by the frightened authorities under cover of night, crowds of black marketeers, pimps, whores and corrupt Allied soldiers thronged the Via Roma. Alan Moorehead, viewing them in disgust, imagined that 'the whole motif was that of a gaudy tropical flower that springs out of decay and smells rotten in its heart'.[6]

With the majority of the Neapolitans eking out a miserable existence on potatoes, chestnuts and figs, GI food could buy anything – and did. Instead of shining shoes, the barefoot urchins now found it more profitable to pimp for their sisters with the GIs. 'You wanna nice girl, GI?' 'Clean girl, GI.' 'Wanna fuck, Joe?'

Black market was the watchword of the hour and the American court at the *Tribunale* was crowded from morning to night with those rounded up by the white-helmeted American military police.

'It included the acquisitive little soul,' the reporter of the *Stars & Stripes* recorded that winter, 'who "borrowed" nine gasmasks; the timid little man who was preparing for the future with 29,000 pounds of GI flour stored away in his cellar; the pink-cheeked pleasant lady who always put sodium bicarbonate in vino bottles so that the cork popping sounded like champagne; the three sad sacks who looked like refugees from a cross-country freight train who were just curious about what was in all those interesting-looking cans; and the skinny shadow

A consignment of food being unloaded, from an American ship at Naples.

edition of Eddie Cantor, pop eyes and all, who kept bawling, "Yes, I did it. I did walk off with those 273 boxes of condensed milk. But please be lenient, please be merciful with me because I have five women and nineteen children to support." '7

The docks at Naples were looted wholesale. Every dockhand and GI employed there, unloading the supplies needed so urgently at the front, took his share – a carton of cigarettes here, a case of C-rations there. Soon organized crime stepped in and whole trainloads of supplies started to vanish.

Deserters also got into the act. Two American enlisted men, Werner E. Schmiedel, alias Lane, and John W. Adams, set up a gang of deserters called the 'Lane Gang' and began to ambush the convoys leaving the docks in grand style; and they did not stop at murder in order to loot those precious shipments of gasoline and Lucky Strikes, worth a fortune on the Italian black market. Once they were apprehended but managed to escape from the Naples Stockade. It was not until March 1945, that they were finally recaptured and sentened to death.

It was not only the Americans who joined in the epidemic of crime and corruption which broke out in Naples and the surrounding area; the English were also involved.

Doctor Lieutenant-Colonel J. Watts had just given a lift to Naples to a cynical GI who told him that they took anyone into the US Army now. 'Why, there's a guy goes up for his medical and he has no arms, but they enlist him and post him to a unit. When he gets there the Adjutant says, "You got no arms. Never mind, son. There's a place for you in this Army. Just go and help those two guys over there, pumping water into buckets." "But I can't help them, I've got no arms." "Never mind. Just tell them when to stop," the Adjutant said, *"They're both blind!"* '8

Next the Colonel was stopped by an RAF officer who told him how he had just led a party of airmen into the hills above Naples to investigate rumours of trouble and had come across an American Military Government Officer who was holding two British Army officers, one of them wounded. The surprised RAF officer, who now wanted Watts to attend to the wounded 'officer', asked for an explanation. The American said he had gone into the hills to investigate stories that two British officers were terrorizing a village up there. He had hidden himself in the back of a car driven by two Italian policemen dressed in civilian clothes. As he had expected, the car was stopped and two Britishers told the Italians that they were 'requisitioning' the car.

The American then revealed himself, but the 'officers'

remained quite cool, telling him they would take him anywhere he wanted to go.

'*You* are the guys I have come to see,' the American snapped.

One of the 'officers' reached for his pistol, but the American was quicker and the 'officer' fell to the ground, shot through the thigh.

Both men were, in fact, deserters, who had made themselves armbands and officers' 'pips' from cardboard and had then headed for the hills. 'Arriving at the village up there they had sent for the mayor and had demanded the surrender of all arms,' Doctor Watts wrote later. 'When this had been done they had settled down as virtual tyrants of the place, helping themselves to anything they wanted and ruling by terror.'[9]

Watts patched the wounded deserter up but, five days later, he stole an RAF sergeant's battledress blouse and, in his pyjama trousers, with the stitches still in his leg, deserted again. Up to the time the doctor left the area he had not been recaptured. Perhaps as an old man, speaking broken English, he is still up in those hills around Naples.

Naturally, as Naples became a leave centre, VD became almost epidemic. Gonorrhoea in a new and more virulent form began to spread at an alarming rate. Even the new antibiotics such as M & B appeared incapable of resisting it, and precious penicillin, the most priceless black market commodity of them all, had to be diverted to the 'pox hospitals' for the treatment of those who had been wounded in a different kind of action.

The Americans set up prophylactic stations throughout the city, where soldiers who had just had intercourse could irrigate their sexual organs with chemicals, just like horses standing in front of troughs. But many were too lazy to use them, nor would they use the pre-intercourse kits, which included squirting chemicals up the penis and then, after the deed had been done, placing the penis in a little antiseptic bag.

But the incidence of VD rose and rose. British soldiers, who did not sign their name and number in their unit's medical room indicating that they had been issued with the standard Army contraceptive, could be sentenced to up to fifty-six days in a military prison if they then contracted VD. But by Christmas the Fifth Army was suffering more casualties from VD caught in Naples than through enemy action at the front. Several hundred cases were reported each week.

All the roads leading into the city were plastered with notices warning leave-men against the disease. 'Pro stations', as the soldiers called the prophylactic stations, were the only places allowed to be illuminated after blackout time. The Military Police cordoned off whole areas of the city in surprise raids, grabbing women between 16 and 60 off the streets without explanation, herding them like cattle into trucks and taking them off for blood tests. Then they were jailed in local prisons until their 'Wassermanns' and 'Kahns'* turned out to be negative. It was even suggested that life sentences should be passed on women *knowingly* giving VD to Allied soldiers. And still the epidemic raged, with nearly a battalion being lost to the Fifth Army each week.

In their scores they entered Naples' US Fifth General Hospital. Officer or enlisted man, black or white, they were stripped of their uniform and given fatigues. On the back of the jacket and on the trouser legs were painted in large smeary letters 'VD'. Everyone in the hospital was going to know why *they* were there.

Inevitably they were welcomed with cheers and boos by those already receiving treatment and by the familiar cry given to all newcomers in the US Army, 'You'll be sor-ry!' But added to it was a new cry, 'Only a hundred and eighty hours more!'

That was the time it took to cure an infected man. Every three hours, night and day, he would receive an injection of penicillin, sixty in all, until his body felt like a pin-cushion. That is, if he had what the British soldier called grimly, 'the full house', both gonorrhoea *and* syphilis. Patients with the former were usually released after two days, for the line was hungry for men.

The male orderlies who ran the place had no intention of making the shots painless, and if anyone missed an injection the medics made the unfortunate soldier begin the painful treatment all over again. In the end he would be sent back up into the line, carrying the little bound 'Syphilis Register' with his name on the cover and a letter to his Commanding Officer making it quite clear why he had been in hospital.

Syphilis patients faced the dreaded spinal tap, or the even more feared 'umbrella' for those who also suffered from gonorrhoea – a catheter inserted inside the penis which was then opened up to scrape away any lesions. Thereafter, as the victims said, 'You pissed five ways at once for the next twenty-four hours!'

The epidemic became so serious that General Clark decreed that only those with jobs to do there would be allowed to enter the city.

So Naples was left to the black marketeers, the crooks and the deserters. No longer would the drunken men from the front stagger through its streets looking for women and more drink – and then yet more women.

One of the last to 'enjoy' Naples, baby-faced Audie Murphy, was awakened at dawn by the girl he had slept with. She told him that he had to leave now; soon her father would be coming home from work. He assured the girl he would write.

'No,' she replied. 'A soldier never writes. Never come back. Eet ees not the first time.'[10]

Out in the street Murphy recognized an old friend from his company, Kerrigan. Kerrigan was drunk and angry.

'What in the hell happened?' Murphy asked.

---

* Tests used to detect VD.

General Mark Clark inspecting men of the US 100th Infantry Battalion, made up of *Nisei* – Japanese-American soldiers.

'*Happened?*' he shouted indignantly. 'That bitch. That gold-toothed slut. Where's my hat? Where's my money? You want to know? That lower than a goddamned snail's belly of a gold-toothed slut! She stole it. Rolled me cleaner'n a whistle.' Kerrigan cackled drunkenly. 'Horseface, that sonofabitch, thinks he knows women. Hell, man, I *invented* women!'

Murphy was not interested in Horseface. He was more concerned with getting his buddy back to the waiting truck which would take them back to the line before the Military Police spotted him. He put his arm around Kerrigan and began to guide him towards the parking lot where the 'deuce-and-a-half' truck was.* They turned a corner and saw a group of Nisei, Japanese-American soldiers, walking towards them. Kerrigan blinked in disbelief. 'My God,' he groaned. 'All is lost. *The Japs have captured Naples!*'[11]

The generals and the staff officers settled in in their vast and ugly headquarters at Caserta. For *them* Naples was still in bounds, while only an hour away men fought and died in the mud and the cold. The contrast was almost too great to be comprehended. The young American writer, John Horne Burns, who spent that winter in Naples as an Intelligence Officer, felt the contrast only too strongly: 'Often, from what I saw, I lost the power of speech,' he wrote in his novel *The Gallery*, published just after the war. 'It seemed to me that everything hap-

* GI name for the standard two-and-a-half-ton truck.

pening there could be happening to me. A kind of madness, I suppose. But in the twenty-eighth year of my life I learned that I too must die.'[12]

Many other, less sensitive, young men learned too that they must die that autumn, as the Allied armies began to crawl up the long boot of Italy. The Italian peninsula is nearly 800 miles long and 100 miles wide. Down its centre runs a backbone of mountains, some as high as 6,000 feet. Out of this backbone branches a never-ending series of mountainous ribs and rivers. In between these ribs ran the roads. Few that they were, they were narrow and winding and almost useless in winter when the floods and the snow came. Not surprisingly the Germans made full use of these ready-made defensive positions. As one Intelligence Officer put it wearily, 'Every 500 yards there is a new defensive position for a company; every five miles a new line for a division.'

So, after the capture of Naples, the war in Italy became always one more river to assault and one more mountain peak to capture. Churchill's 'soft underbelly' of Europe had become a tough old gut!

Winter came with extraordinary abruptness. One moment all had been hot bright sunshine and brilliant white dust; the next everything was mud and snow. With the winter came the pitched battles with hundreds dying, and the corroding cold making it hellish for those who clung to life.

An American Corps Commander wrote: 'It had rained for two days and is due to rain two more ... It is as cold as hell ... I don't see how our men stand what they do.'[13]

Lieutenant Helme of the Coldstream Guards wrote: 'After the first couple of days we had to stretch ground-sheets and gas capes to catch rainwater for drinking. No chance of shaving as any cut would have become infected. But I had a good wash in a shell hole. Men's hands and feet were rather swollen after rain and exposure. ... Had only one blanket each ... and had to sleep two or three together to keep warm.'[14]

In the Guards, as in other British regiments, strict checks on the men's feet were carried out. Officers inspected them daily. Trench foot, which could immobilize a man for days, sometimes even for good, was rigorously fought against. But in the American Army, the most democratic of all Allied armies, the officers took less interest in the health of their men and trench foot now became the main cause of casualties. Many GIs never took off their shoes for days, even weeks. Tissues gradually died, sores broke out and gangrene set in. Shoes had to be cut off swollen feet – sometimes the feet themselves were cut off.

As War Correspondent Ernie Pyle noted: 'Our troops were living in almost inconceivable misery. The fertile black valleys were knee-deep in mud. Thousands of the men had not been dry for weeks. Others lay at night in the high mountains with the temperatures below freezing and the thin snow sifting over them. They dug into the stones and slept in little chasms and behind rocks and in half-caves. They lived like men of prehistoric times. ... How they survived the dreadful winter was beyond us.'[15]

The dead lay where they had fallen, often for days. Lieutenant Mowat of the 'Hasty Pees', now back in action again, helped to bury some of his comrades who had lain on an open road for five days. Despite the chill, wet weather, 'the bodies had bloated to the point where they had stretched their stained, stinking and saturated clothing sausage-tight. They did not look like men anymore. They had become obscene parodies of men. Somebody handed me Gerry's broken spectacles and, for the first time since the real war began for me, my eyes filled with tears. For the first time I truly understood that the dead were ... dead.'[16]

A few days later he wrote in a letter home: 'It's hard for guys my age to grasp that nobody lives for ever. Dying is just a word until you find differently. That's trite, but horribly true. The first few times you almost get nicked you take it for granted you are naturally immortal. The next few times you begin to wonder. After that you start looking over your shoulder to make sure that old Lady Luck is still around. Then, if you're still in one piece, you wonder when she is going to scram to parts unknown. ... A young guy named Swayle came up to us three weeks ago, fresh out from Blighty, and before he really knew what in hell it was all about, he ended up in a pile of perforated meat along with seven of his men. Why him? Why them? And when will it be you? That's the sort of question you ask yourself.'[17]

And when it was you, you were brought down under the cover of the evening darkness on the back of a mule, for no motor transport could take those hills. The dead came back, lying belly-down across the wooden pack-saddles, their heads hanging down one side, their stiffened legs sticking out awkwardly from the other, bobbing up and down as the mules walked. The Italian mule-skinners the Allies were now using were superstitious peasants, afraid to walk beside the dead men, so American and British soldiers had to lead the procession of death.

Ernie Pyle watched one such column reach the bottom of the mountains and recorded that moment of truth: 'The first one came early in the morning. They slid him down from the mule and stood him on his feet for a moment. In the half-light he might have been merely a sick man standing there leaning on the other. Then they laid him on the ground in the shadow of the stone wall alongside the road. ... Then a soldier came into the cowshed and said there were some more bodies outside. We went out into the road. Four mules stood there in the moonlight in the road where the trail came down off the mountain. The soldiers who led them stood there waiting. "This one is Captain Waskow," one of them said quietly. The uncertain mules moved off to their olive groves. The men in the road seemed reluctant to leave. They stood around and gradually I could sense them moving, one by one, close to Captain Waskow's body. Not so much to look, I think, as to say something in finality to him and to themselves. ...

One soldier said out loud, "God damn it!"
Another said, "God damn it to hell anyway!"

Left: American soldiers struggle to extricate a jeep from mud.

Right: An American machine-gun.

Then a soldier said, "I sure am sorry sir."

Then the first man squatted down and he reached down and took the dead captain's hand and he sat there for a full five minutes holding the dead hand in his own and looking intently into the dead face. Finally he put the hand down. He reached up and gently straightened the points of the captain's shirt collar, and then he sort of re-arranged the tattered edges of his uniform around the wound and then he got up and walked away down the road in the moonlight all alone.

The rest of us went back into the cowshed, leaving the five dead men, lying in a line, end to end in the shadow of the low stone wall. We lay down on the straw in the cowshed and pretty soon we were all asleep.'[18]

In truth, the steam had gone out of the campaign in Italy. The invasion of the European mainland, which had started with so much hope, had become a liability. Now the top brass who were to command the invasion of France were beginning to leave for England – Eisenhower first, then Bradley and the disgraced Patton, finally Montgomery himself. They left behind them second-raters such as Clark, in command of the Fifth Army, of whom Bradley wrote: 'I had serious reservations about him. He seemed false somehow, too eager to impress, too hungry for the limelight, promotions and personal publicity.'

Patton didn't trust him either. He thought Clark was 'too damned slick' and 'more preoccupied with bettering his own future than winning the war.'[19]

Montgomery's place in command of Eighth Army was taken by Sir Oliver Leese, a much more experienced general than Clark; but he didn't have Montgomery's charisma, he was slow and the strength of his Army was being seriously sapped. Just as Bradley took with him the 82nd Airborne, the Second Armored, the 9th Infantry Division and 'the Big Red One' for the invasion of France, so Montgomery withdrew the 50th and 51st Division and his 'Desert Rats', the 7th Armoured Division,

for the same purpose.

The Italian front was in danger of becoming a backwater where no spectacular breakthrough could be achieved because of poor generalship and lack of men. Indeed, by now the Germans outnumbered the Allies in Italy. But the campaign still had one important and enthusiastic supporter, Winston Churchill. As he lay ill with pneumonia that winter in North Africa and the 'fever flickered in and out', the problem of Italy remained foremost in his mind; for it was he who had campaigned most strongly for it. 'Were we to leave it a stagnant pool from which we had drawn every fish we wanted?' the old man asked himself.[20] And his answer was – *no*. He wanted a great new offensive, its objective the capture of Rome. The taking of the Italian capital would be, in his opinion, the natural curtain-raiser to the invasion of France. He saw the stagnation of the campaign as 'scandalous'.

Churchill had been a keen advocate of naval landings ever since 1915, when he had been the power behind the disastrous landing at Gallipoli, which had cost him his ministry and sent him out into the wilderness for the first time. Now he wanted to use sea power to turn the campaign in the Allies' favour. He knew that soon nine-tenths of the existing Allied landing craft currently in the Mediterranean would be diverted to the Pacific or to England for the coming invasion. Sick as he was, Churchill advocated that those craft assigned to Britain should be kept a few weeks longer for a great new seaborne operation. While Clark's Fifth Army assaulted the present German frontline positions, known as the 'Gustav Line', another Anglo-American force, under the command of the American Corps Commander, General John Lucas, would turn the Germans' right flank by an amphibious landing to its rear.

Two divisions, the American Third and the British First, would land on a spot only thirty-five miles from Rome itself. The code-name for this bold thrust was, aptly enough, 'Operation Shingle'. But the men who would do the fighting there would soon call it something else – '*Bloody Anzio!*'

'Fortunately ... the escaping gas caused no casualties'

Junkers Ju 88 bombers.

On the afternoon of 2 December 1943, the skipper of the US ship *SS John Bascom*, Otto Heitman, went ashore at the British-controlled port of Bari to report his safe arrival after crossing the Atlantic. On his way he noted there were at least thirty merchant ships anchored in the harbour and knew that there was another convoy expected before nightfall. Obviously the military were building up for a new push. The port was so crowded with shipping that it seemed to him an ideal target for the *Luftwaffe*. But the Britishers running the harbour authority laughed at his fears. Bari was encircled by anti-aircraft guns. He was as safe here as he would have been back in the States.

But even as the Britishers reassured him a high-flying German reconnaissance plane, piloted by *Luftwaffe Oberleutnant* Werner Hahn, was photographing the port, its pilot counting the tiny ships jammed together below. When Hahn had reached thirty he knew Bari was a prime target for a raid. Jerking back the throttle, he banked

northwards, heading back for Northern Italy to make his report. The stage was set for tragedy at Bari.

Earlier that year, in July 1943, ominous reports started to reach Washington and London indicating that a desperate Hitler might resort to the use of poison gas if the Allies invaded Southern Europe. Allied agents verified that the enemy had a quarter of a million tons of toxic ammunition east of the Rhine, including a new and highly secret gas called Tabun. Later the Allies had discovered evidence of possible chemical warfare in Italy. The chemical warfare expert, US Major Stewart Alexander, reported indirectly to Eisenhower: 'Significant amounts of vesicant agent were captured. It seems probable that the majority of the agent is a mixture of fifty percent phenyl dichlorarsine and fifty percent mustard. It is believed that this mixture is of Italian manufacture. There was no evidence of tactical use of this vesicant.'[1]

In August, 1943, President Roosevelt issued a warning. He stated that: 'Any use of poison gas by any Axis power will immediately be followed by the fullest retaliation upon munition centers, seaports and other military objectives throughout the whole extent of the territory of such Axis country.'[2]

The President did not spell out what exactly this 'fullest retaliation' would be, but one month later secret permission was given by the White House for a shipment of mustard gas bombs to be sent for storage at Bari to be used as retaliation in case the Germans used gas. The top brass were thinking the unthinkable!

Thus it was that on that evening of 2 December when the second convoy entered Bari harbour it brought with it an innocent-looking Liberty ship, the *John Harvey*. But the *John Harvey* bore in its hold a weapon much more deadly than any contained in the ammunition ships all

about it in the crowded port. *It had brought with it 2,000 100-pound mustard gas bombs!*

While the *John Harvey* was tying up at the quay, Kesselring was already discussing with his *Luftwaffe* commanders what should be the prime target for a great strike planned by the Air Force. One of them favoured the bombing of the Allied air fields around Foggia. Another suggested strikes against Clark's Fifth Army. In the end Kesselring turned to General von Richthofen, scion of the Prussian military family which had sired the famed 'Red Baron' of World War One.* The dynamic little General, who knew more about the day-to-day operations of the *Luftwaffe* in Italy than the rest, turned down both proposals. Supplies, he insisted, were the key to the current situation in Italy. If the Allies were preparing another landing further up the boot, as Kesselring half-suspected they were doing, then cut off their supplies and the proposed landing would be scrapped.

The Field-Marshal nodded and asked, 'Do you have a specific target in mind?'

Richthofen did. 'Bari!' he answered.

So, as Bari settled down to another December night, its poorer citizens trying to make a meal of their miserable rations, its brothels full of carousing sailors and base personnel, Kesselring ordered all available bombers in Northern Italy to be readied for a great knock-out blow against the Allied shipping now packing the port.

Captain Heitmann of the *John Bascom* was alerted by the cry of one of his look-outs: 'Flare! I see a flare!' He rushed to the bridge and spotted two steady white lights glowing garishly in the sky east of the harbour. He knew that they were parachute flares. Bari was in for a raid. He glanced at his watch. It was thirty-five minutes past seven. Then he shouted, 'Battle Stations!' And, even as he cried, the guns began to thunder. The Germans were coming.

The *John Harvey* was hit and set on fire almost immediately, as the twin-engined Junkers 88 roared over the packed shipping, a bomb-aimer's dream. And the advantage was on their side. For the raid on Bari they used the same secret weapon the RAF had used in the attack on Hamburg five months before – strips of aluminium released from the attacking planes which confused enemy radar. So now it was only the enemy flak which they had to contend with.

Suddenly the *John L. Motley*, close to the ship with its holds filled with the deadly gas, blew up. It produced a chain reaction, the *John Harvey* blowing up a few moments later, the explosion killing the only men who could have warned the authorities of the lethal cargo the ship carried.

Now, as the smoke and fumes from the burning ships started to spread over the embattled harbour where the

* And also Frieda von Richthofen who became D. H. Lawrence's wife.

second greatest loss of Allied ships after Pearl Harbor had just taken place, Captain Heitmann, whose own ship had been sunk, thought he could smell garlic. Why, he wondered. Surely none of the ships had been carrying garlic? There was enough of that already in Italy. Little did Captain Heitmann know it, but mustard gas gives off a strong odour of garlic!

Now the Allied hospitals of the Bari district were inundated with casualties from the burning, sunken ships. Packed though they were with battle casualties, and, in the case of the Venereal Disease Treatment Centre, with VD patients, they started to admit the hundreds of victims of the bombing.

Most of the lightly injured seemed to exhibit the symptoms of bad shock. They were pale, weak, and exhausted. Many complained of thirst. Others were cold and clammy with perspiration. Blood pressure was abnormally low.

The doctors and nurses went to work on the 800 casualties admitted (civilian casualties were never estimated), carrying out the correct treatment to ward off shock. But the patients, even those only lightly shocked or injured, refused to respond.

On the morning of the first day after the raid the first skin lesions were noticed. There was no pain, but extensive blistering began to appear on over 600 of the survivors. The colour of their skin was beginning to change too, turning a striking bronze colour. The doctors were mystified. As the day progressed the condition of the patients worsened rapidly. Their eyesight began to fail. Worse was to come. Their sexual organs started to swell rapidly. In some cases the penis grew to three or four times its normal size and the scrotum was equally enlarged. Now the survivors began to panic. Not only were they going blind, but they were losing their manhood as well.

Sapper Dennis of a railway transport battalion arrived with his company late that evening. Earlier that month he had been witness to a great tragedy when a rickety, patched-up train, packed with Italian civilians, had been trapped in a tunnel and over 300 men, women, and children had been choked to death. He had had the job, with his mates, of clearing out the bodies. Now he was involved in another disaster, though the cause of it was to remain a mystery to him for a long time.

'Our job was to take a trainload of [the victims] by train to another hospital because the Bari ones were already overcrowded. What a poor bunch of sods they were! Most of those we moved were sailors from the Royal Navy, all of them blind, big patches of cotton wool over their eyes, moaning and groaning, just like the pictures of the wounded you've seen of the First World War. We moved them sharpish, because there was something in the air in Bari that set you off coughing so much

The aftermath of the raid on Bari, with smoke and mustard gas fumes drifting across the water.

that you'd think your lungs were going to pack up.

In the Old City Signor Coniglio, then a 14-year-old schoolboy, now an established businessman in Britain, was also worried by the fumes coming from the burning port. 'Frankly, my mother – my father was still a prisoner-of-war – panicked. She got us and a few sticks of furniture and loaded them on an old cart and set us off pulling, telling us we've got to get out of Bari as swiftly as possible. We boys told her, "Mamma, it's only smoke, you know, from the ships!" But she wasn't having it. She said "Do as you are told. You'll be dead if you don't." And, you know, she was right. Hundreds of those who stayed behind must have died – and to this day there are old people in Bari who were young then, who cough up their lungs due to what I thought was harmless "smoke".'

Eisenhower's headquarters, still in Algiers, were well aware of the disastrous air strike on Bari. Eisenhower had been notified of the loss of the supplies vital to the new offensive within hours. Now he was shocked to hear from his Chief Deputy Surgeon for the theatre that the survivors of the Bari disaster were being afflicted by a mysterious malady which puzzled the doctors treating them. He ordered that a specialist doctor in chemical warfare, Lieutenant-Colonel Stewart Alexander, should be flown to Bari to investigate.

Alexander, who had done research into the effects of mustard gas back in 1940, noticed the smell immediately he entered the ward of the first British hospital in Bari that he visited.

'What's that odour?' he asked.

The British M.O. accompanying him answered, 'It's from the oil that most of the survivors had on their bodies and clothes when they were brought in here. We haven't had time to disinfect the wards as yet.'[3]

Alexander then started examining the patients and the pattern began to emerge: the bronzed skins, the blisters, the damaged genitals and eyes. A post-mortem was hurriedly carried out on some of the dead who, in addition to other injuries, had suffered the same contamination. Alexander came to the conclusion that all the victims he had examined, both alive and dead, had been subjected to mustard gas exposure of some kind. It was then that he was informed that a bomb-casing had been recovered from the bottom of the harbour. It had definitely contained mustard. Alexander, who knew nothing of the cargo of the *John Harvey*, was stunned. Had the Germans, for the first time in the Second World War, used poison gas in their attack on Bari?

In the end Alexander discovered that it was the Americans themselves who had brought the gas to Europe which had caused 617 casualties among their own sailors, nearly a hundred of them fatal. (The death toll among the citizens of Bari has never been revealed, if it was ever recorded.) Naturally the Allied authorities clamped down

77

Good advice – Sangro River, November, 1943.

strict secrecy over the whole affair.

Churchill himself was informed of the events at Bari and said that 'the symptoms do not seem like mustard gas.'[4] He ordered that no reference should be made to the tragedy, knowing that Germany would use the incident as propaganda. Dr Goebbels, the German Minister of Propaganda and Popular Enlightenment, would certainly have had a field day. So all references to deaths due to mustard gas were purged from British records.

In his book *Crusade in Europe* Eisenhower does mention the incident: 'We suffered the greatest single loss from air action inflicted upon us during the entire period of Allied campaigning in the Mediterranean and in Europe. ... One circumstance connected with the affair could have had the most unfortunate repercussions. One of the ships was loaded with a quantity of mustard gas which we were always forced to carry with us because of the uncertainty of German intentions in the use of this weapon.' He then added, although he must at least have

known of the military casualties, 'Fortunately the wind was off-shore and the escaping gas caused no casualties.'[5]

As a result of Churchill's – and Eisenhower's – refusal to allow the truth to be known, both the Italian and Allied doctors remained in the dark as to the true cause of their patients' dreadful symptoms. How many of them eventually died because of this is not known, especially among the Italian civilians. Nearly one hundred Allied seamen were recorded as dying of the gas in Bari alone, but many hundreds more had been hurriedly shipped to hospitals all over Italy and also to England and the United States. Nor is it known how many died later of cancer.

So the bombing of Bari passed into the history of the Second World War as the worst shipping disaster to strike the Allies since Pearl Harbor; it remained, too, one of the best-kept secrets of the war. But the high-handed way that the top brass treated both the civilians and their own sailors was symptomatic of the manner in which the

Our chaps – over here – will smash across the Sangro and gallop up the coast to Pescara, then make a left hook into the mountains and pounce on Rome from the east. Our part of the show will open with a colossal crack at the mouth of the Sangro River. ... First Canadian Division will spearhead the advance after the breakthrough has been made. We've bags of tanks and guns so it should be plain sailing.'[6]

As Major Kennedy, one of the 'Hasty Pees' present, commented in disgust afterwards, '*Gallop* up the coast to Pescara, will we? Gallop like a goddamn snail more like!'[7]

Relieving the battered 78th Division, which had made the 'breakthrough' across the River Sangro, Lieutenant Mowat, also of the 'Hasty Pees', was told by the British Division's Liaison Officer, who was weeping with rage, 'We've had 500 casualties crossing this one flaming river! And for what? Haven't any of the high mucky-mucks looked at their frigging maps? There'll be half-a-dozen Sangros before we get to Pescara, *if* we get to Pescara. Thank God you're taking over, Canada. We've *had* this show!'[8]

So, like the soaked and muddy British Fusiliers, 'faces as colourless as wood pulp', who had preceded them, the Canadians slogged into what seemed yet another purposeless battle. For nine days the 1st Canadian Division slugged it out with the Germans. In the 'Hasty Pees' alone one-third of a battalion was lost, dead or wounded. Mowat was wounded and was glad. He was out of it. He was taken to the Dressing Station a happy man; *he had a Blighty wound*! But he was to be disappointed. As the Regimental Surgeon worked on the wounded lieutenant, he chortled, 'You lucky little prick! Shell cut your boot open from end to end and hardly creased the skin. Wait till we get a bandaid on it and you can go right back to work.'

It wasn't a Blighty after all. Mowat turned on his back and yelped with pain. A shell splinter had penetrated his right buttock and the surgeon simply yanked it out with his fingers and said, 'Keep this in memory of me'.[9]

Angrily, Mowat limped back up to the line, his trousers held together with a safety pin.

battle of Italy was now going to be fought. Cruel losses would be suffered time and time again, with young men's lives being thrown away recklessly, even carelessly, by generals who knew nothing of life 'at the sharp end'. In the great blood-lettings to come, the fighting life of those young soldiers would no longer be numbered (for even such things had been worked out by the 'boffins') in months, but in weeks, even in days.

The brigadier from Eighth Army was elegant and fiery. Against the backdrop of a huge map, he explained to the assembled officers of the 1st Canadian Division what they were going to do. 'As you have guessed, gentlemen, our objective remains Rome. Can't let the Hun spend the rest of the winter there, all nice and cosy. So we shall jolly well turf him out. Over on the left – here – the Yanks will burst through the Bernhard Line and streak up the Liri valley past Cassino and pop into Rome from the south.

Even the toughest Allied soldiers engaged in the Italian fighting that winter could not always take it. For the most part the New Zealanders were hard men, brought up on remote sheep farms, used to rough living and thinking for themselves. The Germans rated them as the best soldiers in the Allied camp, though they thought them temperamental. But now the constant fighting and the miserable conditions under which they had to fight and live affected even their will to struggle and resist.

Brigadier Kippenberger, veteran of Greece, Crete and Africa, watched one of his battalions come back down from the line and felt that he had not seen men so exhausted since Flanders: 'Every man was plastered with wet mud up to his neck and their faces were grey.'[10]

Nevertheless he got smiles, cheerful words and ribald comments from every officer and every platoon – save one. The eighteen or so soldiers in that platoon stumbled by him silently, ignoring even his direct questions. An hour later he found out why. The C.O. of his 21st Battalion reported that, when ordered to attack, only the platoon commander and four men had moved; the others had refused to advance.

'Such a thing was unheard of in the Division,' Kippenberger commented later, 'and the C.O. was heart-broken.'[11]

The bitter winter war turned men into animals. Existence was troglodytic. Movement in daylight was often impossible. All supplies, including water (the water on the spot could not be used because it was polluted) had to be brought up during the hours of darkness. The men were as lousy and dirty as their fathers had been in the trenches in the old war. They were angry, bitter and without mercy. One officer came across a German, boots sticking out into the street, head hidden in a doorway. Crouched next to him were two bearded GIs puffing away at their cigarettes.

He asked, 'What about the Kraut?'

'Oh him!' one said. 'Sonofabitch kept lagging behind the others when we brought them in. We got tired of hurrying him up all the time.'[12]

Eric Severeid, the American war correspondent, overheard a 'pink-cheeked' private hesitantly ask a young officer, "Sir, pardon me, I can't find my officer. We've got some civilians in a house back there. What shall we do with them, sir?"

'The lieutenant snapped, "If you can spare a guard, send them back. If you can't shoot 'em in the back! That's what we did in my outfit. Don't take any nonsense from 'em." '

As Severeid commented, 'The pink-cheeked private saluted and left. He had received a simple order for mass murder.'[13]

In the Canadian First Division the survivors joked, as the 1st German Parachute Division fought them to a standstill, 'Four more killing days to Christmas . . . three more killing days . . . ' Most of them thought that they were going to be sent into reserve to celebrate the feast, for they knew the Divisional Commander had told Montgomery that his division 'was worn down to the nub and ought to be relieved'.[14] But that wasn't to be. They were to attack again. And, as it grew closer to Christmas, they were still attacking in the mud and the bitter winter rain.

That Christmas morning Churchill and his wife attended Early Service with Churchill's doctor, Lord Moran, who had safely seen him through his illness. It was held in a barn with a few officers and men of the Coldstream Guards who had been pulled out of the line and sent to North Africa to guard the ailing Premier.

During the service a dove flew in and perched on a rafter and afterwards the Guardsmen said it was a good omen; it meant that there would soon be peace.

One of the officers asked Lord Moran 'a little wistfully' how long the war would last. Moran couldn't answer that question, but he did know that 'as the P.M. grows in strength, his old appetite for the war comes back. . . . The P.M. has a bright idea. He is organizing an operation all on his own.'[15]

Indeed he was. A few days before, he had been on the point of death. Now, with Alexander, Wilson and other top commanders, he was working on his plan at his villa in Carthage. Although an American, General Lucas, who had taken over from Dawley at Salerno, would command the corps to be landed at Anzio, Churchill wanted British troops to participate. He instructed Alexander 'to give full weight to the importance of equality of hazards and sacrifice between British and American troops. I do not like the idea that the first and most risky operation undertaken in the Mediterranean under British command should fall exclusively on American forces.'[16]

On this fourth Christmas of the war for the British, the Great Man and his generals sat down to a magnificent lunch in the African sunshine. There was turkey and plum pudding with all the trimmings. Champagne flowed freely. Over it all presided the 70-year old Premier, dressed in a padded silk Chinese dressing gown decorated with blue and gold dragons, eating with his fingers, slurping his champagne, moon-face glowing. He was a happy man. Not only had he successfully fought off death, but had also shrugged off his 'black dog', the depression which plagued him when things went wrong. Now he would get the campaign in Italy moving once more.

The man who was to command the operation, General Lucas, when he heard that he was being given the task, said, 'The whole affair has a strong odour of Gallipoli and apparently the same amateur is still on the coach's bench.'[17]

'It will astonish the world,' Churchill had boasted at that Christmas lunch.

Lucas's reaction was: 'I feel like a lamb being led to the slaughter.'[18] He was.

That Christmas Eve, as Churchill conducted his 'sick-bed conference', Eisenhower and his private entourage were cruising around that pre-war haven of luxury and escapism, the Isle of Capri. Eisenhower spotted a large white villa and asked, 'Whose is that?'

'Yours, sir,' someone replied.

Pointing to an even larger one, 'And that?'

'That one belongs to General Spaatz.'

Eisenhower exploded. 'Damn it, that's *not* my villa! And that's *not* General Spaatz's villa! None of those will belong to any general as long as I'm boss around here. This is supposed to be a rest center for combat men, not a playground for the brass!'[19]

The Capri story was a good one and was quickly

'leaked' to his men fighting for their lives in the mud.

That evening Eisenhower, Kay Summersby, his 'chauffeuse', and the rest of the crowd celebrated in a hunting lodge which had once belonged to Italy's Prince Umberto. Suddenly the party was alerted by a cry from Eisenhower's orderly, Mickey, 'There's a rat in the General's bathroom!'

The General's dog, Telek, had sniffed out a rat which now sat on its hind legs on the toilet seat.

'I can handle this,' Eisenhower said, grabbing for his glasses and his .45. He fired and missed. The rat jumped up and clung to a pipe. Eisenhower fired again and got part of the rat's tail. He finally tumbled him on his third shot, but the rat was still alive. Finally a sergeant brained the creature with a log, while, as Kay Summersby records, 'the rest of us bent over with laughter.'[20]

'Great marksmanship, Chief,' Lieutenant Commander Butcher congratulated Eisenhower. 'Just what we'd expect from the Supreme Commander.'[21]

The next morning they set off to spend Christmas in Africa, travelling in Eisenhower's brand new B-17, 'fantastically luxurious, like a Claridge's in the sky' as Kay Summersby described it.

That same Christmas morning, as the visiting firemen (VIPs) flew into the sun, their 'tour of the front' completed, an utterly spent Lieutenant Mowat waited anxiously for the latest news of his company attack. The first of the walking wounded, a sergeant wounded in the leg, limped into the cellar where he waited. Mowat offered him a cigarette. Shakily the NCO accepted and told Mowat that the attack had been the usual disaster.

Mowat's friend, Alexander Kennedy, had gone beserk. He had charged the Germans single-handed, firing a tommy-gun. Now he was dead.

'It was the bravest goddam thing I ever saw, and the craziest.'

A moment later the blanket which covered the door to the cellar was pushed aside and a stretcher was brought in. On it lay another old friend, Al Park, face empty under the crown of bandages, barely alive.

Mowat could stand no more. He had reached the end of his own particular road. He broke down and began to cry. Years later he recalled: 'I wonder now, were my tears for Alex and Al and all the others who had gone and who were yet to go? Or was I weeping for myself, and those who would remain?'[22]

A few went to church that Christmas day. In the shell-pocked Church of the Annunziata at Venafro the Italian kids ran about yelling, '*Buon Natale, Americano!*', as the unwashed, unshaven GIs entered for midnight mass.

One was asked later what he prayed for. Private Frank Ryan, a gunner on a 105-howitzer, said, 'I prayed for the same thing at the Queen of Angels Church last Christmas in Chicago, but this time I really felt more deeply what I was praying for. You see this is my first Christmas away from home.'[23]

Outside they threw candy to the kids and shouted 'Merry Christmas' to their buddies as they went back to the waiting trucks which would take them up the line again. It was Christmas night, 1943. Eight Allied divisions had fought for six weeks. The cost had been 16,000 battle casualties and they had advanced seven miles.

Canadian troops with a donkey, used to transport water over difficult terrain.

III:
BLOODY ANZIO

'Poverty, hardship, misery are the school of the good soldier.'

Napoleon.

German propaganda leaflets dropped on the Anzio beach-head.

'A kick in the nuts'

That January there was tension in the air, as from general to private, they waited for the battle to begin. Suddenly Naples was full of troops once again – young innocent-faced reinforcements in bright new equipment, being sent to fill the gaps in the ranks of the divisions which would soon attack; more sober-faced 'old' men in their early twenties, the gold wound stripes on their sleeves or the Purple Hearts on their chests indicating that they had already paid the butcher's bill once.

The main railway station was bedlam. Fat self-important Italian officials in red caps yelling, peasants with bundles on their heads looking lost, the ever-present whores in the shadows, armed Military Policemen on the look-out for deserters, and, of course, the cannonfodder – hundreds of them waiting for the troop trains to take them to the front, staring at the twisted pieces of rusted steel which had once been railway wagons before the Allied bombers had come, whistling at the well-built *signoras*, and more often than not receiving back a look of professional concupiscence.

Soon the whistles shrilled and the Railway Transport Officers, with their red brassards and clipboards, hustled them aboard the trains.

Some didn't go. Lieutenant Telford, recovered from his wound, was also in Naples that January waiting to be posted to his old battalion. With him was another young officer, who had been wounded, 'slick, smart and very glib, a barrister by training'. The ex-barrister didn't want to go to the front. He told Telford, 'Listen, Eric, we've been through more than enough in Africa and Sicily. We won't be lucky a third time. Let's dodge the column. Let's volunteer for one of those new mule companies they're setting up. I'm sure it's going to be a cushy number.'

So the two young officers each volunteered to command a company of French North Africans employed in taking supplies to the men in the mountains. But it wouldn't be the 'cushy number' they thought. The ex-

An Arab muleteer leading his beasts through mountainous country.

barrister was dead before the year was out and Telford wounded yet again, trying to save a bottle of precious whisky during a mortar bombardment!

One man was actually cross that he was not being included in the coming battle. He had fought a bad case of malaria right through the Sicilian campaign and what had followed in Italy and now Audie Murphy could stick it out no longer. His buddy Kerrigan had reported him sick.

'As we wait our turn at the infirmary, I get a fresh hold of my spinning mind. The sweat drips from my face. To Novak I say, "Don't leave me. I'll be back."

'"Damned fool. Don't come back."

'"Wait for me."'[1]

But there was no waiting for the fresh-faced youngster from Texas. His Third Division would soon be going into action. But he'd get more than enough of battle in the months to come, another step on the way to becoming 'the nation's most decorated hero of World War II'.

The 'names' from Hollywood came to Italy to speed the cannonfodder to their deaths. Bob Hope came, skillfully speeding over the corny jokes, stretching out the good ones, keeping everyone laughing. Humphrey Bogart came too. The soldiers pulled his leg about his latest film, *Sahara*, set in the desert during the North African campaign: 'How come you crossed the whole desert without refuelling your gas tank?'

Bogart smiled. 'Hollywood is a wonderful place,' he said. 'They can do anything.'[2]

His wife, who he would soon leave for a cute 18-year-old with a husky voice, finished singing *Stardust* and now it was his turn. 'That's my cue again,' he said, flicking away his cigarette. He stepped in front of the microphone and put on his movie gangster's tough face, 'I'm looking for a new mob,' he growled. 'You guys look like a likely bunch of triggermen.'[3] The cannonfodder loved it.

On 16 January 1944, Fifth Army Intelligence assessed the situation thus: 'Within the last few days there have been increasing indications that enemy strength on the front of the Fifth Army is ebbing, due to casualties, exhaustion, and possibly lowering of morale. ... In view of the weakening of enemy strength on the front, as indicated above, it would appear doubtful if the enemy can hold an organized defensive line through Cassino against a coordinated army attack. Since the attack is to be launched before 'Shingle', it is considered likely that this additional threat will cause him to withdraw from his defensive position, once he has appreciated the magnitude of that operation.'[4]

It was a pious hope. That 'weakening of enemy strength' was a nice phrase when written in the echoing Bourbon Palace at Caserta which housed Fifth Army's HQ, far from the sound and smell of combat.

The land-based attack on the American front would be kicked off by Clark's Texans, the infantry of General Walton's 36th Division. They were to cross the River Rapido above and below the village of San Angelo. It was built on a cliff forty-five feet high and dominated the area where the Texans would cross. It was intended they would come in from both flanks where the river was bent in a tight S and pinch San Angelo out. Another division would then cross the flooded river north of Highway Six, which led to Rome, and wade through two miles of quagmires. If that was not enough, the attacking divisions would first have to cross two miles of perfectly open field before they reached the river, which had been sown with German mines.

Then there was the river itself. Normally in the dry season the Rapido was a mere trickle. But after three months of rain the river was a torrent, in some places nine feet deep. To make matters worse, the German defenders had methodically dynamited the upstream dams, adding to the force and flood of the water.

Because the river was only sixty feet wide, the attackers could not use an artillery barrage to cover the night crossing in case they hit their own men. German artillery had no such problems. They had long registered their heavy guns in on all possible crossing sites. In essence, therefore, the Texans were going to make a night crossing, after fighting their way through the minefield, over a fast-moving river, without the benefit of covering artillery, with the Germans on the high ground being able to observe their every movement. It was a recipe for disaster and it was not surprising that the Texans' commanding general, Major-General Fred Walker, wrote in his diary on the afternoon of the great attack: 'Tonight the 36th Division will attempt to cross the Rapido opposite San Angelo. Everything has been done that can be done to insure success. We might succeed, but I don't see how. ... I do not know of a single case in military history where an attempt to cross a river that is incorporated into the main line of resistance has succeeded. So I am prepared for defeat. ... Clark sent me his best wishes; said he was worried about our success. I think he is worried over the fact that he made an unwise decision when he gave us the job of crossing the river under such adverse tactical conditions.'[5]

Thus, in this mood of doom and gloom, the Texans prepared to attack. The massacre of Walton's 36th Division was about to begin.

Each Texan carried one K-ration, one D-ration, overcoat, cigarettes, rifle, grenades – and part of a boat. If they were lucky, it was of rubber. If they weren't, they were saddled with a part of a cumbersome steel assault boat. They started to plod forward through the wet darkness, their eyes fixed hypnotically on the muddy ground, wading through the fog like legless ghosts. For the engineers had attempted to clear a path for them through the German minefields, lining the safe routes with white tape as was customary.

American artillery bombards German positions.

By eight o'clock that night, 20 January, 1944, there were six battalions – 10,000 men in all – heading straight for what one American military observer called, 'the biggest disaster to American arms since Pearl Harbor'.

The Germans were on the alert. Already they had begun random shelling of the minefield. The shells churned up the mud and destroyed the white guide tapes. Mines began to explode on all sides and the night air was rent by the cries of men with their legs and feet blown off, lying there helpless, bleeding to death.

Even those who had now managed to reach the banks of the Rapido were finding it difficult to begin the assault. As one young officer, Lieutenant J. E. Phillips, recorded after the disaster: 'None of the boats had been designated for any particular unit nor were paddles distributed to each boat. ... Few of the men knew how to handle boats. Some would lift the boats right up and make a lot of noise, half-carrying and half-dragging them over the ground. ... There was a constant jamming of men and boats on the path. Because of the rough ground and clumsy boats one group staggered off the path and set off a mine.'[6]

At 19.30 American artillery started to pound German positions to the rear. For thirty minutes the big 155mm cannon, known as 'Long Toms', thundered. Shell after shell hissed through the dark sky as the horizon exploded in flame.

The Germans were not slow to react. Within thirty *seconds* of the start of the American barrage their guns opened up on the crossing sites! In panic, the Americans scattered into small groups, going to ground, blundering into the minefields, abandoning the boats. Confusion and

panic broke out. 'Everything became disorganized,' a report stated later. In the maze of shell-pocked lanes and roads 'nervous uncertainty prevailed', with the frightened Texans 'not keen for this attack'.[7]

Urged on by kicks and angry shouts from red-faced NCOs and officers, the Texans started to lower their boats into the fast-racing river as the flares soared into the sky on the German side and star-shells exploded in bursts of brilliant silver over the water itself.

Waiting for them on the other side were 400 yards of minefields, barbed-wire entaglements, interlocking fire from machine-guns and multiple mortars and a determined, ruthless enemy.

They started to cross, rowing hard against the current, as the water raced and the shells flung up huge fountains all around them. Boats capsized on all sides, taking the heavily laden infantrymen straight down with them. Men struggled frantically before being carried away by that treacherous current as tracer zipped back and forth across the river.

The engineers did their best. All that night they tried to erect footbridges across the Rapido, harassed constantly by the German fire, taking casualties all the time. One of their bridges was found to be defective on arrival, another had been damaged by a mine on its way up; enemy artillery fire knocked out two others. But by four o'clock that morning they finally succeeded in throwing one bridge across the river. Immediately half a battalion of infantry was across and began to dig in on the other side, as if their very lives depended upon it, which, indeed they did.

'It was easy to dig foxholes in the marshland,' Private Albert Rickett remembered afterwards, 'but we had to stay there and the water seeped through and soon we had water up to our bellies and we couldn't move or get out of there because the guns were shooting right on top of us. We could see the dead and wounded all around us, Americans and Germans.'[8]

A further two companies were pushed across the lone bridge, while medics ran back and forth bringing back the wounded. Some of the reinforcements, who had never been under fire before, couldn't stand it. One G.I. with 'a very young intense' face, began to cry. 'I don't know what happened,' he told the officer who stopped him, 'but it won't happen again.'[9]

Dawn came. The fog was so thick that artillery and air support for the men on the other side was still out of the question. In addition, icy roads on the American side slowed down the arrival of fresh supplies and men. Desperately the engineers used smoke pots to cover their bank of the Rapido from enemy eyes, but the wind was against them. The Germans spotted that lone bridge, the only life-line with the trapped companies on the other side. The artillery growled and a few minutes later it disappeared in a violent explosion.

'These German guns kept going all the time,' Private James Matthies remembered. 'They knocked out every pontoon bridge the engineers tried to put up. They knocked out the footbridges and they knocked out a lot of the boats. It was a tough thing to look at. All of us kept praying and praying that some of the fog would lift so that our planes could come down and dive-bomb the hell out of them and our artillery could spot their flashes and blast their gun positions.'[10]

Finally the fog did lift in the area to the south of San Angelo where Walker's 143rd Regiment had made a relatively successful crossing. It was disastrous for the 143rd's 1st Battalion, commanded by Major D.M. Frazior. From their local observation positions and from the heights of Monte Cassino five miles away, the Germans could see the 1st Battalion's every position. Heavy artillery fire started to fall on them. Tanks moved in. The Texans were now fighting with their backs to the river.

Desperately, Frazior asked for permission to withdraw what was left of his force. The request went through channels right up to General Walker. He refused. He knew what a withdrawal would do for the morale of those still to cross.

But Frazior had already made up his mind. He felt that his first loyalty was to his hard-pressed men and he ordered them to pull back. Some panicked and pushed and grabbed in order to be first back. Others kept their nerve.

'I guess my First Sergeant was one of the last guys to leave,' Pfc Carapelli recalled. 'He had been wounded twice, but refused to be evacuated. When he was finally ordered to leave, he insisted on walking across the broken, heavily shelled footbridge all by himself.'[11]

Others were broken and weary, yet resigned themselves to their fate. An unknown officer, his combat suit sodden with mud, told a senior officer as he reached the American side: 'I've got men still over there.' Then he added slowly, 'This is the worst I have ever seen. I'm not doing anybody any good over there. I'm tired. I haven't got anything in me any more. There's nothing else to do. I'm going back over there.' And so he went, like a lamb to the slaughter.[12]

Some were not so eager to make the attempt. A chaplain who was present recorded: 'Many men became lost; nervous uncertainty prevailed. The situation was no longer in a firm grasp – but out of hand. Quite a few infantry tried in all sincerity to get across the river, some refused to cross, while others deliberately fell into the water to avoid crossing.'[13]

Colonel Martin, trying to put some fire into his badly disorganized 143rd Regiment, sacked a battalion commander, and personally took over. One of his officers saw him standing on the bank shouting orders. 'When I saw my regimental commander standing with tears in his eyes as we moved up to start the crossing, I knew something was wrong.'[14]

He was right. His men were slaughtered on the other side. 'I started out commanding a company of 184 men. Forty-eight hours later, seventeen of us were left.'[15]

Still Clark and Walker wouldn't give up. Both wanted to mount fresh attacks at the earliest possible moment. Clark's aim was to push tanks across and fight through the German positions. Time was running out and the landing at Anzio was almost due to start.

Walker had other reasons. He simply wanted to save what was left of the First Battalion of the 141st Regiment trapped on the other side. He wanted to attack under cover of darkness to minimize casualties. His Corps Commander, General Keyes, overruled him. He wanted the attack to start at two in the afternoon. Walker gave in.

At two o'clock the fresh boats for the two-regiment assault had not arrived. The attack was postponed until three. Colonel Martin of the 143rd protested that it was still too early. Colonel Wyatt of the 141st did not protest to Walker; he simply set the time of the attack back to nine o'clock that night off his own bat.

Back at his CP, waiting for the slaughter to begin once more, Walker noted in his diary: 'I expect this attack to be a fizzle just as was the one last night. The stupidity of the higher commanders seems to be never-ending.'[16]

That afternoon the battlefield was left to the dead. They lay in the churned-up mud, sprawled out in the grotesque postures of those done to death violently.

On the Germans' side they waited. In spite of the smoke, they could see the Americans well enough, for the fields were spread out in front of them like a map, each road and track easily identifiable, with the roofless farmhouses clustered among the shell-shattered trees. They could see, too, the dark, moving shapes of the American supply columns, their gunners busy unloading fresh ammunition outside the gunpits, the infantry sheltering in the ditches and in the wrecked barns.

Then it started again. The valley quaked with the roar of guns. From end to end the horizon blinked with angry red lights. The boom of that tremendous barrage echoed and re-echoed round the circle of hills as the shells slammed into their targets.

Colonel Martin's Regiment started crossing at three that afternoon. The machine guns and mortars opened up at once. They couldn't miss.

'We were under constant fire,' Sergeant Kirby recalled. 'I saw boats being hit all around me and guys falling out and swimming. I never knew whether they made it or not. When we got to the other side, it was the only scene during the war that lived up what you see in the movies. I had never seen so many bodies – our own guys. I remember this kid being hit by machine-gun fire; the bullets hitting him pushed his body along like a tin can. Just about everybody was hit. I didn't have a single good friend in the company who wasn't killed or wounded.'[17]

Still they pushed on with a courage born of despair, but soft flesh was useless against the steel wall of machine-gun bullets. They were mown down by the score, falling in lines, in some cases, as if they were on parade.

Sergeant Rummel was hit in both legs and slammed to the ground. 'I didn't feel any pain,' he recalled afterwards. 'I was just scared to death. There was confusion all around. Two of the boys offered to carry me back but the fire was so intense I told them to get out the best way they could.' Rummel crawled away unaided and 'could hear my bones cracking every time I moved. My right leg was so badly mangled I couldn't get my boot off, on account it was pointed to the rear.'[18]

Further north, one of Martin's battalions also managed to get some men across. But they could not, try as they might, advance further than 200 yards from the river bank. Casualties started to mount steadily. The battalion commander was hit and wounded. In turn, one after another, the three company commanders also became casualties.

Desperately the engineers, working under fire, threw up footbridges at the crossing site, but for the most part these were used by men who had had enough. As one eye-witness recorded: 'These [bridges] seemed for the most part to permit infantrymen to straggle back to the rear bank on one pretext or another – they were ill or carrying messages or helping wounded to the rear.'[19]

Morale slumped. As the situation of the 143rd Regiment became desperate and the enemy artillery fire intensified, the engineers who had been ordered to build a

Engineers use smoke pots to cover the assault on the River Rapido.

Bailey bridge in full view of the Germans virtually went on strike. A regimental officer who tried to get them working radioed back, 'They are dug-in and scared. Work has not begun on the Bailey bridge. Got them out of their holes and started them on their way. Do not anticipate that they will accomplish a thing.'[20]

In the end Martin threw in the glove. At noon the following morning he ordered what was left of his regiment to withdraw.

Wyatt's 141st Regiment kicked off under cover of darkness. But it helped them little. The Germans were waiting and the swift current did not make their task any easier.' The minute the current hit the boat broadside,' one officer said, 'it carried it downstream. I could hear the paddles slapping water and hitting together and then the men yelling when their boat turned over. It curdled your blood to hear those men drown.'[21]

Some made it to the other side and began to dig in frantically. The German fire grew and grew. Orders from above were that there would not be another withdrawal;

they would stay and fight to the end. Two of the battalion commanders said to the regimental executive when they heard the news, 'I know you did all you could, sir. So long.' The other said, 'Well, I guess this is it. May I shake hands?'[22]

Both were subsequently hit and tried to carry on, severely wounded as they were. One finally gave up, after being wounded twice more. The other was found crawling across a bridge on his hands and knees and the man who found him said later, 'It was the only time I saw a man's heart flapping around in his chest.'[23]

It was becoming another Alamo for the Texans, with the Germans playing the role of the besieging Mexicans. By the afternoon all the officers in both battalion headquarters had become casualties. Within the next hour every commander had been killed or wounded. And there was no way back. The survivors either surrendered or fought to the death.

Keyes, Walker's Corps Commander, still wanted him to continue the attack. Walker was in a quandary. It was either carry out the order or resign. He had been a soldier for nearly thirty years and it had taken him all that time to achieve his present rank. Was he going to throw it away just like that?

But shortly afterwards Keyes had second thoughts. He telephoned Walker to cancel the attack by his last remaining regiment. 'Which I did in a hurry,' Walker wrote in his diary the next day. 'Thus many lives and a regiment were saved.'[24]

Now, on the other side of the river, the trapped men were overcome. On the American bank, 'we could hear our American guns gradually diminishing in strength until the only sound was silence.'[25]

His foot clung to his leg by a shred of skin. There was little blood because the heat of the blast had seared his arteries. He had crawled out of his foxhole, pushing with his one good leg, gripping with his nails, fainting several times before he reached the river 400 yards away. He rolled into the icy water, somehow swam across, somehow climbed the steep rocky bank, somehow crawled another 400 yards until the medics found him. At the battalion aid station they wrapped him up and gave him a cup of hot coffee. Gratefully he clutched it in his frozen hands and said, 'My foot's gone, Doc. I know that.' He was twenty years of age and not at all bitter at his fate. Instead he whispered softly, 'I'm all right. I made it. How about the other boys?'[26]

Too many of the 'other boys' had vanished. Colonel Wyatt's First Battalion was never found. Only 100 men survived of those who had crossed the Rapido to assist it. In forty-eight hours of action the two regiments of the 36th Infantry division which had attempted the crossing had suffered 2,000 casualties – a staggering 56 per cent

American infantry advance under fire.

casualty rate.

As for the German defenders, General Rodt's 15th Panzer Grenadier Division, they had been hardly aware that a full-scale divisional attack was underway. Their casualties had been a paltry sixty-four men killed and 179 wounded.

As the German soldiers wandered the battlefield and discovered dead bodies piled everywhere they started to realize the full magnitude of the attack. Some of them were kind and arranged a truce so that the defeated Americans could collect their dead. Others were malicious. When they found some abandoned American signal pigeons, they sent one back with a message. It read: 'You poor nightwatchmen, here is your pigeon back so that you won't starve. Your captains are too stupid to destroy secret orders before being captured. At the moment your troops south of Rome are getting a kick in the nuts. Signed: the German Troops.'[27]

So ended the first phase of the great new offensive in Italy urged by Churchill from his sick bed in Africa. The American 36th Division had well and truly received a 'kick in the nuts'. Clark, of course, being Clark, blamed the Division for the failure on the Rapido, not his own

strategy. He ordered a wholesale purge of divisional command. The Texans lost their Assistant Divisional Commander, its Chief-of-Staff, Walker's own aide, and, naturally, Colonel Martin of the 143rd Regiment who had wept for his men as he had forced them to go into action at that fatal river again.

But the men of the 36th Division wouldn't forget 'Butcher' Clark. From commanding general to private they blamed the Fifth Army Commander for the slaughter on the Rapido. Walker wrote in his diary afterwards: 'The great losses of fine young men during the attempts to cross the Rapido River to no purpose and in violation of good infantry tactics are very depressing. All chargeable to the stupidity of the higher command.'[28]

Unknown to Walker, several of the Texan officers held a secret meeting a few days after the disaster. They came to the conclusion that their great losses had been due to 'Butcher' Clark's inefficiency. They did not know when the war would end, but they decided that when it did they would call Clark to account. They would demand a Congressional Investigation of the battle and of Clark's leadership.

But it would be many a weary month before that came about. In the many battles ahead some of those Texans would fall. Yet the survivors fought on, carrying their

secret with them to the end. They'd get Clark yet!*

But at the time the bitter comments of the officers who had led those men to their deaths were direct enough. The sacked Colonel Martin wrote in a very disjointed passage, 'As long as leaders who have the guts to plunge into hopeless odds such as this operation are sacrificed like cannonfodder, our success in battle will suffer in proportion and disasters will eventually come.'[29]

One of his company commanders was more succinct. Bitterly he told a war correspondent, 'I had 184 men. 48 hours later, I had 17. If that's not mass murder, I don't know what is.'[30]

*In the end they got their enquiry in 1946, but Clark was cleared.

'Between the devil and the deep blue sea'

A thin slice of moon took the edge off the January darkness as the great fleet came to anchor. It was now one o'clock on the morning of 22 January, 1944. The Anglo-American invasion force was less than a mile off the Italian shore. In an hour the British 1st Infantry Division would begin to land to the north of Anzio and Nettuno, and the American 3rd Infantry Division would land to the south. First to go in would be Darby's Rangers who would land directly at Anzio itself. Suicidal, everybody thought.

Indeed, those among the Americans who had taken part in the Salerno landings four months before thought that the whole business, dreamed up by Churchill on his sick bed, would be a blood bath, including US VIth Corps Commander General Lucas.

Now the invaders waited. Any moment they could be discovered. The shore, dark and brooding to their front, could well explode with flame. Out in the bay, packed together as they were, they would be sitting ducks. It would be a massacre.

Suddenly the ominous stillness was broken by a tremendous burst of fire. The British rocket ships opened up, firing 780 rockets within the space of two minutes, blasting away the mines and the wire on the beaches on which the assault troops would land. For those minutes all was noise and confusion. Then, as abruptly as they had started, they ceased firing. Again the waiting infantry tensed.

But nothing happened. Slowly it began to dawn on the watching brass that they had caught the Germans completely by surprise. This was not going to be another Salerno.

Now the first of the British 1st Division began to hit the beaches. Here and there mines exploded. A man went down, his foot blown off, and another. Hastily the sappers were whistled up. They went to work at once, clearing a path for the stalled infantry. But that was about it – a few odd mines. Even the pillboxes, built long before by

An Allied tank coming ashore at Anzio.

the Italians, were not manned.

The horizon sharpened in the winter dawn. Everything was proceeding systematically. Wire nets had been laid and the first vehicles were being driven up the beaches. Men were directed ashore by the beach party under the command of a skinny young officer with a loud rumbling voice, a Major Denis Healey, who one day would live off that voice in the House of Commons.

It was the same on the American beach. General Truscott's Third Infantry Division landed according to plan. Its War Journal for that dawn reads like an account of a peacetime manoeuvre:

0145 Rocket Ships fired.
0220 Second Wave hit Red Beach. Landed dry.
0229 No opposition met by 1st and 2nd waves.
0335 1st Battalion, 7th Infantry reports: all companies now fairly well together. No opposition.

The last entry read simply.
0450 Congratulatory message from Commanding General VI Corps.[1]

Above the Americans of the 'Rock of the Marne' Division, as the light grew brighter, the sky began to fill with more and more Allied fighters and the only sign of German resistance, a lone cannon far inland, was already being engaged by a British destroyer.

Some had thought the task allotted to Darby's Rangers suicidal. Back at Clark's headquarters he had told the planners that his only hope of capturing his objective was to go in quick and fast. 'When I run out of the landing craft, I don't want to have to look right or left, I'll be moving so fast.'[2]

Now, however, as he ran at the head of his Rangers into Anzio, he found there was no opposition – just a few dead Germans, churned to pulp by the rockets, and a handful of dazed survivors, only too eager to throw up their hands and yell *'Kamerad!'* Within the hour all three Ranger battalions were ashore without casualites. It was all too easy.

General Truscott, the Commander of the 3rd US Division, felt there was no need for him at the front. His Division was driving inland without encountering any opposition. It was time to go back to his beach CP and have a good breakfast. Private Hong, his Chinese orderly, went to work with a will and soon the General was eating bacon and eggs on the bonnet of a jeep, watching the invaders pouring ashore by their thousands. Then General Clark and his party arrived from Naples to congratulate him. Hong was ordered to rustle up more bacon and eggs. He muttered angrily as Truscott's supply of precious eggs began to diminish rapidly: 'General's fresh eggs all gone to hell!'

But there'd be eggs aplenty in the march across country to Rome which lay ahead of the Anglo-Americans.

While Hong was cooking eggs, Alexander was wiring to Churchill: 'We appear to have got almost complete surprise. I have stressed the importance of strong-hitting mobile patrols being boldly pushed out to gain contact with the enemy, but so far have not received reports of their activities.'[3]

Delighted that the operation was not going to turn out another Gallipoli after all, Churchill wired back: 'Thank you for your messages. Am very glad you are pegging out claims rather than digging in beachheads.'[4]

It had all been too easy, this landing miles behind the German lines. Darby, for one, was uneasy. It didn't seem right to him, somehow. He told Colonel Churchill of the Commandos, who had also landed unopposed, 'They seem to think it will all be free love and nickel beer. I'm not so optimistic.'[5]

Wynford Vaughan-Thomas, the BBC correspondent on the beachhead, also had his doubts. That night, his first in Italy, he wrote to a colleague further south: 'It is just normal military fuck-up with an American accent. We are commanded by a dear old pussy-cat, who purrs away, that we are all happy on the Beachhead, and in a sense, we are.'[6]

But not for long.

That 'dear old pussy-cat' was VI Corps Commander, General John Lucas. At the time of the landing he was 54 years old, the most senior commander in the Mediterranean except Patton, and he felt every one of those years. As he wrote in his diary on his birthday, 'I am afraid I feel every year of it.'[7]

The following day he confided something more significant to his journal: 'I must keep from thinking of the fact that my order will send these men into a desperate attack.'[8]

General John Lucas, who had succeeded Dawley after the Salerno fiasco, had had no confidence in the Anzio landings right from the start. After the war he told General Gavin, the Airborne Commander, that 'he had told General Clark ... that the troops were inadequate if he was expected to attack Rome. ... Nevertheless Clark insisted that he either take the VI Corps in or be relieved of his command. ... As a consequence Lucas was on the spot. As a career soldier he could not refuse to carry out Clark's orders and thus be relieved of command.'[9]

'The last thing Clark said to me on D-Day,' Lucas later recalled, was, 'Don't stick your neck out, Johnny. *I* did at Salerno and got into trouble.'[10] General Lucas was not about to stick his neck out. Having gained surprise in the landing, he completely disregarded the advantage this gave him. Two days after the landing he was still *thinking* of pushing out from the beachhead. 'I must keep in motion if my first success is to be of any value,'[11] he noted. But in those first forty-eight hours, while Kesselring frantically organized fresh divisions from Northern Italy, France and the Reich to counter-attack the

General Lucas (centre), confers with Admiral Troubridge (left), and General Penney (right), commander of the British 1st Infantry Division.

Anglo-Americans who had landed so far behind his lines, Lucas was more concerned with consolidating his beachhead. He personally supervised the construction of the airfield and air raid warning system and was primarily concerned that his sea route to the Fifth Army at Naples was secured.

Meanwhile, the British Guards of the 1st Infantry Division, who had anticipated a bold dash inland, were kept in reserve, doing nothing. The officers idled their time away playing bridge and the men brewed endless mugs of char. The Irish Guards, in particular, had hoped for a race to Rome. As one of them had declared enthusiastically when they had landed. 'We'll give the Holy Father a holiday and make Father Brookes [the padre] acting unpaid Pope.'[12]

It was little different on the American front. Truscott's 3rd Division sent two reconnaissance troops ahead who prepared all the bridges over the Mussolini Canal to their front for demolition. Otherwise they did little.

Three days passed. Now at last the American force began to move inland, past the farms hastily abandoned by the frightened Italians, noting as they did so what good defensive positions the farms would have made if the Germans *had* held them, with their stout walls and outside bakehouse ovens that could have been turned into excellent pillboxes.

Another day passed in 'maneuvring and displacing', as the 3rd's Divisional History puts it. There were occasional small patrol actions, but that was about all. The Germans were few and far between and there seemed no organized defence.

But in the air the Germans *had* begun to react. Again they used the same weapon they had employed with such success against HMS *Warspite*. While the dive-bombers fell out of the January sky, their sirens howling, the *Luftwaffe* pilots circled the invasion fleet cannily, like sheep-dogs looking for a stray sheep. When they found one they would launch their missile, steering it to its victim by radio beam.

First they sank a military target, the destroyer HMS *Janus*. She went down in twenty minutes, taking with her her skipper and over 150 men. The survivors were picked up, singing 'Roll Out the Barrel'.

Their next victim was definitely non-military. It was the fully illuminated hospital ship, the *St David*. Three hospital carriers were loading wounded and injured when the Germans attacked. The *Leinster* was hit first, but not seriously. Swiftly the crew got the fire started by the bomb under control and calmed the patients. The *St David* was not so lucky. She took a direct hit and began to sink immediately. The harassed sisters and doctors had exactly six minutes to get as many patients as possible up on to the tilting deck, fit them with lifebelts and convince them to jump into the freezing water. One with both eyes bandaged was put into a life-jacket and *thrown* into the sea. He survived. Another who had just undergone major abdominal surgery and who had been receiving intensive care when the ship was hit somehow managed to haul himself onto a raft and also survived.

But time was running out. The stricken ship's bows began to rise out of the water. She was going under stern first.

'Wait for the sisters!' the Captain ordered frantically as the boats started to pull away. *'Wait for the sisters!'*

Then the ship disappeared, carrying with it the skipper, several nurses and the senior doctors, plus most of his staff.

Bobbing up and down in the water, a wounded American soldier, noting the Red Cross brassard worn by the nurses who survived, remarked bitterly, 'Jesus, you must be the only folks around here who still believe in God!'[13]

German attacks on the fleet began to mount steadily as the end of January, 1944, approached. In that last week there were steadily fewer people on the packed beach and harbour who still believed in God. The Germans could hardly miss, for the beachhead was crammed with 18,000 vehicles and 70,000 men in what Berlin Radio called, 'a prison camp where the inmates feed themselves'.[14] Both fleet and beachhead were subjected to air attack and intensive long range artillery bombardments. One of their prime targets was the host of small craft bringing more men ashore. After one near-miss a Pay Corps clerk was heard to cry in astonishment, 'Hey, this isn't on schedule. You ought to push the war further back!'[15]

But there was no rear echelon at Anzio. Anybody could die – clerk or nurse – anywhere.

In one dogfight over a beachhead a German pilot jettisoned his bombs to escape a Spitfire. They landed directly on the surgical area of the evacuation hospital, killing twenty-eight, including three American nurses, and injuring sixty-four others. Later the German pilot who had killed them was shot down and admitted to the same hospital. It was stated at the time that the German was treated like any other patient. But bitterness and resentment began to afflict the men and women who were being subjected to this tremendous bombardment. One survivor of a torpedoed ship told the *Stars and Stripes* reporter afterwards: 'Among the wounded there was moaning but no crying. Mostly they got madder than hell. One man kept shouting into the wind, "God damn those Jerries!" over and over again.'

Another said he had gone into the water with three badly burned teenage sailors. One had died almost immediately. Another began to hallucinate, insisting that the moon was a rescue ship. 'Let's go swim to that ship,' the eighteen-year-old urged the unwounded sailor.

'That isn't a ship. That's the moon,' he replied. 'Just take it easy. Everything will be all right.'

But the boy started to swim with all his might towards the moon. The other man raced after him and caught him. 'I held him for a while,' he told the reporter, 'and then he began to stiffen and I let him go. He was a good man. I hated to see him go. It was a hell of a thing to have one of those boys slip away, then the other.'[16]

Soon teenage boys would be dying at Anzio by the score, by the hundred and, in the end, by the thousand.

It started on the morning of 30 January. Just after midnight Colonel Darby sent in his 1st and 3rd Battalions to kick off the attack on the town of Cisterna, which had to be captured if Lucas was going to advance on Rome. Almost immediately they ran into trouble. The Germans were waiting for them. Machine-gun fire poured from the houses along the road. Tanks and flakwagons, armoured vehicles carrying multiple quick-firing 20mm cannon, came scuttling across the fields. Swiftly they surrounded the surprised Rangers and cut them up into small pockets.

A battalion of German paratroops, the most feared enemy troops in Italy, started to exert pressure. By eight that morning both battalion commanders were out of action, one killed, the other seriously wounded.

Darby attempted to squeeze his reserve battalion, the Fourth, into the area to give aid to his hard-pressed troops. To no avail. They too ran into trouble. By ten it was 'well shaken up', as the *War Room Journal* of the Rangers recorded.

Radio communication began to go. It was reported that Rangers had been seen marching away with their hands up. Darby pleaded with the Commanding Officer of the US 504th Parachute Regiment to send tanks and men to his aid. Over the radio he talked to his old Sergeant-Major, who told the Colonel, 'Nobody is giving up. Shoot them if they come any closer!'

Darby yelled over the chatter of machine guns and the crackle of other frequencies, 'Issue some orders. Don't let the boys give up. Who's walking with their hands up? Don't let them do it! Get the officers to shoot! Don't let them do it. Do that before you give up! You're there and I'm here unfortunately, and I can't help you, but whatever happens, God bless you!'[17]

The radio went dead. Darby went into a farmhouse and wept.

Only six men later returned from the 1st and 3rd Ranger Battalions, while the 4th Battalion lost fifty per cent of its effectives. To all intents and purposes the Ranger Brigade was wiped out and Darby had lost his command, one which he had led through North Africa, Sicily and Italy. For a while he was shattered, but there was no time for sentiment on the beachhead. Almost immediately he was given the command of the 179th Infantry Regiment. He was killed by a shell two days before the German Army in Italy surrendered.

General Truscott, commanding the Third Infantry Division, tried desperately to help. He had heard that Ranger prisoners had been machine-gunned and bayoneted by the German paras. He urged his 'Rock of the Marne' men to ever greater efforts. They attacked with a will, getting within 500 yards of Cisterna, the closest any battalion of the Third would get until the final breakout in May. In that attack two of the Third's men won the

Field-Marshal Kesselring visiting German paratroops in Italy.

Congressional Medal for Honor, one of them, Sergeant Olson, sacrificing his life in the process.

Truscott went up front himself. A shell exploded near his feet and he fell to ground wounded. After his leg had been set in a plaster cast, he continued commanding, hobbling around as best he could; but even Truscott realized that his men could not break through. For Intelligence had now identified eleven battalions from seven different German divisions, five of them armoured, facing the 3rd. Reluctantly he ordered the attack stopped and the 'Rock of the Marne' men went on the defensive.

Lucas tried desperately to keep the momentum of the attack going. When barrel-chested General Ernie Harmon of the US 1st Armored Division arrived on the beach, Lucas put down his corncob pipe and said in his Southern drawl, 'Glad to see you. You're needed here.'

Harmon was cast in the Patton mould, but without the latter's keen intelligence. He affected a lacquered helmet and cavalry breeches like those Patton wore and he had the same tough-guy pose, complete with pearl-handled revolvers. But he was a good man to have in a crisis and he saw he was in the midst of one now.

'Ernie,' Lucas drawled, 'I reckon you got to go places.'

Harmon tugged at his breeches and said, 'Jesus, I'll go places,' and stalked out of the room. He issued his orders, ate a C-ration supper and tried to get some sleep in a freezingly cold truck. At dawn his 1st Armored would support the British 1st Infantry Division attacking out of the beachhead in the Moletta River sector.

Harmon's tanks ran into trouble almost immediately. Four of his Shermans leading the advance got stuck in the mud. An armoured wrecker was whistled up to drag them free, but was ambushed by the waiting Germans. Another four tanks were sent up, and another four, until finally a fuming Harmon had to admit, 'Because I was stupid, I lost twenty-four tanks while trying to succour four.'[18]

That night Harmon convinced Lucas that the area of the River Moletta was no good for tanks and asked to be switched to helping the British in a salient known to both the Allies and the enemy as the 'Thumb'. He was given permission to switch to that area.

The Irish and Scots Guards had already met ferocious opposition in the Thumb and had been badly savaged. Now it was the turn of the Duke of Wellington's Regiment and their comrades in the King's Shropshire Light Infantry and the Sherwood Foresters to keep the attack going. On 30 January they crossed their start-line, the infantrymen bent as if they were facing beating rain. Immediately they were met by murderous German fire. Tanks were everywhere. So were the feared 88s and the 'moaning minnies'. Soon all was confusion, the British infantry cut into small pockets as they tried to take cover in the pouring rain.

'Such a lack of information and no cover in those vines. Shells screaming and whirring like mad vicious witches. Sprays of fire all over the place. Shrapnel like hail. Bullets whizzing from nowhere. And on top of that the bloody

97

rain. We were so cold. Half the soldiers disappeared – mown down, captured, or just fucked off, everything you can imagine.'[19]

As they crossed the high embankments the Foresters made a perfect target. They were shot down by the score. In each house to their front the Germans had placed a tank which fired through the window. Time and again the Foresters attacked. One small group did get through, but lay on the other side like exhausted swimmers and in the end they, too, had to withdraw.

Finally the Sherwood Foresters had to pull back altogether. Their colonel had been wounded in the leg and the face. Their companies were all down to forty men. General Harmon came up in a tank to see what the holdup was. The Sherman climbed a hill and there Harmon got out to walk, for the Germans were on the other side of that same hill. Later he recalled, 'There were dead bodies everywhere. I have never seen so many dead men in one place. They lay so close together that I had to step with care.'[20]

He stopped and called for the Commanding Officer. From a foxhole a corporal with a handlebar moustache, his uniform covered in mud, stood up and snapped stiffly to attention. He was the senior 'officer'.

'How is it going?' Harmon asked, though the answer lay dead all around him.

'Well, sir,' the corporal said, 'there were a hundred and sixteen of us when we first came up and there are sixteen left. We're ordered to hold out until sundown and I think that with a little good fortune, we can manage to do so.'[21]

Harmon ordered the corporal and his fifteen 'gallant comrades' to get on the tank and go back with him. For now he knew that the Allied offensive had definitely failed. The 3rd Division could not take Cisterna and the British 1st and his own First Armored could not thrust through on the Albano Road to Campoleone. The Germans had reacted much more quickly than Lucas had expected.

That night Churchill lamented, 'I had hoped that we were hurling a wild cat on to the shore, *but all we had got was a stranded whale.*'[22]

And as the battered infantry of General Penney's First Division watched Harmon's Shermans pull back to the beaches, they knew what to expect.

All night it had rained, a cold steady downpour, but the waiting soldiers were too tense and nervous to notice. All day they had been expecting the Germans to attack, for an Allied secret agent in Rome had reported that the enemy had selected that day for the great counter-attack which would drive the Allies back into the sea.

Towards dusk the rain began to ease off and the sky cleared a little. A strange silence descended upon the Anzio front. Even 'Anzio Annie' and the 'Anzio Express', the great German long-distance cannon, had ceased firing. Tension rose in the sodden slit trenches as the soaked infantrymen peered to their front, imagining they saw a German in every shadow, trying to locate the enemy in that grotesque landscape.

Another hour passed in tense expectation. Here and there flares hissed into the night sky to hang there in that glowing unnatural light before sailing downwards like fallen angels.

At eleven o'clock reports began to come into the underground headquarters all along the line: increased shelling of the 1st Division's Reconnaisance Regiment and the Loyals; tank and infantry attack on the 45th's 157th Infantry Regiment; attempted penetration of the line between the US 45th Division's 3rd Battalion and the British North Staffordshire Battalion. The German counter-attack had begun.

For nearly a month the Germans would attack and attack at Anzio, flinging in their reserves open-handedly, not counting the cost, determined to throw the Allies into the sea, to carry out Hitler's order – he had helped to plan this operation himself – to rid Italy of the 'sore of Anzio'. Yard by yard the allies were forced back.

'It was the age-old struggle for survival,' the history of the 45th Division recorded, 'not glory or patriotic fervor, that spurred the men into holding the bitterly contested ground.'[23]

Companies, battalions even, were overrun. Some surrendered in face of this overwhelming German might. Others fought on, escaped, and fought on again.

Bringing in the surviving eighteen men of his company, after the rest had been decimated at Campo di Carne, which, ironically enough, means 'field of meat', Captain Sparks watched as they crawled 'to a nearby draw where trickled a stream in which lay the corpses of many dead. The water ran blood red, but many of the men filled their canteens, boiled it and drank.'[24]

A battle-worn British division, the 56th Infantry, was rushed to Anzio to help hold the bridgehead. General Penney, 1st Infantry Division commander, was wounded and out of action for a while. Templer, in charge of the 56th, took over command of the battered First and his own division and fought on.

The crisis came on 18 and 19 February. It was suggested by Lucas that General Harmon's 1st Armored Division, still in reserve and up to strength, should attack and restore the Allied positions.

Just before the artillery bombardment which would precede the attack began, Harmon 'received a message which was responsible for the toughest decision I ever had to make'.[25] His Chief-of-Staff reported that a battalion of the 45th Division found itself directly in front of the place where the barrage would fall.

'To order the artillery attack might mean the death of many fine brave American soldiers. To abandon the artillery attack would be to abandon the sortie upon which, I was convinced, the saving of the beachhead

A British soldier sharing a cuppa with a GI.

depended. The brutal naked choice seemed to be between the loss of some hundreds of men and the loss of many thousands.'[26] Harmon ordered the guns to begin firing.*

His decision showed the gravity of the position as the Germans pressed home their advantage, slowly but surely pushing the battered Anglo-American divisions back towards the sea.

A determined attack by men of the German 147th Infantry Regiment threatened to cut off the Scots Guards and the London Irish. If they could do that, then German tanks would have a clear run down the road which led straight to Anzio. The fate of the whole beachhead was at stake.

Like a latter-day Horatius, Major Sidney of the Grenadiers Guards, a descendant of the famous Sir Philip Sidney, now stood alone, blazing away at the advancing Germans with a tommy-gun as they advanced down a path to the point where they would cut the two British battalions off. His tommy-gun jammed. Two guardsmen began handing him primed grenades which he threw at the Germans. A guardsman pulled out the grenade's pin too soon and disappeared in a flash of violent flame. Sidney was hit in the backside and began to bleed 'like a pig'. Still he continued to throw the grenades as the Germans began to hesitate. He was hit again as a German grenade exploded nearby. Now he was losing blood rapidly. He started to feel faint. Some American paras arrived. Immediately they went into action to help the

*In the end the 'battalion' turned out to be a platoon and it escaped casualties.

handful of guardsmen. Sidney slumped to the ground, weak from loss of blood.

A scared para said, 'Gee, Captain, I don't feel well. I think I'll go back to base.'

'You goddam son-of-a-bitch,' the American Captain snapped, 'you stay where you are!'[27]

And he did. They all did.

That February, Lieutenant Nick Mansell wrote in his diary: 'Oozing thick mud. Tank hulks. The cold, God, the cold. Graves marked by a helmet, gashed with shrapnel. Shreds of barbed wire. Trees like broken fish-bones. Rip,rip,rip of machine-guns. Racket of shells, screeching, snarling, whirring above like furious witches. Earth shudders. Sadistic. Hot shrapnel tearing through what were bushes. The zip of a sniper's bullet. The repellent stench of stomach wounds – human offal! A haystack is burning. Smoke clouds coiling and reeling above poor old Aprilia. A dead gunner, his head squashed by a tank. The terrible sight of seeing men go bomb-happy. "Yellow". Deliberate self-mutilation. Weeping. The worst moment is dusk, a breathless, anxious hush of waiting. Will we or will we not be attacked? *Which of us is to die tonight?*'[28]

And every night at eleven 'Axis Sally', that ugly American woman, working for the Germans in Rome, announced over the radio in her sexy voice, 'Beachhead! *Death's head!* And now I'm gonna play for you boys down there my favourite record.' There'd be a slight pause as she put the needle on the record and over the air from *Radio Roma* would come that catchy little foxtrot, *Between the Devil and the Deep Blue Sea.*

'Go easy, boys ... there's danger ahead'

'We hated the bloody place,' that reluctant soldier Bombardier Castle remembered forty years later. Still refusing to 'soldier' and fighting a losing battle with the British Army, he now found himself in action with the artillery in that shadow of that great peak, Monte Cassino, which dominated the whole battlefield.

'I don't know whether the Germans were up there or not at the time, but everywhere you went, even if you just took your shovel for a walk*, you always had the feeling that somebody was watching you. Bloody uncanny!'

He was right, of course. The main peak at Cassino, Monte Cairo, 6000 feet high, its gullies streaked with snow which ran down from its white pyramid, dominated the whole of the Liri Valley. Nothing could move by day without being spotted by the Germans holding Cassino.

Since the final crossing of the Rapido two months earlier, Frenchmen, Americans, Britons had attempted to capture the feature, and failed dramatically.

'There were bodies everywhere, too many and too difficult to collect,' Castle remembers. 'In March it was all right. It was still cold. But later when the Poles and the Gurhkas did their attacks, Christ how they stank! Some of our gunners, the younger lads, were retching all the time.'

Now it was the turn of the New Zealand Corps to tackle Cassino, defended by Colonel Heilmann's paras; and General Freyberg, the Corps Commander, independent as he was and responsible only to his own Government – 'a prima donna' Clark called him – was not going to sacrifice his men tamely. Freyberg, who had won the VC fighting with the Guards in the First World War, who had defended Crete in the Second and had gained an excellent reputation for his fighting ability in the Western Desert, wanted Cassino, and in particular the Benedictine Monastery, destroyed. As the New Zealand Divisional Commander, General Kippenberg, who was soon to lose both feet at Cassino, wrote afterwards: 'At

*to defecate.

New Zealanders fire a 6-pounder anti-tank gun at German positions at Cassino.

New Zealand Divisional HQ we felt certain that the Monastery was at least the enemy's main observation point. It was so perfectly situated for the purpose that no army could have refrained from using it.'[1]

Virtually all those there that February who were doing the fighting felt the same. Sergeant Evans of the London Irish recorded later: 'It just had to be bombed. Oh, it was malignant. It was evil somehow. I don't know how a monastery can be evil, but it was looking at you. It was all-devouring, if you like – a sun-bleached colour, grim. It had a terrible hold on us soldiers. I don't think I was convinced that the Germans were *firing* from there, but it was such a wonderful observation post. We thought it had to be destroyed. We just didn't know how the place could be taken otherwise. I am sure what I thought was shared by ninety per cent of the lads in our division.'[2]

Fred Majdalany, another infantryman who was there, also experienced that *frisson* of fear that the venerable Monastery towering high above the battlefield occasioned: 'Everybody has experienced the sensation when walking alone past a house that invisible eyes were watching from a darkened interior. Hostile eyes can be sensed without being seen. Monte Cassino projected this feeling over the entire valley. . . . In the cold desolation of winter and fatiguing travail of unresolved battle, the spell of its monstrous eminence was complete and haunting.'[3]

Even that arch-cynic Bombardier Castle was finally convinced that the bombing of the Monastery was justified: 'Didn't matter a toss to me what they did with it then, although I was baptized a Catholic. But afterwards when I saw all our dead, trapped in the rocks and scattered all over the show, I thought they had been right to clobber it. Anyway, all I got out of it was a bloody bad headache from the last barrage and two plaster saints I nicked from the ruins afterwards. Even they didn't do me much good. I left the parcel with them inside behind at Victoria Station in 1945 when I was on my way to be demobbed!'

But, in higher echelons, Freyberg's demand that, before the New Zealand Corps attacked, the Monastery would have to be destroyed met with a mixed reception. General Butler of the US 34th Infantry Division, which had made the first attacks on the Monastery, said, 'I don't know, but I don't believe the enemy is in the convent. All the fire has been from the slopes of the hill below the wall.'[4]

On the other hand, General Eaker, whose planes would be the ones which would carry out the bombing, 'flew over the Abbey in a Piper Cub at a height of less than 200 feet,' according to the US Air Force's Official History, 'and states flatly that he saw a radio aerial on the Abbey and enemy soldiers moving in and out of the building'.[5]

As for Clark, under whose command Freyberg's New Zealand corps now came, his attitude, at the time, was ambiguous. Anzio had been conceived as a means of breaking the deadlock on his Fifth Army front. Now, ironically enough, a major attack was going to have to be made at Cassino to relieve the hard-pressed Anzio beachhead. That February the harassed Clark must have reasoned: 'If I don't agree to Freyberg's request and the Cassino attack fails, the German pressure on Anzio might well turn it into another Dunkirk. If I *do* agree to the bombing of this famous monument, what will world reaction be? What will the millions of American Catholics think of an American general who orders the bombing of one of the greatest Catholic shrines in the world?'

In the event Clark managed to arrange that all the discussions on the subject of the bombing should be conducted by his Chief-of-Staff, General Gruenther. Finally, according to Clark himself, he asked General Alexander for a written order to bomb the Monastery and claimed that this was received at Fifth Army Headquarters.[6] Unfortunately this document was 'lost'.

In any case, after the war Clark was able to wash his hands clear of the whole business. It had been the British, from Alexander down to the Commander of 4th Indian Division, General Tuker, who had wanted the bombing of the Monastery, not he! As he had done throughout the Italian campaign, Clark would fight the post-war analysis of the conflict with his eye firmly fixed on the reaction of the media. He would weather the Rapido débâcle, the bombing of Cassino, the fiasco of Rome – and win those four stars which he coveted.

On the morning of Tuesday, 15 February, 1944, the monks in the great Monastery had just sung the words 'Beseech Christ on our behalf' when the first of a succession of explosions sent a shudder through the thick walls. They were followed by crash after crash which soon joined together into a single cataclysmic roar. Bomb after bomb rained down. Through the long narrow windows, the petrified monks could see the angry yellow flashes of the bombs, the great clouds of black smoke mushrooming up, and hear the rumble of falling masonry. A servant rushed in gesticulating wildly, no sound coming from his pale lips. It was a deaf-mute trying to tell the monks in sign language that a bomb had passed through the frescoed dome of the cathedral. It was the first part of the building to receive a direct hit.

Now treasure after treasure was destroyed – the pipes of the ancient Catarinozzi organ, the high altar, parts of it attributed to Michelangelo, even the tomb of St Benedict, the founder of the Order. One by one, the five cloisters disappeared.

Down below, war correspondent Christopher Buckley of the *Daily Mail* thought he 'could detect little modification in the monastery's outline as each successive smoke cloud cleared away. Here and there one noted an ugly fissure in the walls, here and there a window seemed unnaturally enlarged. The roof was beginning to look ... jagged and uneven ... but ... the building was still standing after four hours of pounding from the air.'[7]

Above: A B-24 Liberator hit by flak over the Cassino front.

Below: The Bombing of Monte Cassino Monastery.

Clark was working at his desk in his Forward Command Post when the attack started, trying not 'to pay much attention to anything that wasn't on my desk, but I suppose I was unconsciously listening all the time.'[8]

A stick of bombs fell close by, sending shrapnel flying all over the place, but 'fortunately injuring no one; except the feelings of my police dog Mike, who at the time was the proud mother of six week-old pups'.[9]

As more planes passed overhead to continue the bombing, Clark knew that he would never see the 'famous old abbey, with its priceless and irreplaceable works of art', so he remained at his CP 'and tried to work'.

Later he told his biographer, Martin Blumenson, that the bombing had made him 'sick at heart'. Those who were at the 'sharp end' had rather different sentiments. Lieutenant Bruce Foster of the 60th Rifles, asked what he thought of the bombing, snarled, 'Since you ask me what I felt about the Monastery, I'll ask *you* something. Can you imagine what it is like to see a person's head explode in a great splash of grey brains and red hair and have blood and muck all over you, in your mouth, eyes, ears? And can you imagine what it is like when that head belonged to your sister's fiancé? I *knew* why it happened. I was positive. It was because some bloody fucking Jerry was up there in that fucking bloody Monastery directing the fire that killed Dickie, and I know that still: to hell with all those Pontius Pilates who pretend they were so bloody innocent and had nothing to do with the bombing. Christ, Dickie was the finest, most upright man you or I would ever meet. I am just glad that he died quickly, which is more than a lot of other poor fuckers did up there. It drove me mad to see those chaps at HQ poring over coloured maps and never dreaming of going up to the front line to see what conditions were really like.'[10]

That evening in Berlin, as Goebbels began to roll the propaganda drum – 'this outrage against European culture by the Anglo-American barbarians' – and sundry higher commanders played the innocent virgin, the Royal Sussex Regiment launched General Freyberg's first attack against the shattered Monastery. In ten hours they lost 140 officers and men out of a total of 328, a forty-three per cent casualty rate. And General Clark at his writing desk was 'sick at heart'.

A week after he had been released from hospital, cured of his malaria, Audie Murphy was among a boatload of replacements heading for Anzio. Fifteen of them, like himself, were recently released from medical treatment, including one man who complained bitterly he was not cured of gonorrhoea and still had a 'run'.

'That's the only kind of discharge you'll get in this army,' someone remarked unfeelingly.[11]

To Murphy the beachhead looked calm enough. Trucks moved back and forth. Boats came sailing in with supplies. But scarcely had they reached the beach when five German bombers came winging in. The men scattered like frightened chickens. But Murphy's experienced eye could see that the attackers were after the ships. He plodded on. A convoy of jeeps came level with them. Arms and legs bobbled grotesquely over the sides of the vehicles. Murphy was seeing what every new reinforcement saw when he landed on the beach – the dead being brought to the cemetery which lay just where the boats bringing the new boys landed.

For at Anzio everyone was in the front line. There was no escaping sudden death even when a man thought he had received that coveted Blighty which would take him back to Naples. Indeed, the evacuation hospital was named by the GIs 'Hell's Half Acre' and was subjected to bombing and shelling throughout the campaign. Some of the forward troops concealed their wounds in order *not* to be sent to one of the most hazardous spots on the beach.

But the nurses could not escape. They had to stay with the wounded, sleeping in slit trenches at night, with the sides covered in blankets to prevent the sand sliding in. But being women they were still mindful of their appearances. Shellfire or not, they went to their slit-trenches with their hair in curlers, faces sticky with cold cream. Once night had fallen, however, no one left his or her trench for any purpose whatever. Daylight would reveal lines of nurses advancing on the open latrines, carrying the tins in which they had carried out their natural functions.

But even the hardest of the nurses could not quite come to terms with the field latrines, constructed right in the middle of the camps. They were roofless and, built with men in mind, were surrounded solely by waist-high strips of hessian sacking. So the nurses had to choose whether to sit it out brazenly or to bend double.

One of these nurses, who confessed to being afraid of the dark, won the George Medal for her courage in tending the wounded, while machine-gun bullets ripped the canvas above her head. Sister Graves was just one of several nurses who won awards for bravery during the Siege of Anzio.

For that was what it had become. As the Anglo-Americans could not break out of the beachhead and the Germans could not push them into the sea, the latter contented themselves with simply cutting their enemies off. From the middle of March, 1944, to the breakout in May, conditions at Anzio resembled the trenches in the First World War. Forward positions were stabilized and remained practically unchanged for three months.

The troops made themselves as comfortable as possible in this great sprawling mess of trenches, caves, dugouts, barbed wire and barricades. But protection from shellfire was more important than comfort. Some of the troops sank huge Italian wine barrels, capable of holding 1000 litres, deep into the ground and slept in them. Many of Harmon's tankers dug holes beneath their Shermans and lived in them. Others dug the tanks themselves in until only the turrets were showing and spent their days in these metal tombs.

As their fathers had done in the trenches, the infantry tried to create some sort of normalcy in this crazy existence. They ran 'races' for example. In the British sector beetle-racing spread like wildfire and large sums of money changed hands in bets. A champion beetle might fetch as much as three thousand *lire*, equivalent to a month's pay for the average private in those days. The system of racing was simple. Various colours were painted on the beetles' backs and runners were paraded around the 'ring' in jam jars. Just before the 'off', the beetles were placed under one jam jar in the centre of the 'course' – a circle of six feet in diameter. At the 'off', the jar was raised and the first beetle out of the circle was the winner.

The Yanks went one better of course. An American engineer, Sergeant Bill Harr, laid out a racecourse, using the white tape the engineers employed to mark the paths through minefields. He collected enough horses and mules for a race and set up a public address system. He even recruited some pretty nurses to give away the prizes to the winners. The odd part of it was that the Derby was in plain sight of the German gunners, but they never fired a single shot at this tempting target. Perhaps they were betting too.

Generals had barbecues, with GI magicians such as Private Roland Ormsby, better known as 'The Baron', who had even brought his own tuxedo to the beach with him! When General Harmon gave a party and invited some British generals, they came with the pipes of the Gordon Highlanders. Before they began to play, Harmon was told that Pipe-Major was always given a 'dram' first. Accordingly he handed the 'great tall Scotsman' a glass filled to the brim with 'not very good whisky'. 'His Adam's apple worked up and down, as he swallowed that whisky in a single gulp. Without a flicker of an eyelid he turned back to the band and struck up the music.' As the General said years later, 'The British seemed to have a lot of old customs. This one was one of which I thoroughly approved.'[12]

All over the beachhead were signs saying '42nd Street', 'Broadway', 'The Good Eats Cafe', 'Beachhead Hotel – Special Rates to New Arrivals'. Crude 'dago red' was sold, bought on the Italian black market, or a potent kind of brandy distilled in makeshift stills, using copper tubing from shot-down German planes. Meals were also served in these places, mainly hamburgers made from Italian cattle which 'just happened to trip over a mine'. Sheep rarely 'tripped over a mine' in the American sector, because the GIs were not overly fond of mutton.

There were underground speakeasies too, run by Italians. The British war correspondent Wynford Vaughan-Thomas described them thus: 'The visitor groped his way down a steep flight of stairs, cut in the slippery rocks to find himself in a huge murky cavern, which reeked of wine, garlic and earthy mould. Enormous vats and barrels

Not the Somme, but Anzio, 1944, where conditions came to resemble those of the Great War.

lined the walls and above them in the flickering light the dark roof was seen to be covered with spiders' webs and dripping with moisture . . . "Al" himself, *il padrone* to his assistants, would usually be found surrounded by his little court of retainers, counting out the greasy *lire* notes of the military currency and issuing his orders to his minions to fill the big glass flasks with *vino bianco* – always the "most magnificent *vino* in Italy, *Capitano*!" The wine was drawn from the casks by the simple process of removing a bung at the top, inserting a rubber tube and sucking vigorously. The lucky purchaser carried it off in a big glass container, set in a wicker basket. No one inquired too closely at the mess where he had got it from, for a "slug of the good old *vino*" before going to sleep gave a good many people on the beachhead enough "catacomb courage" to face the anguish awaiting them next morning.'[13]

Some soldiers walked around in an alcoholic daze for days on end. It is recorded that one GI got so drunk that he staggered right into the German front line. Instead of shooting him, however, the German infantry dusted him off and obligingly pointed him in the direction of his own lines.

In the lulls between the shelling General Harmon was wont to go duck-hunting in some marshy ground only a couple of hundred yards from the Germans. Lord John Hope, a Guards officer on Lucas's staff, on the other hand, indulged in – of all things in that killing ground – *bird-watching*! It was as he was thus engaged that he came across another feature of the beachhead during the Siege of Anzio – deserters.

He was wandering down a deep ditch when he came across some washing hanging out, which he thought 'odd'. Then he spotted a large heap of tins hidden beneath some sticks and told himself, 'My God, those deserter bastards must be in the wood here.'[14] He knew there were an estimated 300 deserters, British and American, at large in the beachhead. He turned a corner and was confronted by two unshaven GIs, one with a red beard, and both armed with rifles. He knew it was touch and go. The deserters were not going to let themselves be captured. 'What are you doing here?' they asked. He told them he was bird-watching which made them laugh. They pretended they had just come from the front and Hope nodded his understanding and went on his way, apparently still seeking bee-eaters and golden orioles. But as soon as he got back to headquarters he reported the men to the American Provost Marshal who promptly sat him on the bonnet of his jeep and raced off to capture the deserters. But as they approached the ditch, 'Red Beard and his companion jumped up and ran like hell into a tobacco field' and that was the last Lord John Hope saw of them.[15]

There were women too. Men who were sufficiently bold or sex-starved would risk sneaking behind the German lines where there were willing farmers' wives or daughters, prepared to indulge them for a tin of corned beef or a bar of chocolate. Indeed there was an outbreak of VD on the beachhead and the hard-pressed medical authorities, their hands full with the wounded, had to set up a prophylactic station to keep the VD rate down. However, the Germans themselves finally put an end to the problem by liberally sowing the gaps in their front with anti-personnel mines.

For the brass and those with money professional sexual services could be obtained in relative safety through Sergeant Walkmeister of the 'Black Devils'. The 'Black Devils', or 1 SS Brigade, were once described as 'the cream of the Army and the scum of the stockade'. They were a mixed bunch, from all walks of life, made up of volunteers from both America and Canada. A forerunner of the American Green Berets, they mostly fought a kind of irregular war behind the enemy lines. At Anzio they took over a remote section of the front where they lived and fought with little official supervision. It was not surprising that when the Black Devils landed in Anzio, one of them, '*Signore Sargente*', as Walkmeister was known to his girls, brought with him an ambulance equipped with drink – and whores.

Lieutenant Stuart of 1 SS Brigade described the vehicle which later became famous throughout the beachhead as 'Walkmeister's Portable Whorehouse', thus: 'A Navy lieutenant was sitting on the edge of one of the bunks holding the hand of a very pretty young lady. Behind her lay one other pretty young lady and on the other bunk lay one – or was it two? more pretty young ladies.'[16]

Old soldier that he was, Stuart asked no questions, but helped himself to medical alcohol plainly labelled 'For the Use of the US Army. Medical Detachments Only', flavoured it with a few drops of pineapple juice and got down to business. It is recorded that for 'Walkmeister's Portable Whorehouse' disembarkation was 'quick and surprisingly efficient. No colonel appeared to ask awkward questions.'[17] Later, when he was established, *Il Sargente* arranged that the girls would be available 'for parties, festivals, or anything needed to take the minds of the Big Brass off their duties for a few hours'.[21] For a small fee, naturally.

Unable to drive the Anglo-Americans into the sea and knowing how lax discipline was in some sectors of the beachhead, the German propaganda companies in Rome stepped up their campaign against the men of Anzio in an attempt to demoralize them and make them surrender or desert. *Leutnant* Thiel, an Italian-speaking staff officer, found an attractive, sultry Roman prostitute named Rita, who was photographed in silk underwear reclining in a seductive pose. An American was added to the picture for the subsequent leaflet, with Rita saying, 'You Americans are so different!' The leaflet was then fired into British positions by the thousand to stir up resentment against the Americans. Surprisingly enough, those leaflets which were not used for more mundane purposes when the supply of toilet paper ran out are still treasured as souvenirs by Anzio veterans.

But it was *Radio Roma*, with its two stars 'Sally' and 'George', which really led the German propaganda campaign against the beachhead. Between playing swing records, Sally, or 'Axis Sally' as she was known to the men, would whisper in her husky voice, 'What are those smart GIs doing to your English women while you are fighting and getting killed here? Easy to guess, eh?' And Sally would spare her audience crouched in their foxholes, receiver placed in a tin pan so that the reception would be clearer, none of the details. That brief encounter back home between the mythical GI and the English rose would be related with no holds barred. Goebbels knew that his propaganda merchants would need more than swing records to grab the attention of the average sex-starved Tommy or GI.

'He opened a can of beer and, after he had had a drink,' Rifleman Bowlby heard one English girl describe such a meeting with a GI, 'he pulled me into the bushes, inned and outed me, wiped his tallywock on my skirt, pissed in the beer can and walked away whistling "God Save the King".'[18]

It was fortunate that there was no television in 1944,

British Infantry clear a building in the battle for Cassino.

for Sally was no beauty. An American by birth, she was short and stubby and at the time of Anzio far advanced in pregnancy due to a brief encounter with a married man who played in the orchestra of *Radio Roma* and who had 'inned and outed' her in a decidedly careless manner.

George, the other star of the show, was full of silky menace and a specialist at the grisly tale: 'Have you heard about Private Fox? He went on a patrol and stepped on a shoe-mine. Nasty things shoe mines. All his guts were blown away. But he went on living another twelve hours. You should have heard him yelling.' Wynford Vaughan-Thomas said his voice had 'a slow, insidious and unnerving quality as he put over his slogan, "Go easy, boys. *There's danger ahead.*" '[19]

And so it went on, day after day. Prince Borghese gave dinner parties for the top brass where the footmen served black market K-rations in white gloves. Visiting VIPs made special day-trips to the beachhead, senators – MPs, self-important journalists. A Colonel Spears came all the way from Palermo in Sicily to snipe at a German so that he could 'hold his own with his son who was a pilot in the Pacific'. The old boy was in luck; he managed to kill a German soldier half his age. Back in Germany some mother had just lost a son.

Clark made periodic visits, always making sure his sorties to the 'front' were well documented by the press. Once he was seen squatting with a GI, apparently sharing a can of K-rations. But when the photographers had taken their shots Clark hurriedly handed the can back to the GI.

But all the time there was death. Eric Sevareid, the American correspondent who had been up at the Italian front since the previous September, wrote in despair, 'One saw so many dead each day, so many bleeding bodies. I realized I was becoming a little obsessed with the tragedy of these youngsters, tending to write about death more and more. Sometimes in the long lovely evenings when we sat by the sea, the old feelings about the death of youth which I had experienced as a college

boy began to steal back, unnerving and frightening me. It would not do; one had to shake off these moods. But it was becoming harder and harder to escape them.'[20]

He wasn't the only one. Coming across a burial party about to inter six new bodies, he asked them what they felt. One of the grave-diggers told Sevareid, 'You get used to it after a while.' His boss, a sergeant, shook his head. 'That isn't true,' he said. 'I never get used to it.' He looked at the six bodies sprawled out in the path. 'With a thousand it would be just a problem of sanitation. with six it seems like a tragedy.'[21]

And all the while the wounded and dying kept flooding in, as the German bombers droned overhead, seeking out their target for the night. A British medical man, Major J. A. Rose, wrote down his impression of the pre-operation ward, a large tent, just after the war, describing the misery of the sodden wounded, lying in the mud: 'The wounded lay in two rows, mostly British, but some Americans as well, in their sodden, filthy clothes; greatcoats, pullovers, battledresses, all of the thickest; soaked, caked, buried in mud and blood, with the ghastly pale faces, shuddering, shivering with the cold.

'Most of them had their first field dressings or shell dressings on. I grew to hate that combination of yellow pad, bloody, dirty brown bandage, and mud-darkened skin.

'Some unconscious, these chiefly head wounds whose loud snoring breathing distinguished them; some (too many, far too many) were carried in dying, with gross combinations of shattered limbs, protrusions of intestines and brains with great holes in their poor frames torn by 88-millimetre shells, mortars and anti-personnel bombs. Some lay quiet and still with legs drawn up – the penetrating wounds of the abdomen. Some were carried in sitting up on stretchers, gasping and coughing, shot through the lungs. ... All were exhausted after being under continuous fire and after lying in the mud for hours or days.'[22]

Well could George, of that silky insidious voice, warn, 'Go easy, boys. There's danger ahead!' There was. The misery and the killing were not over yet by a long way.

'Taking time out of life ... escaping from the war'

One day that March, when the fighting settled down at Anzio, a lone American crouched on a rock behind the German lines surveying the battlefield through a pair of binoculars. He was Lieutenant Winston Sexton of the USAAF, who had been shot down and wounded over Sicily the previous July. Now, although his wounds had not completely healed and his broken leg was still encased in plaster, he had been on the run for months and had covered 500 miles on foot to reach this spot. He had been hiding next to the rock for two days, preparing an approach to the Allied lines, noting any sign of activity on a crude map of the area and thus working out where the front was.

Now he decided that he knew enough. He would have to walk ten miles to the place where he would break through. 'Considering the distance and the very slow speed I would make, I allowed myself four days to get to this position. As for provisions, I took one loaf of bread, two large links of sausage, a couple of ounces of sugar and a pint of alcohol distilled from wine. None of this was to be eaten unless I got pinned down and couldn't move.'[1]

He set out at four o'clock on the morning of 25 March 1944. At daybreak he passed three Germans who took no notice of the shabby, limping 'peasant'; he bumped into an Italian who warned him to get out of the area because the Germans were moving in a battalion of Italian fascist infantry. Finally he holed up for the night in an empty house near the town of Sabodia.

'As dawn came I went back into the house, sat by an upstairs window and looked the situation over. The town of Sabodia was just a half-mile west of me and was separated from the sea by a long lake.'[2] Sexton knew that on the other side of that lake were the positions of his own troops. So he decided he would set out for it as soon

Allied prisoners from the Anzio front being marched through the streets of Rome by the Germans.

as darkness fell. Although he could only move slowly, he determined to swim, hoping the night would allow him sufficient time. So he set off, taking three hours to reach the lake, spurred on by the knowledge that, after nearly half a year on the run, he would soon be with his own kind. He managed to find a hiding place at the water's edge while he prepared for his swim.

'I decided after a time to try swimming dog fashion across the lake. I took off my clothes and hid them, together with my automatic, under a bush. I then got a bottle of alcohol out of my knapsack and consumed the contents, hoping that the alcohol would help to limit the effects of the cold water.'[3] He lowered himself carefully into the water. It was freezingly cold, but he persisted, though his body was becoming colder by the instant. After only a hundred yards 'the startling realization that I would never reach the opposite shore struck like a bolt of lightning!' He couldn't swim fast enough to keep his circulation up and he was beginning to get cramp. He would have to turn back.

Exhausted and frozen, Lieutenant Sexton collapsed on the bank where he left his clothes, knowing that it was 'just a matter of time before I would get caught playing around the front lines. If the Jerries didn't catch me, I'd probably get hit by Allied fire.'[4] So he set off again, trudging north towards Rome, a ragged figure with every man's hand against him.*

Sexton was only one of the many hundreds, perhaps thousands, of British and American soldiers and airmen on the run in Italy that winter. Ex-POWs for the most part, they had officially been told to remain in their prisoner-of-war camps when the Italians had surrendered in September, 1943; the Allied forces would soon rescue them. But that had proved a pious hope and so the *Wehrmacht* had moved in to take over the unguarded Italian camps, sending the prisoners back to the Reich.

Some, however, had not accepted the official advice. From general to private, they seized the golden opportunity offered them by the disappearance of their Italian guards. Many of those who left simply wanted to stretch their legs and had neither the spirit nor the resources to make the journey of many hundred miles to the Allied forces in the south. They set out to find women, better food and a change of scenery.

While some began the long march south in a disciplined fashion, determined to reach their own forces and fight again, others were left drifting through the Apennine foothills. In effect, they lived off the land, begging from the peasantry, lending a hand with the wine harvest, tending sheep or doing any odd job in way of payment. Captain Soames, Churchill's future son-in-law, who was in charge of the Allied escape organization in Italy, found it very difficult to keep these parties moving southwards.

*It was another three months before Sexton got his freedom when American troops marched into Rome.

They had an exasperating tendency to settle wherever they could get 'their feet under the table'. A cushy billet and a pretty and willing girl and they couldn't be moved for weeks.

This close contact with the Italians was an eye-opener for most of them. They had mostly thought of the Italians as lazy and happy-go-lucky, content to live in their picturesque squalor. Now they discovered just how tough and hard-working the peasantry was, scratching a bare living from the harsh mountain country, drinking coffee made out of toasted oats and making meals of the boiled feet of hens. They got to know their simple pleasures – a glass of wine after church on Sunday and a game of cards, a walk over the next hill to eye the girls in the nearest village. They found *their* enemy was not the Anglo-Americans and not the Germans, but authority: *il padrone*, the landlord, *il fattore*, his agent, *il guardino*, the armed keeper who preserved his shoot and woodlands – the whole feudal system and its ally, fascism, which took their grain, their little money and their sons for that remote war in Africa which meant nothing to them.

These share-croppers, *mezzadri*, who the escapers encountered worked long days on the *padrone's* fields, on their own rented ones, to come home to a meal of hard, home-baked bread on which *mamma* had poured a thin mix of tomatoes and onions and a tiny drop of precious oil. Wine they had, but it was without body and stung like pepper.

At four in the morning these humble folk, who still ploughed with oxen, or dug up their sloping stony fields as their forefathers had done two thousand years before, were up once more, feeding their skinny animals, drinking their acorn coffee, and were off again to another back-breaking day of unremitting labour.

Lieutenant Stuart Hood recalled later; 'I did not know how hard life could be until I heard an old man cry to children teasing him with the threat of living to a century, "But I don't want to live. *I want to die!*" I did not know that life could be restricted to one spot, that one's bridal bed could be one's deathbed, that the days could be tied to a cycle of labour and life, mean, squalid, hard. . . . I watched the sudden furies of a woman, beautiful and dirty, with her long hair about her face, as she flung her hoe from her and cursed the fields, the landlord and the hour of her creation.'[5]

Not all, however, who threw in their lot with the Italian peasantry and apparently made no attempt to reach their own lines were content simply to wait for the war to catch up with them. Some joined the newly emerging bands of partisans who were beginning to fight the fascists *and* the Germans, who, now that Italy was officially at war with Germany, were also the enemy.

Sergeant Manuel Serrano, a paratrooper captured in North Africa, was one. He turned up one day at the base of his former unit, dressed in 'British Army shoes,

A band of Italian partisans.

mustard-coloured cotton pants, a torn GI paratrooper's jacket and an Italian straw hat with an orange band'[6] to tell his strange story to his comrades who had long thought him dead.

After Italy's surrender he had gone on the run and joined the partisans. His band had helped more than a hundred ex-POWs to escape back to Allied lines. Then, in March, 1944, Serrano's comrades were informed by a local farmer that Italian fascist soldiers had captured and killed six escapers in the hills near Comunanza. According to the farmer, they had stripped the prisoners and made them dig a ditch. When it was finished, they had machine-gunned them and covered the naked bodies with soil.

'That night,' Serrano told a reporter from the *Stars & Stripes*, 'three of us made for the field. We saw the ditch, but the bodies had disappeared. We checked around and learned the nuns had taken the bodies to the convent of Comunanza after the fascists left. We went to the convent and there were the six bodies, wrapped in white sheets and lying on slabs of wood. . . . I lifted up the covers from the faces and recognized them all. Four were GIs and the other two were British.'[7]

Serrano swore a solemn oath that for each one of the murdered men he would kill a fascist with his 'bare hands'. 'They taught me a lot of tricks at Benning and in England, but fascist-hunting wasn't one of them,' he told the reporter. 'I was pretty nervous.' But in the end he got his fascists and felt it was time that he left the area. But before going, he decided to make a speech in the *piazza* at Comunanza. 'I told them I'd be back some day, and that I would tell the American soldiers what I had learned

from the partisans.'[8] They begged him to stay, offering him the office of mayor and the town's prettiest girl as his wife. 'But,' as Serrano told Sergeant Sions, the *Stars & Stripes* reporter, 'I guess I'll wait till I get back to Brooklyn and find a nice Italian girl there. I like these Eyeties.'[9]

It is not recorded whether the paratrooper who liked 'Eyeties' ever got back to Brooklyn to find his 'nice Italian girl'. Many who fought with the partisans didn't. For the secret war being waged between the partisans and the Germans and their Italian puppets was becoming increasingly murderous, atrocities being carried out by both sides. The bands were growing ever larger, with the communist partisans of the north, mostly made up of workmen from the cities who had no military training, in desperate need of trained soldiers. Thus it was that there were several cases recorded of private soldiers and even a seaman on the run commanding partisan battalions. Two Australians in Piedmont both commanded brigades two thousand strong.

Not all the escapers wanted to join them. Lance-Corporal Dunning, who had escaped from Germany three times by 1944, had taken part in one partisan ambush of a German convoy. Now he was only too glad to leave the partisans and continue his journey. But he didn't get far.

'I was about to rap on the door [of a roadside cottage] when it suddenly swung open. A man of about forty with a broken nose and a twisted grin considered me. . . . Slowly he raised his palm towards us, in a manner reminiscent of a policeman holding up traffic. Imagining the gesture to be some form of salute, I was on the point of imitating it when I saw that his eyes were roving beyond where we were standing. I glanced over my shoulder. Forming a semicircle round us were a dozen men, all wearing red neckerchiefs, covering us with levelled rifles!'[10]

Thereafter Dunning was cross-examined by the partisan leader, who told him finally, 'You are probably see-sawing between a desire to get to your lines and a temptation to try your hand at this unorthodox warfare. I tell you frankly that your chances of wriggling through Kesselring's defences are extremely slender. If you are picked up in civvies, you'll get short shrift and a firing squad. On the other hand, if you throw in your lot with the partisans, you'll be well looked after until the battle sweeps north. What do you say?'

'I'll stick with the partisans,' Dunning answered.

Four days later Dunning, in the company of some Italians, Yugoslavs and four black-bearded Abyssinians, found himself staking out an ambush in the hills, resolved to pay the Germans back for the humiliations and beatings he had suffered in the camps.

'There were roughly twenty of them, all youngsters and as nervous as kittens. They were straggling along in single file, hunched up and peering fearfully in all directions. From the heights opposite a cuckoo called softly. It was an undisguised massacre. The machine-gunners mowed them down with sickening efficiency. One after another the Germans toppled over like toy soldiers. A handful, including the *Feldwebel*, escaped that first devastating burst and rolled behind a low wall. I studied the evasive action of the *Feldwebel* with almost clinical detachment. He crawled on his stomach to a pigsty, pushed open the swinging half-door and wormed his way past the trough. I waited till he had wriggled into an empty pen and covered himself from the shoulders downwards with mud and straw. Then I shot him through the head.'[11]

A week later, to his great surprise, Dunning found himself crossing the Adriatic to continue fighting with the partisans in Yugoslavia. Somehow he survived the months of savage fighting ahead, with its mass executions, reprisals and counter-reprisals; but not all the other Allied escapers he came across during this time did. 'Aussie', one of them, was shot within minutes of leaving Dunning. Another, named Alan, was found shot, naked save for a pair of white cotton pants, after the Germans had abandoned a position attacked by the partisans.

In Rome, seriously ill but still conscious, Lieutenant Sexton, by now hidden in the Vatican City, wondered what had kept him going all those months on the run. 'Was it sheer courage that kept me going' or was I just a damn fool? It would have been easier to stay a German prisoner, I knew that. The Jerries had treated me well and I didn't escape because of fear of ill-treatment. I had lived in a free country twenty-three years and no one had pointed a gun at me there and said, "You do this and that or else!" No one at home had made me hold up my hand and cry, "*Heil Hitler!*" None of my teachers in school had ever taught me to hate, deceive and kill.

'It was taking me all this time to figure out why I had escaped. I guess I never had time to think about it before. I didn't like the idea of being behind barbed wire or being at the mercy of some damned arrogant German. All my life I had heard about the Americans fighting for freedom and here I had been doing it all these months more out of instinct than anything else.'[12]

But Lieutenant Sexton came from an educated, prosperous background. He had been born on the right side of the tracks and it was to be expected of him that, wounded as he was, he would attempt to escape. It was quite natural, too, that he would base his determination on patriotism and the American ideal. But what of Commando Jimmy Faulkney, definitely born on the wrong side of the tracks? When Jimmy was a small baby his father had been posted 'missing believed killed' in France. A few years afterwards his mother died of overwork. Jimmy went into the orphanage and at the age of 14 he was farmed out to a market-gardener. All his teens he worked on farms, off to work at six on a breakfast of dripping-and-bread and cocoa, working all day in the rain and sun, sixty or more hours a week for his keep and a pound.

As soon as war was declared, he joined up. This was freedom and adventure for him at last. But nothing happened. The years passed in garrison duties, almost as if he had joined the peacetime Army; nothing but 'bull' and more 'bull'.

The commandos offered a way out. In 1942 he was captured on some obscure commando raid in the Mediterranean and sent to a *campo* in northern Italy. He was back where he had started, trapped in that square of wire-enclosed dirt just as much as he had been trapped in the market garden.

In 1943 he wrote his last card from the camp to his only sister, now a sergeant in the ATS stationed in Cairo: 'They say the Germans will take us over,' the faded childish scrawl in pinkish pencil reads, 'but they won't get me. When the time comes, I'll be off – *on the trot!*' 'On the trot' is underlined twice, as if he had wished to vent his anger on the paper. When the Germans came, he kept his promise to his sister. He went 'on the trot', and that was the last anyone ever heard of him. He could have stayed behind, like the great majority of his comrades, and survived the war. But he didn't, and, in the end, just like his unknown father before him he was posted 'missing believed killed'.

What had driven him to strike out into the unknown when so many of his better educated, more privileged comrades tamely stayed behind and accepted their fate? A love of adventure? Women? The desire to get away?

Pizzoferato, a typical Appenine village.

After four years of war, he had probably forgotten what it was all about, had stopped bothering about the broad issues, forgotten a time when he had been anything else but a soldier. It had all become a strange, exciting game with a lethal outcome. Perhaps many of those brave young men wandering the remote hills of Italy that winter, vaguely heading for the south and their own forces, were motivated by the same sentiments. The war had become a crazy game. It had all become unreal, as if it were happening to someone else.

'Finally we were shown to bed in the loft, all rather tipsy and hysterical,' wrote escaper Peter Medd later. 'Life seemed good. We were free, we were going home. Soon, any day now, the British would land in Genoa and there would be no more war, but instead unlimited food and luxuries and work for all. Poor self-deceiving Italy!'[13]

Next morning, with a Major Frank Simms, Peter Medd set off for the south. Covering 700 miles in forty days, they finally reached Allied lines. But the young officer would be dead before the year was out.

'In part I was merely taking time out of life,' Lieutenant Stuart Hood, one of those who survived, wrote afterwards. 'Escaping from the war, which is itself an escape from reality. That is why, with one part of their being, men and women welcome it, for its promise of freedom, sexual and otherwise, for its lifting of taboos. In society we build up strong sanctions. You may not smash windows, nor walk into houses nor (decently) read other people's letters. In wartime the censorship is full of unrepressed Paul Prys. The gunners smash with a single round all the virgin windows of their youth. The infantry break down all the doors, ever shut against them, sleep in forbidden beds, rake through drawers, cupboards, chests. Even this was not enough for me. I had to escape

113

from the reality of war into something more romantic. A fugue within a fugue. In the last analysis, I dawdled because I liked it.'[14]

But, as the fighting around Cassino bogged down and Allied progress continued to be counted in yards not miles, the price of that 'dawdling' increasingly came to be paid in blood. Informers and traitors were everywhere. Escapers risked being shot out of hand when they were recaptured. An Englishman was caught selling his fellow escapers to the Germans. They slaughtered him in cold blood. Recaptured prisoners, especially if they were American, were spat on and struck by the mob in Rome. Occasionally the scared *carabinieri* escorting them had to fire over the mob's heads to drive them off. Others were tortured by the Italian policemen in their comic opera hats.

'The *carabinieri* made us lie on the floor,' escaper John Verney wrote of his recapture. 'Then, covering us with pistols and rifles, they set about getting their own back. They concentrated first on Amos, smacking his face, kicking him, spitting and throwing water and one brought a rifle-butt down. . . . Then they withdrew to their corner of the room to sleep, after assuring us that we would be shot in the morning.'[15]

Scared and plagued with dysentery, but not allowed to go to the latrine by the sadistic policemen, they waited for the morning, with Verney feeling 'murder in my heart'. But they weren't shot and in the end Verney and his friend Amos escaped yet again. Verney made it, but Amos vanished. His body was never found. Later Verney wrote: 'In a way it was appropriate that he, the older friend in any young man's life, should have passed out of mine for ever on the day that, according to my perhaps too conveniently tidy theory, I finally grew up. Passed out of it, that is, in the physical sense. The memory remains. Summoned by a chance taste, sight, or smell, by some association of ideas, or for no apparent reason at all, friends from the past reappear in my thoughts arbitrarily, disconcertingly; the dead more vividly, I find, than the living . . . they haunt my dreams, sleeping or waking. That is their revenge.'[16]

By now British Intelligence had built up an escape organization in German-occupied Italy, centred mainly on Rome and the Vatican City, and run by an escaper, Major Derry of the Royal Artillery. He had been part of the mass escape of British officers from the trains taking prisoners to Germany. Their guards had opened fire at twenty yards' range, killing one of his best friends, Captain Short. Short's death had only strengthened Derry's resolve to escape again. The next morning he had done so, jumping from a moving train and injuring his leg. Somehow he had limped south to Rome, collecting en route some fifty other escapers, who, with others already there, he had hidden all over Rome. There Derry ran his escape organization, with help from British Intelligence,

from – of all places – the German College! By the time Rome fell, Derry had passed nearly 3,935 escapers and evaders from a dozen different countries through his network, including 1,695 British, 896 South Africans and 185 Americans. It was highly dangerous work. The German and their fascist allies had informers everywhere. Italians caught aiding an escaped PoW were shot, if they were lucky. If they weren't, they were tortured first and then shot. The problem was complicated by the many German deserters in Rome, some of whom might well be spies sent to infiltrate the escape organization. Every day that the escaper remained in Rome, the greater was his chance of being recaptured.

One such, Wing-Commander Garrad-Cole, was trapped by two SS men in the Via Flaminia who demanded he should accompany them to the feared SS Headquarters in the Via Tasso. Garrad-Cole, who treasured his newly found freedom, having been in the bag since being shot down in 1940, allowed himself to be led down towards the Piazza del Popolo. He saw that the two SS men, who were shorter than he but quite hefty, were armed solely with pistols. 'My only consolation seemed to lie in the fact that they didn't look particularly bright.'[17] He decided to try and escape.

'Suddenly I stuck out my right leg, tripping my right-hand escort so that he staggered forward. As he staggered I struck him behind the ear with all my might. He fell to the ground.'[18]

The RAF man made a run for it. A bullet whined past his shoulder. He saw it strike the wall opposite. More followed. 'By this time women passers-by were screaming and everybody was rushing to take cover.'[19] It was a good thing for the escaper. He could pelt down the street unimpeded by pedestrians. He raced round the corner to a block of flats where he had Italian friends. He dived in and hid himself behind a pillar in the hall. Within seconds I heard the pounding of jackboots on the pavement outside . . . and caught a glimpse of my pursuers as they flashed past the entrance.'[20] He had made it so far, but now the Germans were backtracking. Hurriedly, with the help of his Italian friends, he put the lift out of order and hid in it while the Germans searched the building from top to bottom. For some reason they failed to search the lift shaft and he escaped again. But there were no more strolls through the streets for him. Now he, like the rest, had to wait for the day the Allies would enter Rome.

Some of the escapers were important enough for Allied Intelligence to make an attempt to rescue them from behind the German lines. Under the command of the SOE's representative, Commander G. Holdsworth, who had already infiltrated agents in and out of France by small boat via Brittany and the Helford River, a similar scheme was set up in Italy. From his headquarters at the small port of Monopoli, between Bari and Brindisi, Holdsworth ran arms in to the partisans, mostly communist, and brought out agents and special escapers.

Lieutenant Stuart Hood was present when some escaped South Africans were to be taken off by a submarine sent by Holdsworth. Unfortunately the party also included a German who had deserted because his family had been wiped out by the RAF raid on Hamburg and he no longer wanted to fight. But the South Africans were worried about him. He knew too much. Might he betray them at the last moment? Hood told the partisans who had found the German that they could get rid of him and they had twenty-four hours to do so.

'They shot him over breakfast next morning. Filippo was sitting with his Tommy-gun at his side. Suddenly, without warning, he lifted it and emptied the magazine. The bullets smashed Kurt's breast. They buried him on the hillside a few yards from the bivouac. There were stones and roots everywhere. It was hard work to get far enough down. In the end there was a little mound. They heaped it over with leaves.'[21]

Perhaps one of the most unusual of Holdsworth's rescue missions was that of a party of American nurses whose plane crashed on a routine mission from Sicily to Bari to collect patients. The first attempt was not really successful, as a German armoured unit appeared on the scene just when a plane sent to collect them was about to land. 'If I live to be a hundred years,' one of the thirteen nurses wrote later, 'I shall never forget nor be able to express my feelings when I saw that swarm of planes sent out by the 15th Air force just to rescue us. ... The girls cried and the boys all had lumps in their throats.'[22]

Later they were brought back to Bari by an SOE officer, Gavin Duffy, under Holdsworth's command. Three of them were left behind, unfortunately, and it would be another month before they were rescued under appalling conditions.

By the spring of 1944 it was estimated that there were 11,000 Allied ex-prisoners-of-war or evaders on the run in German-occupied Italy. They included an admiral, an air vice-marshal, a couple of generals and a clutch of brigadiers, all eager to use the 'ratlines', as the escape routes and networks were called. But there were many who had simply gone to ground, found a *signora* and merged into the local populace. Even later, when the Allies reached their remote villages, they never bothered to surface. Some surrendered when the fighting was over. Others stayed on and are still there, old men with blond grandchildren, whose English is broken and interlaced with '*pregos*' and '*subitos*'.

Eric Newby, the author of a celebrated book on the kind of life the escapers lived among the Italian peasants; *Love and War in the Apennines*, was one of those who didn't join the partisans or try to make his way south to the Allies. Indeed he once spent a whole afternoon with

Brigadiers C. H. Boucher, and G. F. Johnson, two of the 'clutch' who made successful use of the escape networks.

an eccentric German officer who, although he knew Newby was a British soldier, chatted with him and continued to pursue his hobby of butterfly collecting.

In the end Newby was recaptured by Italian militia and went back into the bag. But he survived and married Wanda, the Italian girl who had befriended him when he was lying injured in an Italian hospital. Twelve years later he returned to the Apennines with Wanda and their two children to be fêted by the villagers who had hidden him when he was on the run.

Just before the family left, one of his old helpers, Francesco, took him aside and said, 'There's one thing I never told you. ... I couldn't bring myself to. It was a matter of honour.'

To his astonishment Newby learned that he had been betrayed all those years ago, first by a woman and then by a man in the village.

'You can meet both of them if you like,' Francesco said. 'You had dinner with one of them today. He was very, very close.'

Wisely, Newby answered, 'No, thank you. We've all had enough of this sort of thing to last us for the rest of our lives.'[23]

IV:
BREAK-OUT!

'It's jolly to look at the map
And finish the foe in a day'.

A.P. Herbert, 1940

A Sherman tank advances through wooded country.

'Polacks, Frogs and Teds'

It was called 'Operation Diadem'. It was to be the last attempt to break the stalemate in Italy before the coming Invasion of Normandy. On 11 May 1944, with D-Day only three and a half weeks away, four Allied corps would go over to the attack. The American 2nd Corps would attack along the coast. The French Expeditionary Corps would push into the Aurunci mountains south of the Liri Valley. The British XIII Corps would cross the Rapido, aided by the 8th Indian Division and an Italian Motorized Group; for now the Italian Army was fighting alongside its former enemies. This attack would be followed up by the 1st Canadian Corps, plus the British 78th Division. Then, at an appropriate time, there would be a breakout from the Anzio beachhead.

It was going to be a massive operation, with half a dozen nationalities involved. Its aim was the destruction of all German troops south of Rome. It was also intended that, in the second phase of the operation, General Truscott (Lucas had at last been sacked) and his 6th Corps would 'launch an attack on the general axis Cori-Valmontone to cut Route Six (Via Casilina) in the Valmontone area, and thereby prevent the supply and withdrawal of the German Tenth Army'.[1] Subsequently Clark's Fifth Army was expected to 'pursue the enemy north of Rome and capture the Viterbo airfields . . . and thereafter advance on Leghorn.'[2] At that time the Eighth Army would push northwards to Ancona and Florence. There was no mention of any attempt to capture Rome itself!

As they waited for the last great attack to start, some were apprehensive, some were bored, some fatalistic; they had been through it all before. But the really new boys on the Italian front were waiting for the start of the assault with eager fanaticism, for they had been waiting for this moment for four years. They were the Poles of General Anders' Second Corps, who had been given the toughest objective of all – the final breakthrough at Cassino, where Americans, British and New Zealanders had failed so bloodily before them.

They had come a long way to fight this battle. Most of them had been dragged off to the Soviet gulags in 1939, where they had toiled twelve hours a day on a piece of black bread and a handful of dried fish, washed down with water, week in, week out, month after month, for years on end.

'First they took my father, then my brother, then me,' Ludwik Drezniak remembers. 'I was 14 in 1940 and the Russians carried me off to work on the roads, breaking stones with a hammer all day long near Smolensk on a starvation diet. By the time the Germans came in 1941 I was in rags, barefoot, and like a walking skeleton. How I hated those Russians!'

General Anders, their commander, had shared their lot. He had spent years in Moscow's dreaded Lubianka Prison. Together he and his Poles had crossed into Persia, after the Rusians finally released them, and wandered as far afield as Palestine and East Africa, before the Allies finally formed them into a corps of two infantry divisions and one armoured brigade.

Now they were going to fight the *nmetski* once again in Italy and Anders knew that the objective assigned to him would ensure that the new Polish Army would receive international attention. He knew, too, that the efforts of his Corps would give comfort and support to the Polish underground, the Home Army, in their fight against the German occupiers. More, it would encourage them perhaps in the coming fight against another enemy, the Russians, the unlikely ally of Britain and America, who were already crossing into what had once been Polish territory before it had been divided up by the Soviet Union and Nazi Germany in 1939.

As the start of the attack drew near, General Anders prepared his order of the day for Corps. It read: 'Soldiers! The time for battle has arrived. We have long awaited this moment for revenge and retribution. The task assigned to us will cover with glory the name of the Polish soldier all over the world. . . . Trusting in the justice of Divine Providence we go forward with the sacred slogan in our hearts. *God! Honour! Country!*'[3]

General Juin's French were not so new on the Italian front. They had been here since the previous December. They, too, had a debt to pay back. But for them it was more of a debt of honour. For not only had the French Army surrendered in 1940, but it had also passively (and sometimes actively) collaborated with the Germans until late in 1942. Among General Juin's Frenchmen there

Spiritual and material protection: A Polish soldier stands ready to man twin Bren guns while Bishop Josef Gawlina, the Field Bishop of the Polish Army, holds mass for men of General Anders' II Corps.

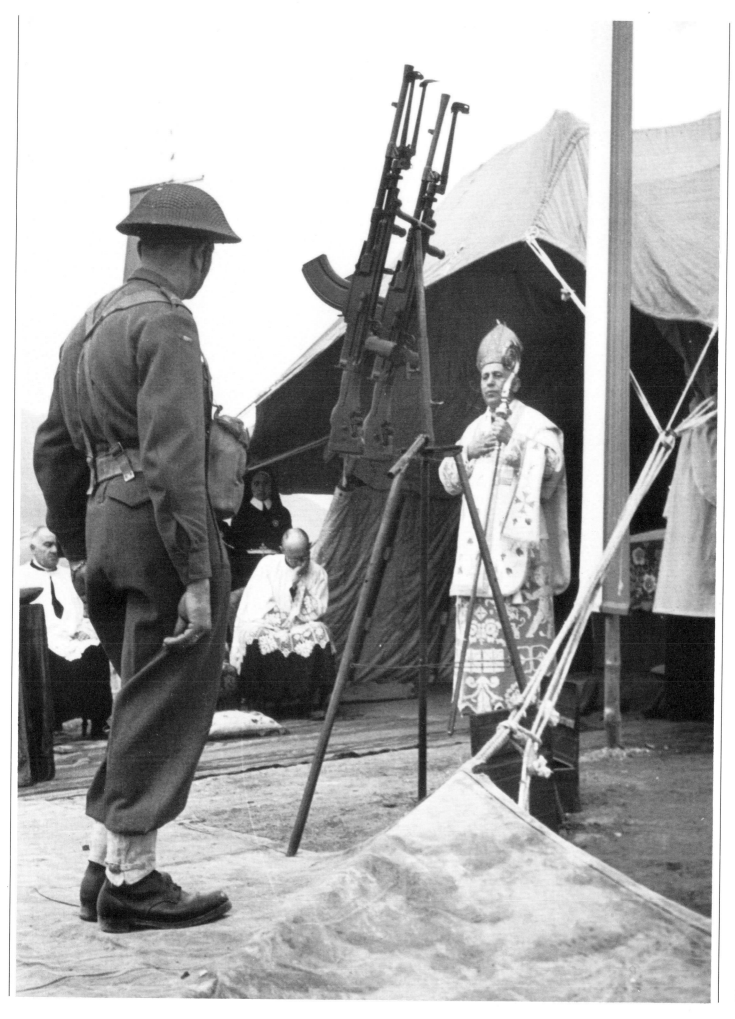

119

were those who had fought against the British and Australians in Syria and those who had briefly fought against the Anglo-Americans in North Africa in 1942. Indeed, the first Americans to be killed in the Second World War in the West were the five hundred-odd who fell in battle against the people they had supposedly come to 'liberate' – *the French!*

Their commander, General Juin, who had also taken part in the initial fighting against the Anglo-Americans in November, 1942, was well aware that the glory of France had been sullied and that it was imperative to restore the honour of the French Army. It was equally clear to him that the Anglo-Americans did not think too highly of the combat capability of his troops. He wrote to his superior, General Giraud, in Africa: 'I have the feeling that we will only make our mark here by showing tact and discretion. The Americans are not people one can hustle. . . . They like us a lot, but they are also imbued with their sense of omnipotence and with a touchiness that you can hardly imagine. . . . The French always seem a little excitable to them and it is important for me to first gain their confidence, particularly before the fighting begins.'[4]

After the first French attempt to take Cassino, in which they had suffered heavy losses, they had gained that confidence and their Anglo-American allies realized that these rag-tag Frenchmen, with their dashing scarves and jauntily cocked *kepis*, could fight. Their black colonial troops, in particular the fiery *Goums*, won universal admiration.

But within their own ranks, especially among the senior officers, there were still plenty of doubts and divisions. Juin did not like Allied strategy one bit. In particular, he thought the constant battering away at Cassino stupid. Nor had he any great opinion of Alexander's or Clark's generalship. There was also dissension among those officers who had joined de Gaulle right from the start and those who had only been converted to the Allied cause after the landings in North Africa had shown that the Anglo-Americans might well win the war after all.

General Juin knew that the old appeals to *la gloire* and *la patrie* were needed it he was going to rally his four assault divisions for an attack which they did not altogether like. He had shown that the coming battle was the first step in the liberation of France. Like that other exile, General Anders, he too issued an order of the day. It was one of those noble, uplifting orders that the French do so well. He spoke of a struggle to come which must be 'implacable and relentless' and ended, '*La France martyre vous attend et vous regarde. En avant!*'[5]

But before Juin's Frenchmen could reach their 'martyred France' they would have to contend with the men who had brought about that martyrdom back in 1940 – the 'Teds', as they were called by the men of the Eighth Army. 'Ted' might be a callow youth of eighteen sent to the Italian front straight from the Hitler Youth or from a *Wehrertuchtigungslager**, as green as some of the Poles who would soon attack him, but these raw replacements were absorbed into formations which had a formidable backbone of veterans, 'old hares' as they called themselves proudly.

The 'old hares' had been fighting since 1939, had seen service in two continents and in half a dozen different countries, in particular Russia. They had a life-style, even a language, of their own that set them apart from normal men. Indeed the 'old hares' from the Russian front told the hoary tale that, in the great final Victory Parade in Berlin, a group of bearded old men would stagger past the Führer to be asked by a shocked official, 'Who are you?' One of the old men would answer, '*Ne ponemyu*'. They had been on the Russian front so long that they had forgotten their own language!

These 'old hares' lived off 'nigger sweat' (coffee) and 'old man' (an Italian meat product with 'AM'† stamped on the can, which they confidently maintaned was made of old men from Berlin's work-houses) and 'roof-hares' (cats) if they were pushed.

Their discipline was much more relaxed than that of the Allies, even though full corporals were saluted in the German Army. Batmen were unknown, except for high-ranking officers. Often the officers messed with the men and addressed them with the formal '*Sie*'. There was none of the 'lads' and 'you men' used in the Anglo-American armies which emphasized the difference in rank. Physically, too, they were usually much tougher than their opponents, the younger men especially hardened by their years in the Hitler Youth and the six-month compulsory training scheme, the *Arbeitsdienst*. The 'wheels', which seemed essential to American troops in particular, were not available to them. They marched everywhere. Nor were their rations so lavish as their Anglo-American opponents. There was no K or Compo Rations for them. They had to do with their sausages and stone-hard *Kommisbrot*, washed down with a slug of schnapps if they were lucky.

Above all, these 'old hares' showed surprising initiative, some of them taking over companies when officers were killed, organizing counter-attacks even, something virtually unheard of in the Anglo-Americans forces, where other ranks and enlisted men were 'not paid to think'.

The parachute formations facing the Poles at Cassino were perhaps the best troops in all Italy. Most of them by now were parachutists only in name. They had never jumped from an aircraft but, in their rimless helmets and baggy overalls, they represented an elite, who had speedily taken over the traditions created in Holland and Crete by the real *Fallschirmjager* who had long ago vanished in the snowy steppes of Russia.

* A para-military training camp for teenagers to build them up for the *Wehrmacht*.

† AM could stand for 'old man' in German – *Alter Mann*.

A German paratrooper, one of the defenders of Monte Cassino.

Colonel Heilmann's men of the 1st Para Division bellowed the *Song of the Paras* often enough during those drunken evenings when they pulled out of the shattered ruins of Cassino for a rest. How lustily and boastfully they sang in those *Kameradschaftsabende*:

> '*When Germany is in danger, there is only one thing for us*
> *To fight, to conquer, to assume we shall die!*
> *From our aircraft, my friend, there is no return.*'

Well, they would not go into this last battle for Cassino from a Junkers. They would fight from behind piles of masonry and brick rubble. And if they could not conquer as they had done in the great days of '40 and '41, they would fight to the very end. The 'Teds' were going to make the Poles pay a stiff price for their final conquest of Cassino and the privilege of erecting a monument there over the 3,784 dead of General Anders' Corps:

> 'We Polish soldiers
> For our freedom and yours
> Have given our souls to God
> Our bodies to the soil of Italy
> And our hearts to Poland.'

The warmth of an early summer had returned to Cassino. Even the man-made destruction of these many months of bitter fighting could not quite spoil the beauty of the Italian countryside. Grass and wild corn had sprung up in the valley once more. The morning sun had coloured the shattered abbey a glowing honey-coloured hue.

Heilmann's paras lurking in the ruins watched the still Liri Valley below, alert as ever, but a little bored. Nothing much had happened here since the New Zealanders had broken off their offensive a month before. Admittedly there was still patrol activity, but that usually took place under cover of darkness and there was a long routine day ahead of them. Slowly, as the day relaxed in the customary schedule of two hours on-duty and four off, they resigned themselves to another purposeless, boring afternoon. Above them the sun vanished and it became overcast. A light drizzle followed and a haze began to drift across the valley below.

Behind the Allied lines below all was hectic in preparation for those who would lead and supply the great assault. While the infantry slept, well-doped in the British lines on an extra tot of 'rum, General Service', fitters and artificers checked the trucks and tanks. Staff officers bustled back and forth. Worried battalion and company commanders checked their maps yet again.

Clark, in the great echoing Bourbon palace at Caserta, pondered what he would do if the offensive succeeded. What kind of personal publicity could he get out of it? For, as Eric Ambler the novelist had written, 'No World War II commander of men had worked more assiduously in the field of public relations than General Clark'.[6]

Once Ambler attended an entertainment at Caserta opera house where the staff officers sang to the tune of a 'well-known patriotic folk song':

121

The Sons of General Clark

Stand up and sing the praise of General Clark,
Your hearts and voice raise for General Clark,
Red, white and blue unfurled upon the field,
Its message flaunts Clark's sons will never, never
    yield
We'll fight, fight, fight with heart and hand,
As soldiers true embattled staunch will stand,
The Fifth's the best army in the land,
FIGHT, FIGHT, FIGHT![7]

Looking down at the slip of green paper he had been given with the words of this remarkable song on it, Ambler could find no mention of a lyricist. Afterwards he 'liked to think it was General Clark himself'.[8]

In essence it boiled down to Rome. Who would have the honour of capturing the Italian capital, if and when the troops going over to the offensive that night broke through the German defences? Alexander had not mentioned Rome in his overall plan. His strategy was based on cutting off the Germans north of the capital. But Clark didn't believe the Britisher was being honest. He confided to his diary that day: 'I know factually that there are interests brewing for the Eighth Army to take Rome, and I might as well let Alexander know now that if he attempts any thing of that kind he will have another all-out battle on his hands, namely, with me.'[9]

As the hour of battle drew closer and the nervous infantry shuffled into position, Clark determined that Truscott's Corps, which would soon break out at Anzio, would be, contrary to Alexander's plan, ordered to march on Rome. As he admitted later; 'We not only wanted the honor of capturing Rome, but we felt that we more than deserved it. ... Nothing was going to stop us on our push toward the Italian capital.'[10]

During the next month more than ten thousand Allied soldiers died in the breakthrough – but all for nothing. Clark would get Rome, but the German Army in Italy would escape to fight on for nearly another year. As Eric Sevareid wrote: 'It was all very dramatic and it seemed like a great victory. In truth we had merely extricated ourselves from our own stupid mistake, committed when we landed on those beaches in January.'[11]

The sun set at a quarter past eight. Now the moon had begun to appear in a bright starry sky, casting its cold silver light on the hustle and bustle below. For some reason the Germans had stopped firing. Only once since Christmas had the guns ceased firing – for a few moments on Easter Morning. Now an eerie silence descended upon the Liri Valley as the infantry waited.

'It was a funny feeling,' Bombardier Castle recalled. 'I'd never experienced anything like it, except at St Valéry when the old div* surrendered back in '40. The guns had

---

* Castle's 51st Highland Division had surrendered to General Rommel's troops at St Valéry in June, 1940.

stopped then and the lads had wondered what was going to happen, when the Jerries came to take them. Waiting to open fire, we was all jumpy and kind of tired at the same time. Perhaps it was tension or something.'

At eleven o'clock, 1,600 guns stretched along a 25-mile front from Monte Cassino to the sea tore the night into shreds. For forty minutes they pounded every known German HQ, battery and defensive position. Clark recorded: 'The ridges in front of the Fifth Army seemed to stand out momentarily in a great blaze of light, sink again into darkness and then tremble under the next salvo.'[12]

Fifty miles to the rear an officer of the British 78th Division was finding it difficult to get to sleep because of the song of the nightingales. Now, as Fred Majdalany recalled, 'Through the song of the nightingales, he sensed rather than heard another sound – a sound that was little more than a faint vibrant shimmering of the atmosphere. He looked at his watch. It was eleven o'clock. It had started.'[13]

'Only numbers count,' Alexander had told his staff before the attack. Now, as the guns blasted the German positions, the attack jumped off. Even as the first shells went whistling towards the enemy, the US 85th and 88th Infantry Divisions sprang into action on the coast. Forty minutes later two French divisions – Juin's 2nd Moroccan and the 4th Alpine – launched their attack on Monte Faito. Five minutes later the British 4th and 8th Divisions began their push, forcing the Rapido River by storm. By midnight thousands of men were advancing across that burning lunar landscape, trying to carry out Alexander's precept that 'only numbers count'. The Poles supported the barrage with their own mortars and light artillery, pouring fire on the paras dug in above them on the mountain.

'We started firing at the same moment as the artillery,' one of their officers recalled later, 'and the men were so quick at handling the weapons that after a while the mortar barrels became overheated. They cooled them off with their own water rations and when all the water had gone they took the only course open to them. They urinated on the hot steel and brought down the temperature that way. Not one of our barrels burst during the action.'[14]

The Poles attacked immediately their own barrage ceased. The 5th Polish Division attacked Colle Sant' Angelo, defended by the 2nd Battalion of the German paras, but the main Polish attack, made by the Carpathian Division and supported by the 2nd Polish Armoured Brigade, was directed at the peak of Calvary Mountain, which had to be taken before they could make the final advance on the Monastery Hill itself.

The Polish attack was a success. Before the paras really knew what was happening to them, the Carpathian Brigade had overwhelmed the company holding Calvary Mountain and the surviving German paras were stream-

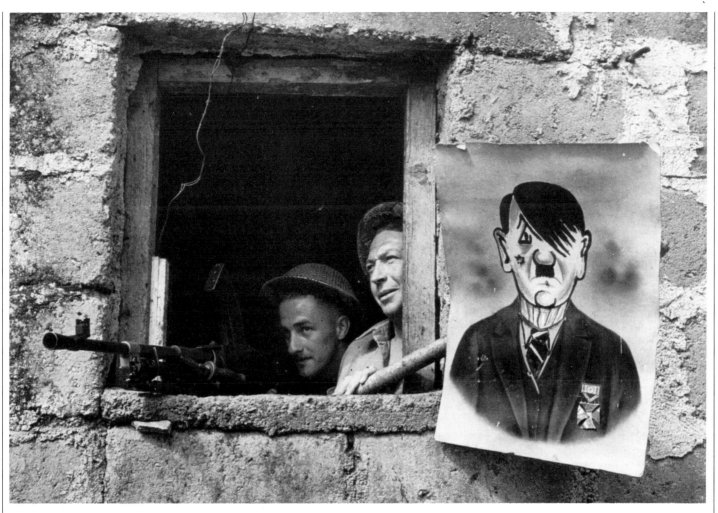

Guardsmen at Cassino, with a cartoon of Hitler, set up to draw fire.

ing down the other side to the safety of their own positions.

As always, the Germans reacted more swiftly than the Allies did to such surprise attacks. Heilmann ordered his 2nd Battalion to counter-attack immediately. But the Poles were waiting. As the leading paras breasted the ridge, they ran into hastily scattered mines and intense fire from Polish machine guns. Desperately the German officers tried to rally their men, but the Poles were too tough. The 2nd Battalion fled.

But the Poles were taking severe casualities too. Ludwik Drezniak, who was in a reserve battalion that night, remembers: 'All the Poles were very angry – Poles can be very angry. One of my friends was so carried away that he ran into the attack with his arm blown off, and when the officer ordered him to go back, he was angry with the officer too. There were dead and wounded everywhere, but we still carried on, we were that angry!'

Captain Majewski, a Polish doctor at a casualty clearing station below, told of the wounded: 'Some crawled to us on their own, others were helped by friends, others were slung over shoulders like sacks. The helpers, the wounded and the dying were all in a state of excitement. At times I thought I was dreaming. There was no fear to be seen in them, only a kind of fury and rage. A corporal came and knelt before me without a word and showed me his back. Through his torn tunic I saw a wound the size of two hands, the shoulder-bone bared. He wouldn't let me give him an injection. I said, "I can't evacuate you without an injection." The corporal stood up and said, "I'm not being evacuated, I must go back. I'll be killed, but I shan't let you evacuate me until I've thrown all my grenades".'[15]

Heilmann was determined to recapture the peak taken by the Poles. He scraped together the remainder of his manpower, including bakers and clerks, and, as dawn broke, attacked again. The Poles, weakened by casualties and lack of reinforcements, nevertheless managed to break up the German attack. But it was not a clear-cut victory. The paras went to ground and began sniping the Poles from seventy yards away. The Poles weakened rapidly. Among the rocks lay 'corpses, twisted human shapes, shattered limbs, bloody bits of bodies,' one Pole recalled afterwards. 'In 13 and 15 Battalions there were only dead and wounded. No one has escaped injury. Captain Jurkowski's Company had ceased to exist.'[16]

'I'd never thought much of Poles until then,' *Oberjäger* Juppi Most remembers. 'I had been brought up to think of them as "*Polacken*" but that day I changed my mind altogether. There couldn't have been braver soldiers than the Poles anywhere in the world. They simply threw their lives away as if it didn't matter a bit.'

As darkness fell Colonel Heilmann ordered yet another attack. Under the command of Sergeant-Major Karl Schmidt an assault squad began to crawl forward, any noise they made covered by the whine and howl of the mortar barrage the Germans were putting down on the Polish positions. They crept on until they could hear the Poles talking among themselves in the intervals between each salvo of bombs.

Suddenly the barrage stopped. The paras rose to their feet, crying as they charged forward. Here and there men struggled back and forth on the edge of holes, momentarily outlined in the glare of an exploding shell. Then the shooting and shouting began to peter out. The paras had won. The position was back in German hands. Of the 2nd Battalion, 15th Carpatian Brigade, which had occupied that position, only one officer and seven men remained alive.

'Juins' Frogs', as Clark called them, did better. His fierce *Goums*, bearded and hook-nosed, wearing their striped robes, plunged into mountainous country that the Germans thought impassable. Using their knives, they quickly disposed of their opponents, men of the demoralized 94th Division, and pushed on, vanishing into the darkness. As Montgomery had once said of them in his clipped manner, 'Dark men, dark night. Very hard to see them coming'.[17]

But the German defences had not been overwhelmed everywhere. The French ran into a well-prepared defensive line, complete with barbed wire entanglements and pillboxes; 'Very soon we came up to the pillboxes, held by battle-hardened enemy, their morale intact, not having been struck by one shell.'[18]

The Germans counter-attacked. The casualties mounted. The situation got so critical that Juin himself came up to direct operations at the front. His presence there was needed: one regiment alone suffering 400 casualties almost before it had begun its attack.

'An ammunition dump exploded nearby. The pass was lit up all red and white by the phosphorescent shells,' one officer recalled. 'The German machine guns increased their fire. Some men began to withdraw, creating further disorganization. The dead were piling up. The battalion commander, already wounded, died bravely an instant later trying to save the battalion records.'[19]

Even the Germans were impressed by the French. One German battalion commander wrote: 'You have no idea of the rigours and horrors. We will not let ourselves become disheartened, but people are tired and have had nothing to eat for three days. Our Free French and Moroccan enemies are remarkably fine soldiers.'[20]

124   The Germans were quite terrified of the *Goums* who

French North African Goums.

were reputed to bugger their prisoners. A British journalist with the 8th Army noted: 'The *Goums* became a legend and a grim joke with the Eighth. No story about their rape, their progress or their other deeds was too wild to be believed.'[21]

They had closely cropped crinkly hair, with a plaited pigtail at the back. They said it was given them so that the Lord had something to grab on to when He yanked them to Paradise after they had been killed. Practically all of them wore beards, for they maintained that 'a man who has not seen action and does not wear a beard is not a real man'. According to the rumours in both the Ger-

man and the Allied camp, they were paid to cut off German ears with their big ten-inch knife, the *koumia*. It was also said that their favourite trick was to sneak up on a couple of sleeping Germans, whip the head off one and steal away, leaving the other to wake to the spectacle of a headless comrade. Like the Germans, the Italian peasants upon whom they were billeted lived in mortal fear of the *Goums*. One civilian told a correspondent: 'We suffered more during twenty-four hours of contact with the Moroccans than in the eight months under the Germans. The Germans took away our goats, sheep and food, but they respected our women and our meagre savings. The Moroccans flung themselves upon us like unchained demons. They violated, threatening with machine guns, children, women, young men, following each other like beasts in rotation; they took our money from us, they followed us into the village and carried off every bundle, our linen, our shoes. Even those of their officers who tried to intervene came under their threats.'[22]

The steady pressure of the Poles, the French and their savage *Goums* was beginning to tell. The German High Command changed the name of their defensive line across Italy from 'Hitler' to 'Dora'. The ignominy of defeat could not be associated with the name of the Führer.

'Thus did the human body fight to the very end against death'

One night while the men at Anzio were waiting for the Huns to crack and the order to make their own breakout, a young officer, making a routine inspection near the beach, was startled by a deep voice growling in the darkness, 'Whoa boss!' He turned round, surprised to find himself staring into an inky black face.

'Don't you know how to challenge?' he demanded sternly. 'Weren't you going to challenge me?'

'No, boss,' the black replied with a disarming grin. 'I wasn't goin' to challenge. I was goin' to shoot!'[1]

The young officer has just encountered the 'invisible soldier', the only one of that multi-racial army, which included a score of different nationalities from Brasilians to South Africans, whose history is not recorded – the black American soldier.

That spring there were thousands of them serving in Italy in every capacity from fighter pilot to grave-digger, but it was as if they did not exist; they were the invisible soldiers of that great Allied force. It was not altogether surprising in an army which was at that time strictly segregated.

Ironically enough the first US soldier to be killed in combat in the Second World War was a black man, Robert Brooks, after whom the parade ground at Fort Knox was named. As one of his comrades recalled after the war, 'He lied about his race. We was all white, see? And he lied to get in a white outfit. He was yellow-complected, had kinda kinky hair. I called him "Nig" all the time and I didn't know he was a nigger, see.'[2] When his parents were invited to attend the ceremonies at Fort Knox to honour their dead son killed in action in the Philippines in December, 1941, they wouldn't come. They didn't like it that their son had lied about his race to join a white combat outfit.

Until December, 1944, when Eisenhower, desperate for infantrymen, appealed for blacks to join combat units, there was little chance of blacks being able to fight for their country. For the great majority of black Americans

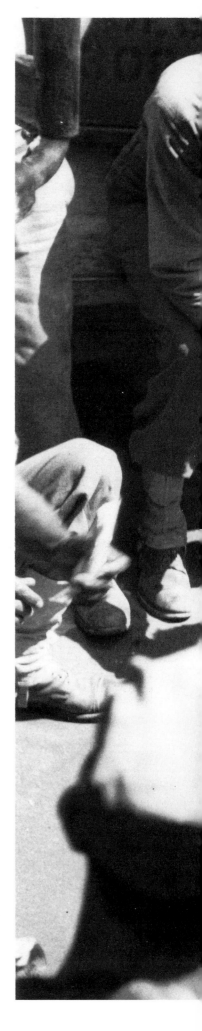

Black American soldiers shooting 'craps'.

drafted during the war the only jobs available were menial ones such as drivers, cooks, grave-diggers and the like. They were allowed arms for training; otherwise their rifles were locked up for the night. In the South they were, more often than not, not allowed to go into town. Those from the north bold enough to speak to a white woman were threatened with lynching. Beatings at the hands of white troops were frequent; and in Italy Negroes who did come in contact with white women, even if they were mostly prostitutes, were often waylaid and beaten up by their so-called comrades in arms.

Indeed the blacks were thought of so lowly by the white authorities in the US Army that when the Hollywood star Lena Horne, herself a black woman, was sent south to entertain the troops she was asked to give two concerts at one camp. The first performance was to be for white soldiers; the second for black troops – *and German prisoners-of-war*! It is said that Miss Horne entertained the black troops and the Germans, and then left.

But, in spite of all the threats, the humiliations, the violence, there were some blacks prepared to fight for a segregated America. In Italy there were the fighter pilots of what they called the 'Spookwaffe', the all-black 332nd Fighter Group.

There were four squadrons of planes, piloted by 200 blacks, a token representation of the Negro in the Army Air Corps. One of these squadrons, the 99th Fighter, first saw action at Anzio in January. The pilots had experienced the miseries of segregation during their training at Tuskegee Air Base. On one occasion one of the trainee pilots had been saved from lynching by British cadets, training in America, who protected him. On another occasion the black Orderly Officer was thrown out of his official car and his driver had a tooth knocked out. Both went back to base on foot. 'Sassy negras' didn't ride in cars in the South! When the news spread round the base, the men were all for storming the city, weapons or no weapons, to exact retribution. Fortunately, cooler heads prevailed.

One pilot, Lieutenant Heber Houston of the 99th, became the butt of his fellows because of the number of times he was shot down over the beachhead in the four months of the 'siege'. A former colleague said, 'The fellows of the 99th were always ribbing Heber about Anzio. They said that every time they saw Heber he was crash-landing on Anzio, shot down, or he was arriving back at the base via a vehicle on which he had hitched a ride. Then he climbed into another plane and was off again to repeat the process. Houston actually was shot down two or three times at Anzio. I think one might safely say he was shot down more than any other guy at Anzio and lived to tell the tale. As far as I know he was never seriously hurt.'[3]

One morning at the beginning of the battle of Anzio the 99th shot down five German planes without loss.

That afternoon they shot down a further three. As one of the black pilots recalled after the war, 'This was something all black pilots felt: we had to prove ourselves. We had to be good. No, we had to be better.'[4] Now all of those in the Anzio beachhead were going to have to prove themselves, whatever their nationality or colour. The time to break out was approaching and General Truscott was finalizing his plan.

Day by day the situation reports poured into Truscott's HQ in Nettuno as rumours swept the beachhead. The British had crossed the Rapido . . . the French had passed the mountains . . . it wouldn't be long before the Poles finally took the Monastery. Then Sixth Corps Intelligence reported that two German divisions were being pulled out of the ring around Anzio and sent back to the next fortified German line, the Gustav Line. This meant that the Germans were having to strip troops from Anzio to bolster up the sagging front at Cassino. It couldn't be long now.

During the months of the 'siege', Truscott and his staff had prepared four different plans for the breakout. In the second week of May Alexander visited him and told the American Commander that he was interested in only one of them: the one which would place the Sixth Corps squarely across the line of retreat of the beaten Germans. 'This is the plan I want and I reserve for myself the decision as to the timing of launching it.'[5]

Next day Clark appeared at the beachhead. He had other plans for Truscott's Sixth Corps. He heard what Truscott had to say and then phoned Alexander to tell him firmly that all orders to his subordinates in the US Fifth Army had to go through him. He, for his part, wanted to feel free to direct his Army as he wished. Alexander withdrew gracefully. So we have the curious picture of the Supreme Commander refusing to put his foot down at the most decisive part of the long Italian campaign. Later, when Alexander's biographer quizzed Mark Clark over the matter, the latter said, 'To censure me for thinking only of the glory of capturing Rome is sheer nonsense. I know Alex didn't like the way I was doing it, but he issued no ultimatum to me to make me do it differently. He left it to me. I told him exactly what I was going to do, and he acquiesced.'[6]

With a lazy, apparently easy-going Supreme Commander allowing Clark to do what he pleased, Truscott, who was one of the few American generals who understood and liked the British, realized which way the wind was blowing. He decided to use mainly American troops for the breakout, using as his excuse the fact that the British were tired and understrength. So it would be his 1st Armored, 3rd and 45th US Infantry Divisions which would attack and, of course, have the honour of entering Rome first. The capture of Rome was going to be an exclusively American affair. The men who had been fighting alone for two long years before America had even entered the war were going to be denied the privilege of helping to capture the first enemy capital in mainland Europe. It was going to be Patton and Messina all over again, with, this time, General Mark Clark in the role of conquering hero.

Fresh troops were moved in to the attack on the Eighth Army's front. Both were battle-experienced divisions, the 1st Canadian Infantry and the British 78th.

The only French-Canadian unit serving with the 1st, the Royal 22ᵉ Regiment, known throughout the Canadian Army as the 'Van Doos', went straight in without even attempting to dig in. But some thought the Quebeçois were pushing that Gallic *sangfroid* to the point of foolhardiness. Other Canadian battalions, such as 'Hasty Pees' were more circumspect in a battle where, as the Regimental History records, 'German and Canadian sub-units became intermingled,' as 'Regimental jeeps and stretcher-bearers hurrying forward to evacuate the wounded wandered into enemy lines, then out again unscathed.'[7] The battle 'quickly degenerated to the platoon and company level and became a savage mêlée of infantry against infantry.'[8]

The 48th Canadian Highlanders pushed forward, supported by tanks of the Royal Armoured Corps. But the infantry and the tanks were split by a river and the Germans soon seized the opportunity presented them on a silver platter – tanks without infantry support. Immediately they employed a new weapon that would be the bugbear of all tankers until the end of the war – the *panzerschreck* – an anti-tank weapon consisting of a long tube, operated by one man, which fired a percusion bomb. The 'tank-frightener' knocked out three Churchills immediately, then a further two sent to assist the ambushed tankers. The rest of the troop 'wisely retreated'.

But, if the Germans were weakening, they were making the Canadians and British pay dearly for every yard of ground gained. In the 78th's Irish Brigade, for example, Colonel Goff, commanding the London Irish, was killed on the first day of the attack. The next day his comrade, Colonel Bala Bredin, C.O. of the Inniskillings, was badly wounded in both legs and refused to be evacuated until he fainted and could not command any more. The following day, Colonel John Loveday, commanding the 16th/5th Lancers, was killed in action – three out of four commanding officers put out of action in 72 hours.

Losses among the rank and file were equally high. The leading companies of the Lancashire Fusiliers, fighting across the littered, ridged fields, lost heavily, leaving the ground behind filled with their dead. In C Company, for example, forty men out of ninety were killed and wounded and the losses would have been higher if young Fusilier Jefferson had not tackled the advancing German infantry and tanks with his PIAT. Fighting it out alone, a David against an armoured Goliath, he knocked out

General Alexander on a visit to the Anzio front.

the lead German tank and saved his company. It won him the Division's third Victoria Cross.

The Buffs suffered similar losses and their C.O. was killed. The Argylls were no different and their Commanding Officer was wounded but refused to be evacuated. One by one the bold and the brave were being put out of action as the bloody butcher's bill in Italy mounted once more.

The 6th South African Armoured Division was thrown into the attack, regiments moving into battle bearing names from the Imperial past – Natal Mounted Rifle, Prince Alfred's Guard, Imperial Light Horse. A great multi-national army, drawn from three continents and a dozen different countries, moved forward. There were even contingents of Belgians and Greeks mixed up in this huge force, which spoke every language from Afrikaans and Iroquois to the manifold languages of the sub-continent of India.

The Canadian 5th Armoured Division was ordered in. Lord Strathcona's Horse, the British Columbia Dragoons, Princess Louise's Hussars thrust forward into the fray. The Germans, as always, were waiting. Well-sited and camouflaged, their 57mm anti-tank guns took up the challenge. Solid AP shells zipped through the air. The big Shermans were easy targets. That day they well deserved their name of 'Ronsons', after the lighter. Even a graze from a German shell could turn them into blazing infernos. In a matter of minutes one Canadian unit lost seventeen Shermans. Soon the battlefield was dotted with the blazing wrecks of Canadian tanks.

The British 8th Hussars were brought up and en-

Right: Polish troops in action near Monte Cassino.

countered what was left of Lord Strathcona's Horse: 'We met some Straths coming back from their shelling. They were in awful shape. They told us they'd lost a lot of men,' an officer of the Hussars recalled. 'We found a lot of them in a Field Dressing Station.'[9]

Soon it was the turn of the Hussars, then that of the British Columbia Dragoons, who went forward into devastating German fire. The 88mms thundered and the 57mm anti-tank guns slammed shell after shell into the Canadians's Shermans.

'We were ordered forward. Steve Coppinger kicked off and then I was ordered to go with him. He went about fifty yards when I saw his tank burst into flames and I saw Steve fall out of the turret. I stopped my tank as I thought I was still in the hull-down position. I reported what had happened when, wham, my tank was hit. My driver pulled the fire control switches for the extinguishers and I reported that we were hit and told the crew to bail out. I then climbed on to the sergeant's tank. I got up on the back of the tank and hit the sergeant on his helmet to get his attention. Sergeant Singbeil was traversing his gun to the right when his tank was hit. The round really hit hard. I had only one foot on the back deck as I was reaching over into the top of the turret to talk to him.

The concussion from that solid shot hitting his tank was so severe that it broke a bone in my foot and knocked me off the tank. I landed in among the crew of my own tank who were crawling down our tracks towards the river. My driver . . . was hit with a piece of steel that flew off the sergeant's tank. Subsequently the corporal's tank was hit. There were bad casualties in both of these tanks.'[10]

And so the slaughter went on. The Hussars had little chance against the superior German guns. Their Shermans were under-armoured and outgunned. Even as their line finally began to crumble, the Germans were exacting a heavy toll on the attackers. As one Hussar wrote of that afternoon: 'I think we all grew up a lot that day. We discovered that if necessary higher command would throw in a squadron of tanks to stop a counter-attack, regardless of consequences. The 'Y' Camp days of soldiering were gone, the grim reality that we could get hurt took over.'[11]

The Poles went into their last attack against Cassino. That once holy site was now a place of dread and fear. Everywhere among the smoking ruins, bloated in the

May sun, were the dead bodies of those who had gone before. A chronicler of the Carpathians described the Poles' approach: 'It's so quiet, oh Lord – how time crawls! Though our boots are wrapped in rags, every step is a strain on the nerves. Then ... crash ... a man has carelessly knocked against a stone. Everyone lies flat on the ground, listening tensely. They haven't heard. We can go on. Slowly, very slowly, stooping, the soldiers make slower and slower progress. They look like ghosts. But suddenly, one, two, then a third spandau starts spitting out their lethal bullets.'[12]

The Poles charged, carried away by their reckless, defiant pride. A couple of tanks rumbled to their assistance, systematically blasting away at the wrecks of Allied tanks to their front which were being used by the defenders as machine-gun posts.

The infantry ran into the first German minefield. They had been planted hurriedly, some still above the ground. 'Teller mines!' the infantry called to one another and pushed forward through the minefield. But the Shermans stalled, for the mines, which could not injure infantry, were designed to be set off by the heavier pressure of a tank. Hurriedly the sappers were called up. The Germans spotted them. There was the howl and thud of mortar

bombs. Here and there a sapper went down as he prodded for mines with his bayonet. Red-hot shrapnel flew everywhere. Gingerly, inch by inch, their engines howling in low gear, the thirty-ton monsters edged their way behind the engineers. Suddenly a mortar barrage landed right in the middle of the sappers.

Now the infantry were on their own, the tanks unable to reach them. 'We were in utter despair,' one tank commander said later, 'being unable to reach our comrades dying in front of Albaneta. With real fury we blasted away at the ruins and at every suspicious bush or pile of stones.'[13] But in the end the tankers' ammunition ran out and they had to scuttle to the rear for safety like impotent metal beetles.

The Cassino battlefield had become the Inferno. There were dead and dying everywhere. Captain Smerecznski, taking a rest in a cellar, found he was lying near a dead Indian. 'The corpse ... was buried under a few loose stones, as were the dozens of other bodies we found scattered everywhere. ... The place was alive with rats, big, bloated creatures that scurried about with impunity while we slept. The sickly sweet smell of decaying flesh

131

was nauseating and we could do nothing to rid ourselves of it. We even sacrificed blankets, employing them as shrouds for the corpses we discovered but we could not eliminate the pestilential odours that clung to the whole area.'[14]

The casualties mounted and mounted. Down below the hospitals were swamped. The Poles alone sent back 3000. The crowded wards represented a little League of Nations. There were even Italians in the British wards and by the time the fighting was over, there would be 975 of these Italian 'co-belligerents' buried at Cassino.

Every effort was made to fly the gravely wounded back to Africa for specialist treatment. Others went by train and boat, a pain-racked ordeal lasting three days – frost-bitten Free French troops going to Africa to have their feet amputated; men riddled with amoebic dysentery and recurrent malaria; blinded soldiers soon to be released into a strange unfamiliar civilian world.

'One of the happiest convoys we ever had,' remembers Sister Hilda Edwards, one of the nurses who accompanied these trains of misery back to Africa, 'was of Grenadier, Welsh and Coldstream Guards. They were so happy to be going home that they sang all the way from Tunis to Algiers. ... Yet all of these men were blind, some in one eye, some in both. One who had my unbounded admiration had lost both arms and was totally blind. I asked him one day if he would like a cigarette and, since he occupied one of the lower bunks, I sat on the floor to hold it for him. This gave him the chance to talk, which was what he needed more than anything else. His fifth child, whom he would never see, had been born while he was in Italy. I hoped that he would not detect the emotion in my voice. I admired these men so much because they had the will, an unconquerable spirit and a sense of dignity which even mutilation could not destroy.'[15]

Others lay out among the dead, gravely wounded, in no-man's-land, locked in a personal nightmare that cannot be described, spending hours, even days, racked with pain and tortured by the thought that they would never be picked up, or that they would be killed first.

Such an unfortunate was an unnamed Pole who was wounded and trapped in the wire during the first Polish attack. His leg was pulped and looked, according to the British source, like 'a black pudding'. Eventually the wound turned into one enormous scab and it ceased to bleed. ... His cells were attacked by bacteria and pus flowed out of the wound. ... It was turning gangrenous.'[16] For six days and nights the Pole stayed out there, with no food, no water, no attention. 'His body was smashed but he was not defeated; he did not want to die. Even after six days of waiting he still did not want to die. ... He began to hallucinate ... delirium followed. He came out of his coma. The British found him covered all over with flies and took him to a first-aid post. Thus did the human body fight to the very end against death by degrees.'[17]

The unknown Pole survived, as did Private Jackson, wounded on the slopes of Monte Cassino. After a youth spent in the fierce German air raids on Hull, convoy duty in the North Atlantic, fighting in North Africa, Sicily, and Southern Italy he had been wounded at Cassino fighting with the 6th Battalion, the Black Watch. But his wound turned him bitter about the whole waste and futility of battle. Forty years on he wrote: 'So ended six years of war, home and abroad, probably the best six years of my life wasted, fighting a war that proved nothing.'

For the Poles who were fighting so bravely at Cassino nothing would be proved either. Their victory, bought at a cost of nearly 4,000 dead and wounded, would be a hollow one. It would not enable them to return to their Homeland for which they were shedding their blood so prodigally. Most of them, including their Commander, General Anders, would die in exile. But they did not know that then. They fought, they died, pushing ever closer to their objective across that ravaged landscape.

Early on 18 May a handful of Polish Uhlans of the Podolski Lancers, under the command of Lieutenant Casimir Gurbiel, entered the ruins of the Abbey. From below their silhouettes could be seen moving through the shattered debris. The Germans had gone. The Uhlans could find no Polish flag, so they raised their red-and-white regimental banner as a signal that the Monastery was Polish at last.

'Mouths dropped open with emotion,' wrote one of the watchers, Sergeant Choma.[18]

Then a bugler played the medieval Polish military signal, the Krakow *Hejnal*. Choma recorded, 'There was a lump in my throat as, through the echo of the cannon's roar, the notes of the *Hejnal* rang out from the Abbey. ... These soldiers, hardened by numerous battles, only too well acquainted with the shocking wastefulness of death on the slopes of Monte Cassino, cried like children, as, after years of wandering, they heard not from the radio, but from the previously invincible German fortress, the voice of Poland, the melody of the *Hejnal*.'[19]

'Today,' wrote the reporter of the *Stars & Stripes*, who went to visit the place immediately after its capture, 'there is nothing left of Cassino. It stinks with the dead bodies of horses, dogs, mules, cattle, civilians and soldiers still in the rubble. Its water mains are wide open. Its fabulous tunnels are cleared of the Nazis, as are its hotel and railway station and its hills. Allied soldiers and Italian civilians, if they want to, may now roam its streets by daylight for the first time in safety since last November, when Allied guns first brought the town within their range. Cassino now belongs to the engineers and grave-diggers. Cassino belongs to the past.'[20]

Another visitor at that time was Sister Kitty O'Connor,

who had attended many of the victims of that great slaughter over the last months. She went up to have a look at the place where the men had fought for so long and found, 'hardly one stone remaining on top of another. The tin hats of the dead soldiers lay about under dead trees where no birds sang. There was total silence. Then a poor peasant went by with a donkey pulling a cart in which sat his wife, his child and a sewing machine.'[21]

But now Cassino didn't matter any more. It was just a name on the map. The entire might of the Eighth Army was streaming across the bridges over the Rapido along Highway Six on the way to Rome. There was a constant stream of nose-to-bumper traffic heading north and Cassino was no more than a passing curiosity. The soldiers packed in their trucks might gaze in wonder at the piles of rubble for a few moments and then pass on to new battles. Cassino was no longer important.

So they passed on, leaving the battlefield to the dead, interred in their hundreds and thousands, without the benefit of 'taps' or the 'last post'. There was no time and there were too many of them. But they weren't altogether forgotten. For now the story of the secret truce between the men of 36th Texan Division and the Germans opposing them could be told – how both sides had allowed a ceasefire back in January, 1944, in order that the Texans could go back across the Rapido to bring back their dead.

'What was it like?' one of those who went over was asked.

'Strange,' he replied. 'All of a sudden when the truce was called, all was quiet. The field was as silent and dishevelled as a fair ground after a Fourth of July picnic, only nobody was going home from this "picnic". The Jerries had stuck rifles up in the ground where the dead soldiers were lying. The Germans with us helped carry the litters from the foxholes back to the river. There we loaded the bodies on a boat and pulled it across the water. Soon after that the shooting and killing started all over again and the noise was just as bad as ever.'

The *Stars & Stripes* reporter who interviewed the young soldier recorded that, as he left, 'Pfc Jones settled more comfortably in his chair, like a man getting set to daydream. He stretched out his feet in front of him. He clasped his hands behind his head and his eyes had a far away look. ... The soldiers who had just listened to his story knew Jones's thoughts had drifted back to that bleak January afternoon on a death-strewn battlefield shrouded in a ghostly quiet and with his mind's eye the young veteran was reviewing the personal tribute he and his buddies paid to our honored dead there.'[22]

On the other side of the Mediterranean that day the Swedish MV *Gripsholm* was docking at Algiers, bringing with her hundreds of Allied PoWs exchanged by the Germans for their own men because both parties were too sick ever to fight again. As the white-painted Swedish

The Polish and British flags flying at last over the monastery of Monte Cassino.

vessel drew level with the quay, steaming slowly by the drab grey battleships of the Royal Navy, the band of an armoured division struck up that trite, yet moving song of that year, *There'll Always Be An England*.

For a moment on the packed deck, filled with men who would be invalids for the rest of their lives, nothing happened. Then a lone voice took up the melody and 900 other voices drew breath and joined in. As the gangways to freedom started to rattle down, the full-throated roar of those last poignant words echoed back and forth among the docks:

If England means as much to you
As England means to me.

133

US tanks waiting for the order to advance.

'Clark said he would have his troops fire on the Eighth Army'

A strange silence crept over the dark plain as zero hour approached. Infantrymen, laden with equipment like pack animals, waited. Tanks and trucks were crammed into farmyards and orchards. The gunners sat tensed by their cannon, beside them great piles of shells. Further back the ambulance drivers waited for it all to start; and in their tented hospitals the surgeons and nurses laid out their instruments, preparing for what was to come.

Even the top brass went up front, talking in whispers, somehow afraid to break the heavy brooding silence as dawn approached with a threat of rain in the air.

Over 160,000 British and American troops were crammed into the beachhead. Wynford Vaughan-Thomas, waiting up there at the front for the breakout from Anzio to begin, thought of Milton's lines as zero hour approached:

'Oh how comely it is, and how reviving
To the spirits of just men long opprest,
When God into the hands of their deliverer
Puts invincible might'.

But he admitted that 'the GIs getting ready for the advance had other things on their minds than apt quotations from the poets.'[1]

Vaughan-Thomas was right. Pfc Gerold Guensberg, eighteen years old and born in Germany, crouched in a ditch with other men from the US 3rd Division, listening to the older soldiers talking about sex. How English women liked it best standing up, whereas Italian women preferred if from the back. Now, as zero hour came closer and the talk dried up in the prevailing tension, young Guensberg's greatest fear was that he would die before he had 'become a man'.

Audie Murphy, back in the line again after yet another spell in hospital, was not far away with his platoon of the Third. He was confident. 'We no longer feel like orphaned underdogs. Our forces are driving up from

135

the south and the beachhead bristles with accumulated power.'[2]

Clark was there too. The day before he had told the assembled newspaper correspondents in Truscott's HQ at Nettuno that the forthcoming attack was under his 'personal command'. Reporters there felt in no doubt that, after the Third Division had captured Cisterna, Clark's objective would be the Valmontone Gap, thus cutting off the Germans, as Alexander planned. Clark, however, maintained that he was going to remain 'flexible'. How flexible he would be would come as a shock to the reporters – and to the British Supreme Commander.

Having risen at four thirty, Clark squatted in his forward command post waiting for the attack to start. As usual he wore his steel helmet. But today he did not remove it and replace it with his overseas cap for the sake of the photographers to show how contemptuous of danger he was. Today there was death in the air and he was taking no chances. The Fifth Army Commander's sole experience of 'combat' had been an afternoon in the line back in France in 1918. He had been ushering his men into the trenches when he was hit and wounded, without ever having fired a shot in anger. Thereafter he had spent the rest of the war sending up supplies to the fighting men. He wasn't going to chance being hit again.

At fourteen minutes to six the beachhead artillery thundered into action. It was a tremendous bombardment with 5000 guns pouring shells down upon the surprised Germans. Vaughan-Thomas thought it 'awe-inspiring'. Eric Sevareid felt the earth 'begin to tremble. . . . Shells passed over our heads and our jackets flipped from concussion.'[3]

Now the dive-bombers joined in. Silver streaks fell from the dawn sky. Hurtling down as if they were about to smash into the earth, the pilots shrieked straight for the German positions, only to level out at the very last moment, tiny black eggs tumbling from their bellies.

'Through a break in the clouds we saw their tight formations,' Sevareid reported, 'the fighter bombers wheeling and darting and disappearing in the curtain dividing the two armies.'[4]

The infantry started to move out. With an explosive roar, polluting the morning air with the stink of gas, the engines of 1st Armored Division burst into life.

'Around us now sleepy men crawled from their holes in the ditches and grubbed for cigarettes with stiff and dirty hands. They were waiting for the first violated bodies to be passed back into their care. The tanks came clanking up the highway, moving very slowly and well apart, their radio antennae nodding behind like drooping pennants of armoured horse and knight, jolting slowly to take the field. In and out of their ranks courier jeeps scuttled like agitated beetles.'[5]

Guensberg noted, 'While we were waiting to advance down the ditch the first wounded began filing past in the opposite direction. Those with light wounds seemed to have a silly smirk on their faces, as if they had won their tickets back to the US.'[6]

It was six thirty. The infantry had been committed and it was now irrevocable. The top brass could only wait and hope they had got it right this time. Sevareid and the other correspondents 'slid down into a ditch and drank coffee with the medics. One man read and re-read an old American newspaper that lay on a sandbag. The black headline said "Joan Sobs on Stand" and the story had a Hollywood dateline. Another man studied and restudied a single page in a book on photography. Nothing portentous was said. One remarked, "They can hear this in Rome maybe". A shell screamed too close overhead and we slid deeper into the ditch. A lad grinned at us and said, "Are you noivous in the soivice?" '[7]

In the British sector they definitely were. For there two battalions of the British 5th Division were engaged in a diversion at the strangely named village of L'Americano, which was to draw off the German attention from the main American attack. The Green Howards and the Northamptons, fighting against a battalion of German paras, were in trouble right from the start. Mines, snipers and German machine-gunners took their customary toll. Whole platoons were wiped out. Still they plugged on doggedly.

The German paras counter-attacked. Still the Green Howards and Northamptons fought on. The whole weight of the divisional artillery was brought down on the enemy. The paras were stopped at grenade range and finally the two British battalions managed to establish themselves on the opposite bank of the River Moletta below L'Americano and dig in, thus pinning the German 4th Parachute Division down and preventing them from influencing the breakout of the Americans. But again the butcher's bill had been high. In the Green Howards alone, the battalion lost, in four hours' fighting, six officers and 149 other ranks, exactly one quarter of its strength.

The Americans were taking casualties too now. Guensberg remembers how his column 'had to make our way gingerly between remains of corpses, dismembered limbs, scraps of bodies. A shell must have dropped short. We were too numbed to give this any thought. . . . We climbed out of a ditch and crossed a field. A few German soldiers began running towards us waving their hands high in the air and calling out "Kamerad". They were terrified.'[8]

Further back they were receiving the first casualties. Sevareid noted that 'the man with the book, who had not yet turned the page, carefully marked his place and got up. The soldier lay unmoving on the grass floor of the tent, staring at the roof. Blood was seeping rapidly through the bandage on his head. His helmet lay on the grass, the steel bent back from the hole the shell fragment had caused.'[9]

Sevareid bent down and said, 'You're going to be all right.' There was only the faintest flicker in the wounded boy's eyes. 'Everyone talked now. The man sterilizing instruments began to whistle. Another ambulance bumped into camp. The familiar routine of war and systematized suffering was well under way.'[10]

Crouched in a ditch up front, Audie Murphy watched fascinated as another platoon sergeant of the Third charged a German position. 'Motioning his men to follow him, he rises and, with a sub-machine gun, he charges head-on toward one of the enemy positions two hundred yards away. On the flat, coverless terrain, his body is a perfect target. A blast of automatic fire knocks him down. He springs to his feet with a bleeding shoulder and continues his charge. The guns rattle. Again he goes down. Fascinated we watch as he gets up for the third time and dashes straight into the enemy fire. The Germans throw everything they have at him. He falls to the earth. When he again pulls himself to his feet, we see that his right arm is shattered. But wedging his gun to his left armpit, he continues firing and staggers forward. Ten horrified Germans throw down their guns and yell "*Kamerad*".'

Carried away by the sergeant's reckless courage, his men stormed and captured the German emplacement, but by then their leader was dead.

'This is how Lutsky, the sergeant,' Murphy wrote after the war, 'helped to buy the freedom that we cherish – *and abuse*.'[11]

That day a fellow member of the Third Division won the Congressional Medal of Honor, the medal Murphy himself would win a year later. Private John Durko was advancing with his company when it came under concentrated machine-gun fire, supported by a mobile 88mm gun. The infantrymen hurriedly flopped down and took cover.

'We had been sitting there about thirty minutes, helpless, unable to do a thing about the situation, when the BAR* man in my squad, Pfc John Durko shouted to me, "Toothman, I'm going to get that 88 with my heater",' Durko's platoon sergeant, Cleo Toothman, related afterwards, adding, 'He always called his BAR a "heater".'[12]

'Before I could say a word he took off like a ruptured duck. He made the first hundred yards in a dead run. Machine-gun bullets were striking the ground only a foot or two behind him, but he was running faster than the Krauts could traverse. The Kraut 88 crew let a couple of fast shells go at him also, but they exploded about thirty yards from him and he dived into a shell hole which one of our own guns had conveniently made a split second

* A light machine gun.

Men of the Green Howards search a captured German paratroop.

before he got there. I told myself that he would never make it. The enemy fire, coupled with our own artillery, was the heaviest that I had ever seen in such a small area. The enemy machine-gunners converged their fire on the shell hole occupied by Durko, making it, in my opinion, impossible for him to advance farther.'[13]

But nothing was stopping Durko now. His blood was up. Followed by Private Charles Kelley, he jumped up and raced in a wide circle for the 88mm gun, the bullets slicing the air all around him. He closed with a machine-gun pit. With his free hand he lobbed a grenade into it. The crew died a sudden death. Now Durko was only yards away from the 88.

'Durko was a madman now,' Kelly said after the battle. 'He jumped to his feet and *walked* toward the 88mm, firing his BAR from the hip. He ignored the other two machine guns. He reached a point within ten yards of the weapon and wiped out the five-man crew with one long burst of fire. Durko then wheeled on the second German machine gun and killed its two-man crew with his BAR.'

'The third German machine gun opened fire on Durko. The gun was only twenty yards away and its first burst of fire wounded him, making him stagger. But like a wounded lion he charged this gun in a half-run. Durko killed both the gunner and assistant gunner of the enemy weapon with a single burst from his BAR and, staggering forward, fell across the dead German machine-gunner. When I reached him he was dead.'[14]

Durko was not the only member of the 3rd Infantry Division to win the coveted award. The same afternoon Pfc Patrick Kessler was also awarded the Medal of Honor for his bravery in single-handed combat.

He survived. Many didn't. By the end of the war the US 3rd Infantry Division had won more Medals of Honor than any other unit in the US Army. But the cost was high – 30,000 dead and wounded. The division had suffered approximately *300 per cent casualties.*

The offensive was going well. After thirty-six hours the Americans had taken 1,000 prisoners and the key town of Cisterna was about to fall. But all attention was now focused on the progress of the American Second Corps on the southern front. They had already passed Terracina and were pushing rapidly up the coast towards Anzio and the juncture with the Allied forces there. Once they did so, there would no longer be a beachhead. There would be a solid front across Italy.

The actual link-up, when it came, caught everybody by surprise. At a small bridge which had been blown by the retreating Germans Captain Ben Souza of Truscott's 6th Corps encountered a Lieutenant Francis Buckley strolling casually up a road.

'Where the hell do you think you're going?' Souza asked.

'I've come to make contact with the Anzio forces,' Buckley answered.

'Well,' Souza snarled, 'you've made it!'[15]

Clark's publicity maching sprang into action. He himself hurried to the beachhead and the whole ceremony was re-enacted for the benefit of the photographers and newsmen.

'The Fifth Army publicity machine promptly issued a statement saying that Anzio was now justified,' Eric Sevareid, Clark's arch-critic, wrote that day, 'and broadly implying that the commanders responsible for the landing there had been right all along, always knew they were, and that, in fact, the whole operation proved the wisdom of the high command, whose subtle methods were frequently misunderstood by grosser minds. ... If any correspondents sent off the statement, I did not observe them.'[16]

They all knew just what a blunder Anzio had been and how near it had come to disaster.

Military commentators in London and New York chortled that there were up to 100,000 Germans trapped in the coastal lowlands as a result of the link-up. Now the Allies had a connected front allowing for much more mobility and, after the four months of the siege, there were huge piles of stores awaiting the troops advancing from the south. But again Sevareid was not impressed. Driving down to Naples that day, he observed only a few captured Germans; the rest had escaped northwards. He

US M-10 tank destroyer in action during the advance on Valmontone.

concluded: 'It was all very dramatic and it seemed like a great victory. In truth, we had merely extricated ourselves from our own stupid mistake, committed when we landed on those beaches in January.'[17]

On the evening before that historic link-up Clark had asked Truscott, 'Have you considered changing the direction of your attack toward Rome?'[18]

Truscott was puzzled by the question. His attack was going well. Why not continue the drive towards Valmontone, which had as its objective the cutting-off of the German 10th Army, as planned in the original strategy? It was only later that he was to realize the significance of Clark's question.

Meanwhile Harmon's leading elements of the 1st Armored Division were now only ten miles from Valmontone, while the British of the Eighth Army were forty miles away. Colonel Howze, in charge of the point, knew that he was faced by a mere eight German tanks. Still he was twelve miles deeper into the German position than any other unit of Truscott's 6th Corps. He radioed back to

Harmon, 'I am in a soft spot. For Pete's sake let the whole 1st Armored come this way.'[19]

Harmon agreed instantly and passed on the news to Truscott. The information made Truscott 'feel rather jubilant', but not for long. Back at his HQ he was met by Colonel Dan Brann of the Fifth Army's staff. Brann said, 'The Boss wants you to mount the assault you discussed with him to the north-west as soon as you can.'[20]

Truscott was 'dumbfounded'. 'This was no time to drive to the north-west where the enemy was still strong,' Truscott wrote after the war. 'We should pour our maximum power into the Valmontone Gap to insure the destruction of the retreating German Army.'[21]

At first Truscott refused to obey the order. He told Brann that he 'would not comply with the order without first talking to General Clark in person'.[22] But Brann told him that was not possible. Clark was neither on the beachhead nor could he be reached by radio. Just like Patton before him, Clark had cut himself off in order to avoid any complications. So Truscott prepared to turn the bulk of his Corps towards Rome, leaving only a weak force to carry on the fight to Valmontone, consisting of the depleted 3rd Division and 1st SSF.

Trying to feign some enthusiasm, he met his commanders and told them that the new direction of attack would bring them easy gains. General Harmon and 'Iron Mike' O'Daniel, commanding the 3rd, were particularly bitter about the change, while Colonel Howze called it 'one of the worst decisions I ever knew'.

Clark's formal order to Truscott reached him on 26 May and on the same day a copy of it was sent to General Alexander. That morning Alexander suddenly appeared at Clark's HQ to be told that the General was somewhere near Anzio. So, just like Truscott, Alexander had to deal with subordinate officers, in this case, Gruenther, Clark's Chief-of-Staff.

Alexander had come for clarification of the new order. Would Clark continue to drive towards Valmontone?

'Certainly, Sir,' Gruenther replied, explaining that 6th Corps would now engage in a two-pronged drive, one heading towards Rome, the other keeping on for Valmontone. What he did *not* tell Alexander was that that second prong was made up of two weak and under-strength units.

Alexander seemed satisfied. 'I am for any line of action which the Army Commander believes will offer a good chance to continue his present success.' But he wanted to be absolutely 'sure that the Army Commander will continue to push toward Valmontone.'[23]

Gruenther reassured Alexander. Clark, he said, had Valmontone thoroughly in mind, which was a clear untruth. With the forces available, Clark could not possibly cut off the retreating German Army. Victory in Italy that summer was now going to be sacrificed for the sake of General Clark's personal prestige.

For, although Alexander had laid down the boundaries between the British Eighth and the American Fifth Armies well before the battle began, with Rome being allocated to the Fifth Army sector, Clark was now haunted by the fear that the British would 'get in on the act', as he called it. He confided to his diary: 'First the British have their eyes on Rome, notwithstanding Alexander's constant assurances to me that Rome is in the sector of the Fifth Army. ... The Eighth Army has done little fighting. It has lacked aggressiveness and failed in its part of this combined Allied effort.'[24]

When Eric Sevareid tried to make his resentment at the drastic change of plan public in a radio broadcast, the sentence 'There is a question whether the two aims [of getting Rome and of destroying the enemy] are compatible or mutually exclusive'[25] was cut out by the censor. At the morning conference attended by all the journalists accredited to the Fifth Army, Clark referred to 'a broadcast' that suggested the Allies might cut off the bulk of the German Army and said, 'That is sheer nonsense!' The Germans could escape easily, whatever he did. Yet, Sevareid maintained, it had always been the Allied objective to cut them off. 'Now the General spoke in a manner that seemed to deny that the idea had ever entered his head. Some of us remained puzzled and sceptical.'[26]

Truscott wrote after the war: 'There has never been any doubt in my mind that, had General Clark held loyally to General Alexander's instructions, had he not changed the direction of my attack to the north-west on May 26th, the strategic objective of Anzio would have been accomplished in full. To be first in Rome was poor compensation for this lost opportunity.'[27]

So the opportunity was lost. Alexander had twenty-eight divisions chasing twenty-one German, of which more than a third had been reduced to virtual impotence. For nearly five months the Allies had fought at Cassino, a battle which had cost many nations many lives. It had inspired courage of high order and endurance of a kind not known since the trenches of the First World War. But it had ended with a crowning act of strategic folly which ensured that the Allies were deprived of victory just when it seemed it was within their grasp.

Now, to cap it all, Clark's new drive for Rome was running into trouble, slowing to an almost stop, embarrassing for Clark, deadly for the men at the sharp end. Clark had sent Harmon's First Armored across the flat coastal plan below the Alban Hills. From their observation posts up there the German spotters could pick the Shermans out easily. Within the space of ten minutes the First lost twenty-five.

While Clark chafed at the slowness of the British Eighth Army, his own 34th and 45th Divisions had come to a standstill. His 36th, Walker's unlucky Texans, had also bogged down. Suddenly the front was hardening. It almost looked as if the Germans were going to do it yet once again. Kesselring seemed to be stabilizing his line before Rome. Suddenly worried Clark even began to consider waiting till the British Eighth Army caught up with him and helped him to break the German line.

Then he struck luck. General Walker, 'the Old Man' as he was known to his Texans, came up with a plan to break the deadlock. The Texans had now come to be regarded as a hard-luck outfit by the rest of the Fifth Army. But the Rapido débâcle had also turned them into a trigger-happy bunch who shot first and asked questions afterwards, or so men from other units thought. Walker knew how his division was regarded throughout the Army. Now he determined to redeem its reputation. If they could scale Monte Artemisio, then the town of Velletri, which was holding up further progress, would be cut off. He put forward his idea to the top brass. Both Clark and Truscott saw the plan's potential. But both felt the Texans couldn't do it. Clark said to Walker, 'Fred, I can't OK this. If you do it and succeed, we are on our way to Rome. But if you fail you will have to bear the brunt of what comes with the failure and your action will be without my approval or the approval of Truscott.'[28]

Clark was making himself pretty clear. If Walker succeeded, he'd give him a medal. If he failed, Clark would have known nothing and Walker's head would roll. It was as simple as that.

Walker didn't hesitate. He drew up his plan immediately. One of his regimental commanders, Colonel Lynch, knew that the success of the operation depended upon complete surprise. He briefed his Texans before they set off: 'I told them that in order to minimize the chance of new men disclosing our show by firing at noises in the dark, all troops were to move with loaded magazines but no ammunition in the rifle or pistol chambers until the break of dawn. Any killing was to be done by bayonet, knife, or other quiet means. Travelling between the two leading battalions all night, I did not hear one single shot until after dawn.'[29]

'We marched all night,' one of those men remembers. 'It seemed to me that almost all of this march was through one large draw. We had all been cautioned to maintain absolute silence, and when the troops learned what we were doing this became the quietest bunch of guys I have ever seen. All night long I never heard as much as a small clink from a piece of equipment.'[30]

The few German sentries they encountered had their throats deftly slit and by dawn the Texans were in position. A clever ruse at daylight destroyed the German positions ahead. American aircraft zoomed in from the *north* and the Germans, thinking they were their own planes, sent up flares to indicate their positions. The bombers dived to the attack, the enemy line clearly illuminated by their own flares. The Texans pushed forward down the road that led to Velletri. Suddenly eighteen German tanks appeared 'with a German officer standing in the first turret, arms folded Hitler-style'.[31]

But the American bazooka men were ready. They blasted the armoured column with their rockets and, as one of the officers there commented afterwards, 'The thing I will always remember about this incident was the German officer in the lead tank. When the bazooka round hit he squirted out of the turret like a cork out of a champagne bottle!'[32]

Now Velletri fell and German resistance started to crumble. Clark was overjoyed. After so many days of frustration, this news, as Clark said, 'caused us all to turn handsprings'.

Alexander nearly turned 'handsprings' too, when he finally learned what Clark was about. The two of them met on 2 June, as the Fifth Army now started to push in earnest on Rome. Clark began by demanding that Juin's Frenchmen should take over more of the Eighth Army's sector, thus keeping the British at a safe distance. In his memoirs Clark writes: 'Rather expected an argument but Alexander said I should not worry. If my attack didn't go through, he would bring in the whole Eighth Army to assure success. I replied our attack was going through.'[33]

Clark also told Alexander that it was going to be made quite clear in a final communique that it was 'Fifth Army troops' who had entered Rome. What he doesn't mention in his memoirs is that the future boundaries between the Eighth and Fifth Armies were discussed at that meeting. Alexander's Chief-of-Staff, Sir John Harding, recalled that this issue was the nearest they ever were 'to coming to blows'.

After the war, interviewing Clark on the Rome issue, journalist Sidney Mathews recorded Clark's comments: 'Everybody was anxious to get to Rome or to take part in its capture.... The French Expeditionary Corps, Clark said, wanted to be in on it (as did the Poles). ... When Alexander told Clark he wanted the Eighth Army to take part in the capture, Clark got pretty sore. He told Alexander that if he (Alexander) gave him (Clark) such an order he would refuse to obey it and if the Eighth Army tried to advance on Rome, *Clark said he would have his troops fire on the Eighth Army!* Alexander did not press the point.'[34]

The German enemy had been forgotten. The battle was now between the Americans and the British.

A German Panther tank, knocked out during the advance on Rome.

A British outpost near Ardea.

'On this historic day I feel like vomiting'

The Germans were pulling out. As the heavy guns rumbled in the hills, the long, camouflaged columns of tanks and trucks, packed with weary infantry, rolled through the sun-baked streets of the Italian capital, heading north.

Some were sorry to see them go – the toadies, the hangers-on, the handful of convinced fascists, the titled mistresses of high-ranking German officers. As they left, the pro-German fascist police went into a frenzy of sudden raids and arrests. Day after day they rounded up key resistance figures and those they suspected of helping the partisans in the hills outside Rome. But soon they too would flee.

But the great majority of Romans were too hungry, too apathetic, too worn out by four years of war to care about anything but an end to the conflict and the return of peace – and food! Old people were collapsing of hunger in the streets. Ragged beggars were everywhere. Discharged Italian soldiers, still in uniform, ran the risk of being rounded up and deported to German labour camps in the Reich.

Those few still strong enough to do so worried whether the Germans would simply abandon the city, or whether they would attempt to make a fight for it. On 2 June Pope Pius XII, who had been Papal Nuncio in Munich in the twenties and who was thought by some to be pro-German, broadcast to the world on his Name Day. He maintained that 'whoever raises a hand against Rome will be guilty of matricide to the whole civilized world and in the eternal judgement of God'.[1] But neither the Allies nor the *tedeschi* paid much attention to the Pope's pronouncements.

Wing-Commander Garrad-Cole, still on the run in Rome and now being hidden by an Italian officer, 'went for a walk around the city the day before it fell. We still did not know whether or not the Germans intended to defend it. But there were very few German soldiers about and the complete absence of any defence works seemed to us to confirm the rumour that Rome was to be declared an open city.'

The Italian and the Briton walked down to the Tiber, but there were no signs of German sappers preparing the demolition of the bridges there. They passed along the river bank to turn up the Piazza del Popolo into the Via Flaminia. There 'we saw the first Huns pulling out. They were all heading north in an odd assortment of transport, some German, some Italian, and even the odd bullock cart, piled high with equipment of all kinds. Here was the Master Race in full retreat!'[2]

But the 'Master Race' were not gone yet. Kesselring was keeping his options open. The day after Garrad-Cole went down to the Tiber, he ordered all important bridges across the river to be covered by machine guns, thus effectively cutting the city in two. In fact, Kesselring was intending to withdraw, but he feared a popular uprising by the Roman population. The manning of the Tiber bridges was ordered to convince the citizens that the Germans might well make a fight for the capital. He also ordered 'the King of Rome', General Kurt Maeltzer, a popular figure in Rome's high society, to attend a gala performance of Gigli singing in *Un Ballo in Maschera*. This was intended to quash suspicion of an immediate withdrawal. Maeltzer was not overjoyed at the prospect. An allied spy in the capital heard he was 'stinking drunk' and that his headquarters was in complete confusion.

It was no better at Fifth Army HQ. On the third Gruenther, Clark's Chief-of-Staff, wrote, 'The CP has gone to hell. No one is doing any work this afternoon. All semblance of discipline has broken down. Although the G-3 War Room purposely shows only a moderately conservative picture ... everyone ... who has come from Anzio this morning has brought back a pair of pants full of ants with the result that this unsuppressable wave of optimism and expectancy has swept through the headquarters.'[3]

Up front the position was less rosy. On the same day Harmon and Truscott, standing in the shadow of a factory on the outskirts of Rome, came under sudden machine-gun fire.

'This I thought was the ultimate anticlimax,' Harmon wrote later. 'The two of us who had gone through so much together were to be killed by fire from an Italian privy!'[4]

Harmon ordered up a passing tank. The Sherman didn't bother to use its gun. Instead it charged across the field and butted squarely into the privy where the German gunners were hiding. 'When the tank had finished, there was neither maching gun, outhouse – nor German!'[5]

On the same afternoon the men of the 5th British Infantry Division on the right wing of the Fifth Army attacked the small town of Ardea. The Division was weakened and depleted by the four months they had spent in the trenches at Anzio. Only the day before a whole company of the Division's 6th Seaforths had been annihilated by an unexpected German counter-attack. Now the 2nd Wiltshires attacked the high ground to the north-west of Ardea. They didn't get far. The battalion was pinned down by the heavy fire coming from the positions of men of the 4th German Parachute Division. The two leading companies suffered particularly heavy casualties and could advance no further.

The battalion commander threw in his only reserve, a platoon under the command of Sergeant Maurice Rogers, a handsome young man who had already won the Military Medal. Now, with Corporals Boyland and Cuddle, Rogers led his little band under heavy fire right up to the German wire. At 100 yards range seven German machine guns blasted at them and they were forced to go to ground – all save Sergeant Rogers.

Grabbing a sub-machine gun, he fought his way through the wire, bullets cutting the air all around him. In that mad fury of battle which carries a man away so that he forgets all fear, Rogers killed the crews of the first two machine-gun posts. The appearance of this mad Englishman in their midst threw the Germans into confusion. Their firing started to flag.

Rogers' platoon seized their opportunity. Inspired by his courage, they successfully crossed the wire and began to catch up with the lone NCO. Then things started to go wrong. As he doubled forward for the third machine-gun post, Rogers was hit in the leg and he went down. But somehow he struggled to his feet again and, still firing from the hip staggered towards the German post, blood streaming down his leg. But there he was shot at point-blank range. He was awarded a posthumous VC.

On the same day, 3 June 1944, while Clark's staff officers downed tools, carried away by the 'unrepressable wave of optimism and expectancy' two other young men also won their country's highest award for bravery posthumously.

As always the Third was in the van of the attack. Up at point was a patrol of the Third's 15th Infantry. They were advancing along Route Six when they ran into German infantry, supported by flak waggons and tanks. They had walked straight into a German ambush.

The platoon leader was killed immediately and Sergeant Raymond Bunning took over the badly shaken survivors.

'The only way out,' he recalled after the war, 'was to the rear. I ordered everyone to lie low until I could figure the lay of the land. While we were lying there I saw two of my men jump up and walk toward the enemy. Pte Elden Johnson, my BAR man, and Pfc Herbert Christian, a tommy-gunner, had elected to sacrifice themselves in order that the rest of us could withdraw from the trap. They motioned to me, indicating that I was to take remainder of the patrol to the rear.'[6]

'Almost at once,' another member of the trapped patrol, T/5 Douglas Bragg, recalled, 'Pfc Christian was hit just above the right knee by a 20mm slug which completely severed his right leg. . . . I was almost sickened by the sight. Blood was gushing from the stump. Shreds of flesh dangled from his leg. This man Christian was like a wounded animal. Instead of calling for aid he took his Thompson sub-machine-gun and made his way forward on one knee and the bloody stump, firing his weapon as rapidly as possible. He was raking the Kraut and succeeded in killing or wounding at least three.'[7] This momentarily paralysed the Germans. For a moment or two they forgot to keep on firing.

Now it was Private Johnson's turn. Pte Robert Wriston recalled: '[He] advanced a total of about twenty yards reaching a point within five yards of the enemy. He killed the crew of the machine gun which had killed our patrol leader with one burst of fire. . . . Reloading his weapon, he turned on the riflemen to the left and fired directly into their position, either killing or wounding four of the enemy.'[8]

Moments later he was was hit by a burst of fire. He slumped to his knees and, balancing thus, he killed another German before he pitched forward dead.

Meanwhile Pfc Christian had continued to hobble forward, trailing his shattered leg behind him, until he reached the Germans. He cut down a German armed with a machine pistol. Then the Germans turned the whole weight of their fire on him, blasting him apart with a furious salvo of 20mm shells. He died on the spot.

Both were awarded the Medal of Honor.

On the same day General Clark, for his part, was still fighting determinedly to keep anyone from entering Rome apart from himself and his own troops. While they brought in Sergeant Rogers' dead body and Pfc Christian and Pte Johnson stiffened in the dust where they had died so bravely, Clark pondered a message from Alexander. It requested that a detachment of Anders' Polish troops should participate in the entry into Rome.

'Apparently,' Clark wrote in his memoirs, 'the idea has spread around that we were going to have a formal parade into the capital.'[9]

But Clark wasn't having that. He signalled Alexander: 'Please politely tell everybody, including the Swedes if necessary, that I am not framing the tactical entrance of troops into Rome. God and the Boche are dictating that. I wouldn't know where to put anybody anyway. . . . So let everybody know that there will be no detachments of Greeks, Poles, Indians or anybody else entering Rome until the formal parade is held. Also try to keep visiting firemen from running up here as soon as the capture of Rome is imminent.'[10]

Up front, Eric Sevareid encountered 'a soldier who seemed no more than a boy in his teens, the artless, helpless type which ought never to be taken into the army'. His eyes were unnaturally large and his hands were twisting a towel rapidly, senselessly.

'Do you know where the aid station is, sir?' he asked Sevareid and his companions. They told him and asked him if he had been hit.

'No Sir,' he replied, 'it's my nerves, I guess.'

They left him, Sevareid telling himself the boy was 'a casualty as surely as any man with a bullet through his head.'[11] All the same he was sentenced for desertion.

A little later he came across the company from which the boy had deserted. 'In a sun-speckled grove the men lay sprawled on their backs oblivious of the traffic's dust or the spasmodic machine-gun fire so close at hand, catching any moment that fortune provided for precious sleep.'[12] A soldier walked past, going downhill, he held up his hand to show the blood-stained bandages covering what was left of his thumb. 'How's that for a cheap Purple Heart?' he quipped before disappearing.

One GI grunted, 'He's got the war made.'

Another said enviously, 'Lucky bastard!'[13]

Sevareid knew what they meant. The wounded GI would 'never have to fight, sleep in mud and be frightened again'.[14]

Sevareid and his companions pushed on past a dead German sniper wearing American boots.

'That guy shot two of our medics,' an angry officer explained. 'That made us sore.' So when they captured him they told him to make a run for it. Sevareid counted thirteen tommy-gun bullets in his back.

Further along the road to Rome lay a dead American colonel; in his notebook: 'I got through the last war alright, but I will not survive this one.'[15] An Italian was kicking the dead body of a German soldier, while his son tugged vigorously at his boots. GIs were looting German prisoners, using their rifles on those who were too slow to empty their pockets. Dead Germans lay by the verges their faces made whiter by the dust thrown up by the constant stream of traffic. Rome was close now.

'Please take Rome soon,' Clark's ageing mother wrote to her son. 'I can't stand the wait much longer. I'm all frazzled out.'[16]

On 4 June General Clark tried to oblige his mother. He, too, was exceedingly anxious to capture Rome. The Normandy landings were only a matter of a day and a half away. If his troops had not taken the Italian capital by then, he would fail to gain the headlines he coveted so greedily. Time was running out.

His top generals knew it too, for while Clark was flying towards the front, General Frederick, commanding a column of tanks and his own Special Forces unit made up of American and Canadian troopers, had just seen his first attempt to rush the city stopped by German artillery fire. Frustrated, he pulled back a little along Highway Six and was studying his map near a large blue and white sign labelled 'Roma'. It was then that his Corps

Mark Clark's 'historic' photograph, standing below the 'Roma' sign that was later removed for him, as a souvenir.

Commander, General Keyes, jeeped up and demanded, 'What is holding you up here?'

'The Germans, Sir,' Frederick replied.

'How long will it take you to get across city limits?' Keyes asked.

'The rest of the day,' Frederick estimated, explaining that he was opposed by several self-propelled guns that he would need to outflank.

'That won't do!' Keyes snapped. 'General Clark has to be in the city by four o'clock.'

'Why?' Frederick asked.

'Because he has to have his photograph taken,' Keyes answered solemnly.

Frederick stared at his Corps Commander, amazed. Was Keyes serious? Keyes' face remained impassive.

Frederick shrugged and said, 'Tell the General to give me an hour.'[17]

Just then Clark himself appeared. Almost immediately he spotted the 'Roma' sign which had, as he wrote later, 'a great appeal for me'. Together with Keyes and Frederick, he crawled down a ditch, followed by photographers,

to get the picture of himself posed in front of the sign.

For a moment or so he dared to stand erect in front of it while the photographers snapped away. Then a sniper hidden on the other side of the road opened up and, according to General Clark's account, put a 'bullet through the sign with a bang'. The three generals fled for cover, while Frederick sent a soldier back to remove the sign as a souvenir for the Army Commander. Later he shipped it back to the States where it adorned his home until he died.

So Clark obtained his 'historic' photograph, but the capital was not to be his that day. The resistance on Route Six was too intense and Frederick's men couldn't take Rome within an hour. Clark departed for the safety of his headquarters, leaving Frederick to ask Keyes why it had been so important for Clark to capture Rome that day.

'France is going to be invaded from England,' Keyes snapped in disapproval, for he had no time for Clark's mania for self-publicity. 'We've got to get this [the capture of Rome] in the newspapers before then!'[18]

It couldn't be much longer now. Kesselring was pulling his troops back ever more rapidly. Indeed, after being ambushed twice, the First Battalion of the 3rd Division's 7th Regiment had penetrated the city at nightfall on the 4th, setting up their camp at the San Lorenzo railway yards and establishing a perimeter around the station.

That night men of their sister regiment, the 30th, started a three-battalion push into the city heading for the river. They had been ordered not to use anything but small-arms fire in order not to damage the capital's monuments. There was going to be no second Cassino here; General Clark was very strict about that.

Consequently they were held up until the afternoon by a handful of last-ditch defenders and a few tanks until engineers could be sent forward to check the bridges across the Tiber and all public buildings. For the top brass was frightened that the retreating Germans would do what they had done in Naples the previous autumn and plant delayed-action bombs and booby traps timed to go off weeks later.

But not a single mine was discovered. Rome was fit to receive it conquerors, its citizens, as a cynical German noted, eager to 'fling themselves at the feet of their liberators'. Cautiously the Romans started to emerge from their cellars. Only weeks before they had been spitting at the British and American prisoners from Anzio whom the Germans had deliberately marched through Rome. Now they offered wine and flowers to the incoming Americans.

Wing-Commander Garrad-Cole and his Italian benefactor went into the dark street to meet the Americans, Both of them smoking.

'Welcome to Rome,' the Briton shouted. 'I'm a British prisoner of war'.

American troops pass the Colosseum.

The reply he received was not quite what he expected. The tired GI cursed, 'Put that goddamed cigarette out! Don't you know there are planes about?'[19]

His reception was no better at the Grand Hotel, already taken over by the Americans, although there were still German snipers on the roof. Trying to get in for a drink, he was stopped by an American MP guarding the door. He told the American, 'I have been in the habit of using the bar in this hotel in spite of the German occupation.'

The MP was unimpressed. 'I still don't believe you,' he drawled. 'Beat it.' The Wing-Commander beat it.[20]

More and more American troops were pouring into the city. Driving past the Colosseum, one of them whistled softly and pointed to the ruins, saying, 'Gee, I didn't know our bombers had done *that* much damage to Rome!'

In fact there had been little damage done to the city, and there were girls and wine a-plenty for the taking. American dollars bought *vino* at five cents a bottle and a prostitute for twelve cents. The restaurants opened up immediately and started serving wine and prime cuts of horsemeat to the weary GIs just as they had been doing the previous week for the Germans.

In the long months that Murphy and his comrades of the Third had been bogged down on the beaches at Anzio, there had been talk of 'wholesale drinking and fornication'. In Rome the reality was different and Murphy wrote later that 'we prowl through Rome like ghosts, finding no satisfaction in anything we see or do. I feel like a man briefly reprieved from death; and there is no joy within me. We can have no hope till the war is ended. Thinking of the men on the fighting fronts, I grow lonely on the streets of Rome.'[21] In the end he and his men pitched their tents in a public park and 'we sleep until our brains grow soggy and life oozes back into our spirits'.[22]

War correspondents swarmed into the city to record the historic moment. Bodies littered the streets, as Sevareid vividly recorded: 'I had smelled the sharp sweet gaseous odor of death before, but nothing like this. It inflamed the nostrils and I could even taste it in my mouth. Each breath drew it in deeply. I began to choke and water streamed from my eyes. ... I stayed sick for hours afterwards. The sight of death is nothing like its smell.'[23]

A staff officer of the 6th Armoured Division of the South African forces, trying to obtain permission for his tanks to cross one of Rome's bridges, was held back at gunpoint by an American MP, as was Major Sidney of the Guards.

Clark was not allowing anyone but Americans in Rome that day.

Meanwhile the correspondents waited for the Conqueror to make his appearance. The population was going wild. Men were grabbing and kissing the GIs' hands. Women threw flowers and burst into tears. Young boys and girls begged to be allowed to ride on the passing vehicles. Sevareid felt that he should 'remember that they had been our recent enemy, that they were happy because the war was over for them as much as because we had driven out the Germans. ... But one tried in vain. I felt wonderfully good, generous, and important. I was a representative of strength, decency and success.'[24]

But where was General Clark?

General Clark and his small jeep party were, in fact, lost. For over an hour they had been wandering around the capital. Finally they came across a priest in St Peter's Square who asked in English, 'Is there any way in which I can help you?'

'Well,' Clark replied, 'we'd like to get to the Capitoline Hill'.

The priest, who was in reality a leading member of the Allied PoW escape organization, gave the General the instructions he required, then said, 'May I introduce myself,' gave his name and asked what the American's name was.

'My name's Clark', the Fifth Army Commander replied with undue modesty.

The priest did a double-take. He shouted to some bystanders that here was the American Army Commander and a boy on a cycle volunteered to take Clark and his party to the Capitoline Hill, where, when Clark had still been an obscure major looking forward to retirement, Mussolini had thundered to his 'Romans' from that celebrated balcony.

Clark pounded on the door of the Town Hall. Perhaps he anticipated some Roman mayor, in a frock coat with a sash of his office across his portly chest, opening it and ceremonially handing him the key to the city. But it was locked and no official could be found. So he set off for the *Stampa Estera* where the photographers and correspondents would be waiting for him by now, reflecting that 'It had been a curiously varied as well as an historic day. We had been lost in the ancient capital which we entered as liberators after a long and unprecedented campaign. We had been welcomed and taken in tow by a priest and a boy on a bicycle. We had almost been mobbed by excited, cheering crowds. But now we couldn't even get into the town hall. ... Anyhow, I thought, we got to Rome before Ike got across the Channel to Normandy.'[25]

The correspondents were waiting when Clark's Chief Public Relations Officer burst into the room with the information that the Conqueror would hold a press conference at the Campidoglio building immediately.

The Conqueror was lounging against the balustrade which overlooked the square when they reached the building. There was a jam of people all around him. Already the newsreel photographers were grinding away, photographing the victor against the vista of a captured Rome spread out below.

Truscott arrived, then Keyes. They regarded the jostling newsmen 'with a questioning look in their eyes,' as Sevareid saw it. General Juin followed and obviously felt the same distaste for this publicity-crazy Army Commander and the crowd of photographers and correspondents out for a 'scoop'.

'Well, gentlemen,' Clark began, smiling modestly, 'I didn't really expect to have a press conference here. I just called a little meeting with my Corps Commanders to discuss the situation. However, I'll be glad to answer your questions. This is a great day for the Fifth Army.'[26]

'That was the immortal remark of Rome's modern-day conqueror,' Sevareid commented acidly. 'It was not, apparently, a great day for the world, for the Allies, nor all the suffering people who had desperately looked toward the time of peace. It was a great day for the Fifth Army.'[27]

Then Clark spread out a map and made a great show of pointing out this and that on it while his Corps Commanders glowered with embarrassment. As Truscott was to say later, 'I guess it was [a great day for the Fifth], but I was anxious to get out of this posturing and on with the business of war.'[28]

In the three and a half weeks since the breakout had started the Americans had suffered 18,000 casualties, the British Commonwealth forces and the Poles 15,000, and the French some 11,000 dead and wounded – nearly 44,000 in all. And to what purpose? The Germans had got away. The war in Italy had not ended. The Germans continued to fight for almost another year. By the end of 1944 the Allied armies would have fought their way through yet another fortified line at the cost of another 20,000 casualties and the end would still be no nearer.

For the combat soldier after Rome Italy would still be the same giant minefield, the same miserable war of mud, mules and mountains. But now, with all attention focused on events in Normandy and North-West Europe, it would become the forgotten war. Cynically the infantrymen slogging through the mud to yet another attack would sing, 'We're the D-Day Dodgers, out in Italy, always drinking vino, always on the spree ... in sunny Italy.'

Watching the 'Clark show' on 5 June 1944, as the Army Commander postured in front of the map for the benefit of the newsreel men, one of Sevareid's colleagues, bitter and sickened by it all, leaned over and whispered: 'On this historic day ... *I feel like vomiting!*'[29]

A surrendering German passes the wreckage of a Panzer Mark IV tank.

Epilogue

'I've tried to describe the things I have seen,
Panorama of Italy, the brown and the green.
I've neglected the war scars, visible yet,
But those things we want to forget.

I'm glad that I came and damned anxious to go.
Give it back to the natives, I'm ready to blow'.

Panorama of Italy, written in the winter of 1943–44
by six anonymous GIs. Three were killed in action
and three were taken prisoner.

Monte Cassino – after the battle.

Not many of the Americans, Canadians and British who
had landed in Sicily on that July day when it all started
survived to see the Allies' triumphant entry into Rome.
So many of them had been killed, wounded, broken in
body and spirit along the way.

Audie Murphy did. But if he wasn't broken in body
like so many of the rest, he was in spirit. The war had
marked him. To the end of his short life, he could not
sleep without a loaded forty-five beneath his pillow. Just
before his death, he told an interviewer: 'I really identified with soldiering. That's my problem, I'll admit. To
become an executioner, somebody cold and analytical,
trained to kill and then to come back to civilian life and
be alone in the crowd – it takes an awful long time to get
over it. Fear and depression come over you.' As his
interviewer said, 'The most decorated soldier in World
War II . . . was also a casualty – so much of his spirit had
been killed in action.'[1]

Murphy was one of the few originals left. Telford, the
infantryman who had seen his platoon butchered on the
road to Etna, was out of it. So was the Canadian Mowat
of the 'Hasty Pees'. Pinder was out too, wounded and
very ill in hospital in North Africa. Only Bombardier
Castle of the originals, that reluctant hero who had refused to soldier from the very start, had made it. That
summer he found the cushy number he had been looking
for all the while. He was made swimming instructor at
the Eighth Army rest camp near Amalfi.

The gaps they left had been filled with men of many
races, creeds and nationalities, from Basutos to Zulus.
They would continue this unnecessary war to its bitter
end. The brave Poles who had sacrificed so much never
saw their beloved homeland again. Although the British
had purportedly gone to war on their account in 1939,
the British Government did nothing to support their
national aspirations in 1945. Indeed it almost seemed as
if the British wished to forget in that year of victory that
the Poles even existed.

'Those of us who fought at Monte Cassino, Falaise,
Arnhem, did our duty,' one Pole pointed out. 'Many
never saw the end of these battles. . . . When the war was
over, there followed a victory parade in London where
all nations took part save one . . . *The Polish Army was
not invited!*'[2]

It was little different for the French. An inquiry by the
First Free French Division in November 1944 found,
'that the soldiers of General de Gaulle were regarded as
an alien element, motivated above all by a taste for
adventure and that . . . the battles in which they had
taken part were known only vaguely. . . . My men were
disappointed to find out that no one seemed interested in
them nor in what they had done.'[3]

All those who had fought on that long march to
Rome, especially the infantry, whatever their nationality,
felt the same sense of waste, loss, purposelessness. What
was it all about? Why were they fighting this useless war
in Italy? Their losses were tremendous, especially in the
infantry. In the British and Canadian rifle companies
thirty-one per cent of the fighting men were knocked out,
either killed or wounded. In American rifle companies
the losses were forty-one per cent; and the Poles suffered
even worse, nearly forty-three per cent. That meant that
nearly every second Polish soldier engaged in combat was
killed or wounded. That summer you could follow the
route they had taken to Rome by the simple white crosses,

or just by a bayoneted rifle stuck in the earth with a helmet dangling on the butt. 'K.I.A.' was chalked on the crosses with a bit of pencil or charcoal – 'Killed In Action'.

Once, one of the hard-pressed infantrymen slogging his way to Rome was told by a correspondent that he was making history. '*History, hell*!' he snapped back angrily. 'I wish to hell I was back in Iowa running my butcher's shop!'[4]

Some were doomed to go on fighting long after the shooting war had ceased. Irving Peltz, an American veteran who had lost an arm, a leg and an eye at Anzio bitterly told an official inquiry: 'I wanted to prove to myself and to everybody else that, even though I was disabled, my biggest obstacle was people. Yes, I said people. They practically broke down everything I was trying to accomplish. I'd walk down the street and almost everybody would stop and stare. On the train, bus or trolley, it was always the same. In restaurants they'd look up from their food. Damn them all! Can't they leave a wounded veteran alone? Haven't they got any sense? *Don't they realize they make me feel like a freak?*'[5]

The Andrews Sisters, of the wartime '*Boogie Woogie Bugle Boy of Company B*' fame, also met a veteran of the Italian campaign whose fight would continue long after the war ended, till the day he died indeed.

'A few months later at the Golden Gate Theatre,' Maxine Andrews recalled, 'the doorman came in and said, "You have a visitor." We were just about to do our last show. In walked a serviceman. On his back was another serviceman with no arms and no legs. One we had seen in the ward. He had this artificial arm on. He said, "I never asked you for your autograph because I said that one day I was going to give you mine." He leaned over on the dressing table and he signed his name on it. It was Ted.'[6]

And some have only the memories of the men dead these forty-odd years. 'Two days had to be snatched for shopping and affairs generally,' Mrs McCracken, widow of Colonel McCracken, who died of wounds in Italy that winter of 1943, recalls. 'The other twelve I shall never forget. The weather was extraordinarily kind all the time. However tired we were it was often difficult to go to bed on those lovely warm nights because hanging out of the window listening to the silence that was only broken by the occasional gentle plop of a feeding fish, was so fascinating. Sometimes the war gave us a distant reminder of its existence. From our own quiet darkness we could see the flash of guns and the searchlight streaks and knew that the town twenty-five miles away was having an air raid....'

'A fortnight can be a very small part of a person's life, but this particular fortnight was much more than merely fourteen days.... It was to be a memory that could make the difficult times ahead easier for both of us.... Angus could forget the heat and the dust in remembering the water lapping against the old boat as we drifted home down the lake.... Even the flies conjured up the sweep of the moors ... and a start at dawn was a reminder of other cooler early mornings when a fussy little moorhen bobbed across the lake on her mysterious but obviously urgent business.'[7]

And in the end memories were about all that year-long struggle to reach Rome amounted to. There is little to show today for all the effort and blood shed by those young men. Those beaches where they stormed ashore in Sicily and on the Italian mainland have been swallowed up in the great coastal sprawl of tourist hotels and villas. Do those trendy young men with their sunglasses and gold chains or the topless beauties tanning themselves a golden brown there know that once, in another life-time, other young men fought and died on those beaches? I doubt it. Nothing marks the spot where Walker's Texans were slaughtered on the Rapido. The only memorial to the 'Hasty Pees' is the remote mountain village they once stormed, some of its crumbling houses still pocked by shrapnel and bullet holes.

The real and only monuments to them all, friend and foe alike, are the cemeteries which stretch across Italy. In the one at Monte Lungo dedicated to the dead of the 'War of Liberation 1943–45' Italians who fought for the Allies lie next to other Italians who fought for the Germans. One can well ask what *did* they die for, fighting for both sides. It is a question for which one can find no easy answer.

And, of course, there is Cassino, with its cemeteries, German, Polish and American. An ex-officer of the US 36th Division, visiting the American cemetery many years after the war, recorded: 'I wandered out into the paths, stopping now at this grave, now at another, hoping that by reading the inscriptions, by busying my mind, I could control my emotions. But I could not keep back the tears, even when with one desperate effort, I recalled the great ode of Catullus* who two thousand years ago had come to the tomb of his brother to pay honor to his memory. ... Yet groping for the words helped me to discipline myself to say hail and farewell in a dignified way to men who had been my brothers years ago in a common struggle. The struggle now is half-forgotten, and perhaps finally, in the larger perspective of history, it was unimportant. But it was for these men that this story was written.'[8]

This one too, to the men of many nations who fought and died, and those who survived that *LONG MARCH ON ROME*.

* Even so, accept this tribute handed down, According to the old parental custom, Moist with a brother's tear. And, forever, brother, hail and farewell.

Reference Notes

A German Tiger tank knocked out in the fighting in Sicily.

Introduction
  1 Ewen Montagu: *The Man Who Never Was*, Lippincott, Philadelphia, 1967
  2 ibid.
  3 ibid.
  4 William Shirer: *The Rise and Fall of the Third Reich*, Simon and Schuster, New York, 1960
  5 Charles Whiting: *Canaris*, Ballantine, New York, 1975
  6 A. Kesselring: *Memoirs*, Kimber, London, 1960
  7 ibid.
  8 W. S. Churchill: *Great War Speeches*, Corgi, London, 1953
  9 Nigel Nicolson: *Alex*, Pan, 1973
 10 ibid.
 11 Martin Blumenson: *Clark*, Cape, London, 1985
 12 ibid.
 13 Edited: *Combat*, Dell, New York, 1958

 14 ibid.
 15 Blumenson, op. cit.
 16 ibid.
 17 ibid.
 18 Eric Ambler: *Here Lies Eric Ambler*, Weidenfeld and Nicolson, London, 1986
 19 ibid.
 20 Nicolson, op. cit.
 21 F. Majdalany: *Cassino*, Longman, London, 1957

BOOK ONE/One
  1 E. Mowat: *And No Birds Sang*, Cassell, London, 1979
  2 ibid.
  3 R. Lamb: *Montgomery in Europe*, Buchan and Enright, London, 1983

4 ibid.
5 Ladislas Farago: *Patton*, A. Barker, London, 1966
6 A. Cunningham: *A Sailor's Odyssey*, Hutchinson, London, 1951
7 ibid.
8 D. Eisenhower: *Crusade in Europe*, Doubleday, New York, 1948
9 James Gavin: *On to Berlin*, Bantam, New York, 1978
10 ibid.
11 *Reader's Digest* March, 1980
12 Mowat, op. cit.
13 B. Fergusson: *The Black Watch and the King's Enemies*, Collins, London, 1950
14 D. Flowers: *Taste of Courage*, Harper, New York, 1968
15 *45th Division News*, 13 July, 1943
16 Edited: *Eyewitness Account of World War Two*, Bantam, New York, 1960
17 A. Murphy: *To Hell and Back*, Corgi, London, 1950
18 Lee Eisenberg: *Fifty Who Made the Difference*, Villard Books, New York, 1984
19 R. Martin: *The GI War*, Little Brown, Boston, 1967

BOOK ONE/Two
1 Omar Bradley: *A General's Life*, Simon & Schuster, New York, 1983
2 Cunningham, op. cit.
3 Farago, op. cit
4 ibid.
5 B. Jacobs: *Soldiers*, Norton, New York, 1958
6 Farago, op. cit.
7 Bradley, op. cit.
8 Edited: *The Fighting Forty-Fifth*, Army and Navy Publishing, Baton Rouge, 1946
9 ibid.
10 Bradley, op. cit.
11 ibid.
12 Farago, op. cit.
13 *Daily Telegraph*, July, 1943
14 Martin, op. cit.
15 P. Stainforth: *Wings of the Wind*, Falcon Press, London, 1949
16 ibid.
17 ibid.
18 ibid.
19 ibid.
20 ibid.
21 Hilary St George Saunders: *The Red Beret*, Four Square, London, 1958
22 Stainforth, op. cit.
23 Bradley, op. cit.
24 Martin, op. cit.
25 Flowers, op. cit.
26 Martin, op. cit.
27 Edited: *History of the Durham Light Infantry in the Second World War*, Gale & Polden, 1950
28 ibid.
29 ibid.
30 ibid.

BOOK ONE/Three
1 Bradley, op. cit.
2 ibid.
3 ibid.
4 Farago, op. cit.
5 Gavin, op. cit.
6 Murphy, op, cit
7 ibid.
8 *Stars and Stripes*, August, 1943
9 *History of 45th Division*
10 C. Codman: *Drive*, Little, Brown, Boston, 1957
11 Farago, op. cit.
12 Bradley, op. cit.
13 Fergusson, op. cit.
14 Mowat, op. cit.
15 ibid.
16 ibid.
17 ibid.

18 ibid.
19 ibid.
20 ibid.
21 John Gunther: *D Day*, Hamish Hamilton, London, 1944

BOOK ONE/Four
1 Bradley, op. cit.
2 Codman, op. cit.
3 ibid.
4 Farago, op. cit.
5 ibid.
6 ibid.
7 ibid.
8 ibid.
9 Quentin Reynolds: *The Curtain Rises*, The Right Book Club, London, 1945
10 Bradley, op. cit.
11 ibid.
12 ibid.
13 ibid.
14 Martin, op. cit.
15 Bradley, op. cit.
16 Farago, op. cit.
17 David Irving; *War Among the Generals*, Allen Lane, London, 1981

BOOK TWO/One
1 Mowat, op. cit.
2 ibid.
3 Alan Moorehead: *Eclipse*, Hamish Hamilton, London, 1945
4 ibid.
5 H. Pond: *Salerno*, Pan, London, 1960
6 Saunders, op. cit.
7 ibid.
8 Stainforth, op. cit.
9 Blumenson, op. cit.
10 Pond, op. cit.
11 Flowers, op. cit
12 Pond, op. cit.
13 Moorehead, op. cit.
14 ibid.
15 ibid.
16 R. Butler: *Hand of Steel*, Hamlyn, London, 1980
17 ibid.
18 Reynolds, op. cit.
19 ibid.
20 Martin, op. cit.
21 Reynolds, op. cit.
22 ibid.
23 Butler, op. cit.
24 Blumenson, op. cit.
25 Moorehead, op. cit.
26 J. Steinbeck: *Once There Was a War*, Heinemann, London, 1959
27 Martin, op. cit.
28 ibid.

BOOK TWO/Two
1 Saunders, op. cit.
2 ibid.
3 Pond, op. cit.
4 ibid.
5 ibid.
6 ibid.
7 ibid.
8 ibid.
9 Stephen Roskill: *HMS Warspite*, Collins, London, 1957
10 ibid.
11 *History of the 45 Division*
12 ibid.
13 ibid.
14 ibid.
15 Blumenson, op. cit.
16 Nicolson, op. cit.
17 Blumenson, op. cit.

18 Nicolson, op. cit.
19 Pond, op. cit.
20 ibid.

BOOK TWO/Three
1 Gavin, op. cit.
2 Martin, op. cit.
3 Gavin, op. cit.
4 ibid.
5 Mark Clark: *Calculated Risk*, Harper, New York, 1950
6 Moorehead, op. cit.
7 Martin, op. cit.
8 Flowers, op. cit.
9 ibid.
10 Murphy, op. cit.
11 ibid.
12 John Horne Burns: *The Gallery*, Secker & Warburg, London, 1948
13 Ellis, op. cit.
14 ibid.
15 Martin, op. cit.
16 Mowat, op. cit.
17 ibid.
18 *Stars and Stripes*, December, 1943
19 Bradley, op. cit.
20 Nicolson, op. cit.

BOOK TWO/Four
1 G. Infield: *Disaster at Bari*, Hale, London, 1971
2 ibid.
3 ibid.
4 ibid.
5 Eisenhower: *Crusade in Europe*, Doubleday, New York, 1948
6 Mowat op. cit.
7 ibid.
8 ibid.
9 ibid.
10 Flowers, op. cit.
11 ibid.
12 Martin, op. cit.
13 ibid.
14 Mowat, op. cit.
15 Lord Moran: *Winston Churchill, The Struggle for Survival*, Sphere, London, 1966
16 Nicolson, op. cit.
17 H. Baldwin: *Command Decisions*, Harcourt Brace, New York, 1959
18 ibid.
19 S. Ambrose, *The Supreme Commander*, Doubleday, New York, 1970
20 K. Summersby: *Past Forgetting*, Collins, London, 1979
21 ibid.
22 Mowat, op. cit.
23 Martin, op. cit.

BOOK THREE/One
1 Murphy, op. cit.
2 Martin, op. cit.
3 ibid.
4 ibid.
5 Ellis, op. cit.
6 Martin, op. cit.
7 Ellis, op. cit.
8 Martin, op. cit.
9 ibid.
10 ibid.
11 ibid.
12 ibid.
13 ibid.
14 Ellis, op. cit.
15 ibid.
16 ibid.
17 ibid.
18 ibid.

19 ibid.
20 ibid.
21 ibid.
22 ibid.
23 Martin, op. cit.
24 Ellis, op. cit.
25 Martin, op. cit.
26 ibid.
27 Ellis, op. cit.
28 ibid.
29 ibid.
30 ibid.

BOOK THREE/Two
1 *History of the Third Infantry Division*, Infantry Journal Press, Washington, 1947
2 ibid.
3 Nicolson, op. cit.
4 ibid.
5 Saunders, op. cit.
6 Wynford Vaughan-Thomas: *BBC War Report*
7 Baldwin, op. cit.
8 ibid.
9 Gavin, op. cit.
10 ibid.
11 Baldwin, op. cit.
12 Vaughan-Thomas, op. cit.
13 B. McBryde: *Quiet Heroines*, Chatto & Windus, London 1985
14 Martin, op. cit.
15 ibid.
16 ibid.
17 *History of 3rd Division*
18 E. Harmon: *Combat Commander*, Prentice-Hall, New Jersey, 1970
19 Raleigh Trevelyan: *Rome '44*, Secker & Warburg, 1983
20 Harmon, op. cit.
21 ibid.
22 Vaughan-Thomas, op. cit.
23 *History of the 45th Division*
24 ibid.
25 Harmon, op. cit.
26 ibid.
27 Trevelyan, op. cit.
28 ibid.

BOOK THREE/Three
1 F. Majdalany, op. cit.
2 Ellis, op. cit.
3 Majdalany, op. cit.
4 Ellis, op. cit.
5 Majdalany, op. cit.
6 Clark, op. cit.
7 Majdalany, op. cit.
8 Clark, op. cit.
9 ibid.
10 Trevelyan, op. cit.
11 Murphy, op. cit.
12 Harmon, op. cit.
13 Vaughan-Thomas, op. cit.
14 Trevelyan, op. cit.
15 ibid.
16 Adleman and Walton: *The Devil's Brigade*, Corgi, London, 1968
17 ibid.
18 A. Bowlby: *The Recollections of Rifleman Bowlby*, Corgi, London, 1969
19 Vaughan-Thomas, op. cit.
20 Edited: *Combat*, Dell, New York, 1958
21 ibid.
22 Vaughan-Thomas, op. cit.

BOOK THREE/Four
1 Eric Williams: *Great Escape Stories*, Peacock, London, 1958
2 ibid.
3 ibid.
4 ibid.

5 Hood: *Pebbles from My Skull*, Hutchinson, London, 1963
6 Martin, op. cit.
7 ibid.
8 ibid.
9 ibid.
10 G. Dunning: *Where Bleed the Many*, Elek, London, 1955
11 ibid.
12 Williams, op. cit.
13 ibid.
14 Hood, op. cit.
15 John Verney: *Going to the Wars*, Collins, London, 1955
16 ibid.
17 Garrad-Cole: *Single to Rome*, Digit, London, 1955
18 ibid.
19 ibid.
20 ibid.
21 Hood, op. cit.
22 Foot and Langley: *MI9 Escape and Evasion*, Futura, 1979
23 Newby: *Love and War in the Apennines*, Penguin, London, 1971

BOOK FOUR/One
1 Nicolson, op. cit.
2 ibid.
3 Trevelyan, op. cit.
4 ibid.
5 ibid.
6 Ambler, op. cit.
7 ibid.
8 ibid.
9 Blumenson, op. cit.
10 ibid.
11 Sevareid: *Combat*, ed M. Miller, Dell, 1952
12 Clark, op. cit.
13 Majdalany, op. cit.
14 ibid.
15 Ellis, op. cit.
16 ibid.
17 Trevelyan, op. cit.
18 Ellis, op. cit.
19 ibid.
20 ibid.
21 ibid.
22 ibid.

BOOK FOUR/Two
1 Vaughan-Thomas, op. cit.
2 S. Terkel: *The Good War*, Hamish Hamilton, London, 1985
3 Edited: *The Invisible Soldier*, Wayne State University Press, Detroit, 1975
4 ibid.
5 Blumenson, op. cit.
6 Nicolson, op. cit.
7 Ellis, op. cit.
8 ibid.
9 ibid.
10 ibid.
11 ibid.
12 Trevelyan. op. cit.
13 ibid.
14 Ellis, op. cit.
15 McBryde, op. cit.
16 Trevelyan, op. cit.
17 ibid.
18 Ellis, op. cit.
19 Trevelyan, op. cit.
20 *Stars and Stripes*, June, 1944
21 McBryde, op. cit.
22 *Stars and Stripes*, June, 1944

BOOK FOUR/Three
1 Vaughan-Thomas, op. cit.
2 Murphy, op. cit.
3 Sevareid, op. cit.

4 ibid.
5 ibid.
6 Trevelyan, op. cit.
7 Sevareid, op. cit.
8 Trevelyan, op. cit.
9 Sevareid, op. cit.
10 ibid.
11 Murphy, op. cit.
12 *History of the Third Division*
13 ibid.
14 ibid.
15 Sevareid, op. cit.
16 ibid.
17 ibid.
18 Blumenson, op. cit.
19 Harmon, op. cit.
20 Trevelyan, op. cit.
21 ibid.
22 ibid.
23 Blumenson, op. cit.
24 Clark, op. cit.
25 Sevareid, op. cit.
26 ibid.
27 Ellis, op. cit.
28 Trevelyan, op. cit.
29 ibid.
30 ibid.
31 ibid.
32 ibid.
33 Clark, op. cit.
34 Trevelyan, op. cit.

BOOK FOUR/Four
1 Ellis, op. cit.
2 Garrad-Cole, op. cit.
3 Trevelyan, op. cit.
4 Harmon, op. cit.
5 ibid.
6 *History of Third Division*
7 ibid.
8 ibid.
9 Clark, op. cit.
10 ibid.
11 Sevareid, op. cit.
12 ibid.
13 ibid.
14 ibid.
15 ibid.
16 Trevelyan, op. cit.
17 Blumenson, op. cit.
18 ibid.
19 Garrad-Cole, op. cit.
20 ibid.
21 Murphy, op. cit.
22 ibid.
23 Sevareid, op. cit.
24 ibid.
25 Clark, op. cit.
26 ibid.
27 Sevareid, op. cit.
28 Trevelyan, op. cit.
29 Sevareid, op. cit.

Epilogue
1 L. Eisenberg: *Fifty Who Made The Difference*, Villard Books, New York, 1984
2 Ellis, op. cit.
3 ibid.
4 Martin, op. cit.
5 Martin, op. cit.
6 Terkel, op. cit.
7 Flowers, op. cit.
8 Ellis, op. cit.

INDEX

Numbers in *italics* refer to illustrations

US Ranger preparing to go out on patrol.

PHOTOGRAPHIC

ACKNOWLEDGEMENTS

The publishers are most grateful to the Imperial War Museum for permission to use the photographs which appear on pages 2, 7, 11, 12/13, 14/15, 19, 21, 22, 25, 27, 28, 30, 31, 32/3, 35, 36/7, 39, 44, 45, 47, 48/9, 50/1, 55, 57, 61, 63, 65, 66/7, 69, 72, 73, 74/5, 77, 78/9, 81, 82/3, 84/5, 87, 89, 90/1, 92/3, 95, 99, 100/1, 103 (below), 105, 107, 108/9, 111, 113, 115, 116/7, 123, 124/5, 126/7, 129, 130, 131, 133, 137, 138/9, 141, 142/3, 146, 147, 149, 152, 157; to the Associated Press for the photograph appearing on page 9; to Peter Newark's Western Americana for the photograph appearing on page 23; to Robert Hunt Library for those appearing on pages 40/41, 58/9, 71, 97, 103 (above), 121, 134/5; and to the Sikorski Museum for the photograph appearing on page 119.